KEOLADEO NATIONAL PARK, BHARATPUR

Birds in Paradise

KEOLADEO NATIONAL PARK, BHARATPUR

Birds in Paradise

SUNAYAN SHARMA

NIYOGI
BOOKS

Published by
NIYOGI BOOKS
Block D, Building No. 77,
Okhla Industrial Area, Phase-I,
New Delhi-110 020, INDIA
Tel: 91-11-26816301, 26818960
Email: niyogibooks@gmail.com
Website: www.niyogibooksindia.com

Editorial and Design: Write Media

ISBN: 978-93-89136-36-4
Year of Publication: 2020

Printed at: Niyogi Offset Pvt. Ltd., New Delhi, India

With

great honour, I dedicate this book to

Maharaja Surajmal Jat, the legendary king of

Bharatpur State, for the creation of this unique

World Heritage Site

Keoladeo National Park

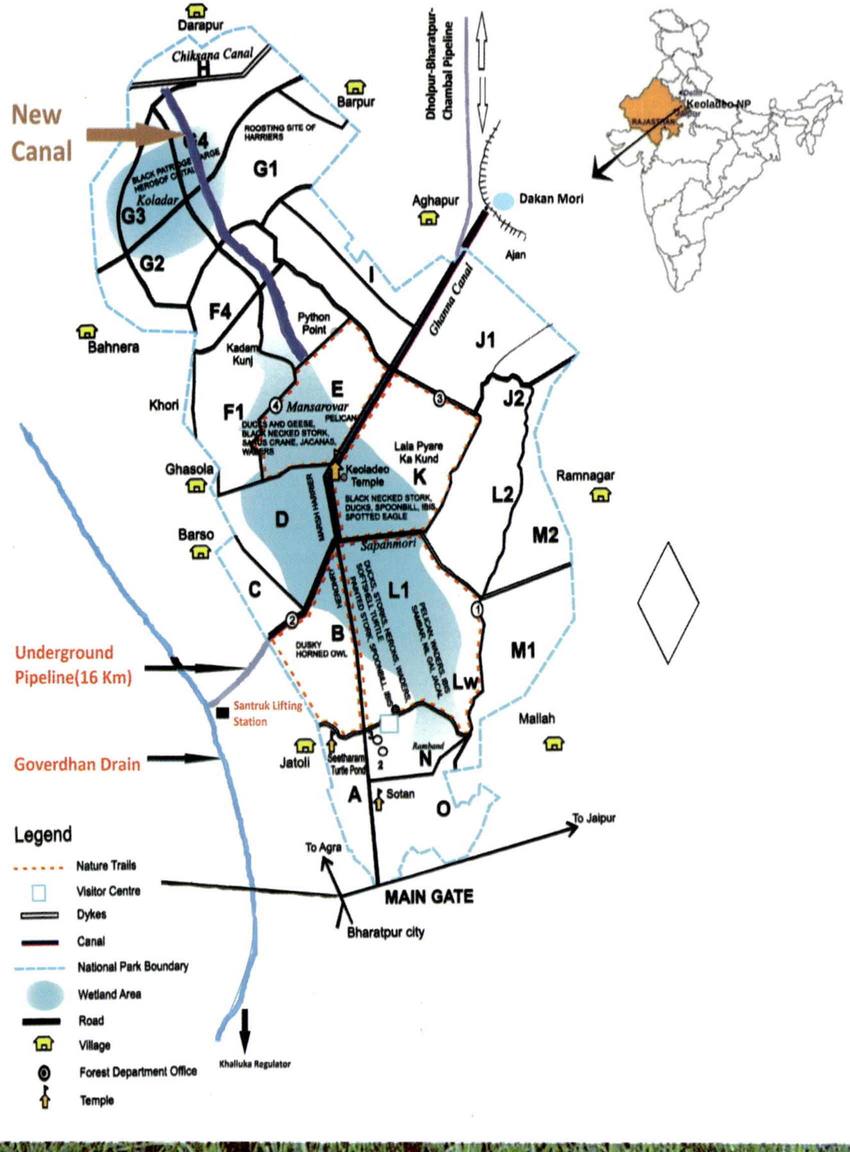

CONTENTS

Message 9
Foreword 11
Preface 13

PART I
Nature's Playground 21
Overview 23
Dynamic Wetlands 39
Bewitching Heronries 49
Resident Ducks, Rails and Jacanas 65
Where do the Birds Come From? 75
Migratory Water Birds 81
Majestic Cranes 95
The Star Attraction 101
Birds of Prey 113
Terrestrial and Arboreal Birds 125
Non-Avian Fauna 143
The Park and its People 171
Challenging Nature 177

PART II
Debacle in Keoladeo 187
Where Has All the Water Gone? 189
Habitat Devastation 193

PART III
Rebuilding Keoladeo 197
Managing a Growing Menace 199
Creating New Water Resources 209
Debatable Issues 223
Going Down the Park's Memory Lane 231
Acknowledgements 236
Appendix 239
Bibliography 280
Index 281

NAVIN SHARMA

MESSAGE

The Keoladeo National Park, formerly known as the Keoladeo Ghana Bird Sanctuary Bharatpur, is a highly dynamic yet fragile ecosystem. This national park records over 380 species of avifauna along with other fauna and flora. A protected area that requires continuous strategic interventions for maintaining the wetlands and their natural inhabitants, gaining an insight into the issues faced by the management is a key lesson for any naturalist. It is important to know how, for years, the Rajasthan State Forest Department and the District Administration have been upholding the ecological integrity of this fascinating wetland habitat in the face of anthropogenic pressures and climate variability.

In this book, Sunayan Sharma provides an insight into the effort that contributed to the revival and management of the national park from a declining condition. The author relates the complexities and issues of managing a wetland ecosystem. Controlling the wildly spreading invasive species *Prosopis juliflora*, regulating water levels in the park during prolonged seasonsofdrought,gatheringthesupportoflocalcommunitiesand searching for new water resources in times of crisis are issues that continue to be relevant. A salient feature of these memoirs are photographs that bring to life the scenarios of wildlife and their habitats.

Continuing in the practice of India's forest officials writing of the experiences of their time, I trust that this book will be useful for all readers, bringing to salience the importance of this national park, and to bring forth future advocates for conservation.

Ravi Singh
Secretary General and CEO
World Wide Fund for Nature-India (WWF-India)

Spoonbill couple on nest being threatened by another spoonbill to evict

NAVIN SHARMA

FOREWORD

Indian forest officers get a hands-on experience of managing a park or a forest reserve. The trials and tribulations, departmental intrigues, covert and overt political interference, pressure of non-government organisations, aspirations of the local communities and personal commitments—all come into play while on duty. Yet, few know about the immense pressure a senior forest officer has to work under, particularly when political and administrative support is lacking.

Despite having a ringside view of a protected area, not many officers sit down and write their memoirs. Sunayan Sharma is an exception. He has done a tremendous job by sharing his experience of running the world-famous Keoladeo National Park during the three years of his tenure as Research Officer and then two years as Director. This was a tumultuous time when the famous *jheel*s (lakes) of the park had little or no water. In the chapter titled, 'Creation of New Water Resources', he has given details of his struggle to bring water to the park. It reveals the kind of behind-the-scene activities that a forest officer has to engage in to get things done due to intractable bureaucratic tangles.

Over 200 research papers and two major books have been written on Keoladeo but Sharma's work is commendable as he has presented an excellent historical description of the park and the equally famous town, Bharatpur. Most of the research papers deal with the birds of the park,

A pure breeding colony of the openbill stork

but Sharma has dug out legends, folklores and history, which no one has done. This book, right from the Overview itself, is an interesting read. The comprehensive details the author has given about the complex ecology of the wetland is a reflection of his deep knowledge of the ecosystem of the park. Wild creatures such as fish, turtles, pythons, dragonflies/damselflies and butterflies play an important role in the ecology of the Keoladeo National Park but these have found, for the first time, due place in a book on Keoladeo. This clearly shows that the author is committed to present the park in totality to the readers. Mesmerising scenes and animal behavioural acts, displayed in the form of beautiful pictures taken by Sharma and a few other wildlife enthusiasts, add huge value to the book.

Each chapter of this book is informative and gives a new perspective to the problems of the park. Sharma's ground action to remove the pernicious weed, *Prosopis juliflora*, highlights that, if there is determination, anything can be done. It is also an example for future park directors to keep the area cleared of *Prosopis* and *Eichornia*. Resources are not a problem if the willingness to act is there. Sharma shows this very clearly in his book.

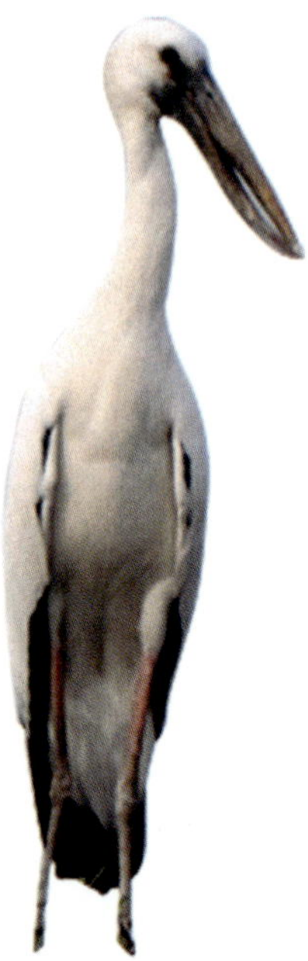

In his five-year tenure, Sunayan Sharma was able to understand the fundamental problems of the park. I hope *Keoladeo National Park, Bharatpur: Birds in Paradise* will set a trend and more senior forest officers will come forward and write about their experiences. We need better documentation of India's protected areas and wild species. This book is a good example.

Dr Asad Rahmani

Ex-Director, Bombay Natural History Society, Mumbai

PREFACE

My fascination for nature turned me into a forester even though basically I am an engineer. The management of the Aravalli forests was my first assignment, which I thoroughly enjoyed, but a serious dearth of wildlife in these luxuriant forests disappointed me. I questioned: 'Can't we manage these forests in a way that protects wildlife as well?' Perhaps this brought me to the Wildlife Institute of India, Dehradun, in 1985, where I was trained in wildlife management for nine months. My first visit to the Keoladeo National Park was from this Institute, after a few months of joining the

A pair of Sarus cranes mating; these birds are known for their fidelity

NAVIN SHARMA

course. What I saw before me was simply amazing—lakes full of multi-coloured beautiful ducks, geese and fish-eaters probing the shallow waters. The sudden take-off by hundreds of birds from the water surface on the approach of an eagle or a harrier, and then their landing back after taking a few rounds in the sky, was a breathtaking drama. It was mesmerising.

After the completion of the course, I got posted to Jodhpur where my chief responsibility was to ensure protection to the precious desert wildlife. Though I enjoyed my work here, the grandeur of Keoladeo was luring me all the time. The exciting memories of my last visit kept haunting me till, in 1988, I was posted to Keoladeo as a Research Officer. With my residence and office inside the park, I was in the lap of this heavenly abode all the time. The job demanded that I wander in the park day and night and that totally matched my desire. Hence, during these three years I combed not only every single inch of the park but also availed the opportunity of learning about the various elements credited for the creation of this haven. As a Research Officer, not wearing the cap of the top boss, I had the best opportunity to mingle with all kinds of people and minutely identify the ever-growing potent threats to this fragile ecosystem. The existence of the park depended upon the supply of water from the Ajan Dam and the farmers located all around the dam wanted this water for their crops. The politicians were standing in support of these voters. Many other problems needed to be addressed. Perhaps, as Director, with several other administrative duties, I would not have learnt about the root causes of these problems, but as a Research Officer I could do so quite easily.

I had no dearth of time to devote to a study of not only the ecology of the various habitats but also the individual species of birds and other wildlife inhabiting the park. The Bombay Natural History Society (BNHS) was carrying on a long-term research project here. Dr V.S. Vijayan, Project Scientist, along with several researchers, were working on different animals and habitats, covering almost all aspects of the park. This proved fortunate and I am indebted to them for generously sharing their knowledge with me. The atmosphere inculcated a researcher's approach in my way of working,

NAVIN SHARMA

A spoonbill collecting material for the making of a nest

which benefitted me hugely later on in my career as a wildlife manager, especially during my second tenure here as Director.

Field visits on foot and regular cycling gave me ample opportunity to collect exclusive evidence, in the form of notes and photographs, pertaining to nature and the behaviour of animals, which I treasure even today. This opportunity lasted for three years, till I was assigned the job of managing the Sariska Tiger Reserve as Field Director. And even though I enjoyed my stint at Sariska and other later assignments, my memories of Keoladeo refused to fade and I kept myself abreast of the developments there. The raising of the height of the Panchana Dam, thereby killing the flow of the Gambhiri river, the main feeder of the Ajan Dam, had shaken me. In 2004 and 2006, Keoladeo got no water as a consequence of this development.

NAYAN KHANOLKAR

Taking advantage of this water shortage, *Prosopis juliflora*, a perennial weed, engulfed the entire park, including the lakes and grassland.

The danger of getting delisted from the World Heritage Sites started lurking. This time, under these hostile conditions, it was like a punishment posting for me. The park, where I had received my first lessons in birdwatching and management, was dying before me. Perhaps I was sent here as its last Director. It was too painful to bear and I was desperate to find a genuine solution for its salvage and was determined not to leave any stone unturned. God was merciful. The knowledge I had gained during my earlier posting about this park, Bharatpur's drainage system, people's nature, the requirement of the villagers located all around the park and my associations with the people who mattered inside and outside the park all helped me hugely in finding solutions to these key problems.

Short- and long-term projects were initiated to mitigate this water crisis; a new canal was dug inside the park, for the first time after 1896, to utilise drainage water, which otherwise was going waste, chiefly to save the world-famous heronries. This proved successful. In addition, another new source (the Govardhan drain) was found to ensure the fulfilment of the remaining water requirement of the park; this mega project is now literally its backbone. An innovative scheme was launched to eradicate the menace of *Prosopis juliflora* forever, by rooting out its plants, big and small, through people's participation. Not a penny was spent from the government exchequer. This benefitted the neighbouring villagers, thus helping the park management in improving relations with them.

Facing page: *A yellow-footed green pigeon perched in its nest, looking after its little ones*

This was, perhaps, a lone example of this kind globally. The World Heritage Centre and the International Union for Conservation of Nature (IUCN) showered praises on these achievements. The Bharatpur media, which otherwise is known for its severe criticism of government officers, applauded me for these activities; they even honoured me at the time of my transfer to Sariska Tiger Reserve later.

In 2010, after the successful completion of the tiger rehabilitation task at Sariska Tiger Reserve, I retired from my job as an extremely satisfied wildlife manager. I am pleased to have contributed to saving the World Heritage Site, Keoladeo, a birds' paradise and the pride of Bharatpur and India. I had seen this nature park in its prime glory, then its fall when it faced the threat of extinction and then again its revival. Friends, especially the Keoladeo-Ghana wildlife lovers, wanted me to share the told and untold stories of these three phases that the Keoladeo National Park had passed through. Thus this book was born, appropriately divided into three sections—its uniqueness, debacle and revival.

NAVIN SHARMA

A playful mood—the rhesus macaque is one of the best-known species of the Old World monkeys. **Facing page:** *A grim sight of a python eating a monkey*

ANSAR KHAN

Though Keoladeo is basically a birds' park, every single plant and animal found here, small or big, has added to its beauty. They have helped to make it unique and thus the park enjoys the status of a World Heritage Site as well as a Ramsar Convention Site. Therefore, in the first part, I have also written about fish, pythons, odonates, butterflies and turtles. I hope this effort will also help in their easy identification and accord due importance to these species, which otherwise remain unnoticed under the shadow of the major fauna that can be found here. These chapters have been especially written for the benefit of the park personnel, nature guides and other wildlife enthusiasts.

Buffalo-grazing, which was stopped in Keoladeo after it became a national park, has been a point of controversy among ecologists, wildlifers and the

A pure breeding colony of painted storks

park management. Some eminent scientists have been holding the stoppage of this grazing responsible for the destruction of habitat, thus causing the loss of the Siberian cranes as winter visitors to Keoladeo. I feel that it is my earnest duty to present the facts before the wildlife fraternity. A separate chapter, 'Debatable Issues', has been dedicated to this discussion. The object of writing this book is to share my field observations and intimate experiences, which have been full of challenges and excitement, with people, in general and wildlifers, researchers and foresters, in particular. The intent is to add something new to the existing valuable literature on Keoladeo. As a veteran wildlife manager, I am hopeful that it will be useful for those foresters who are rendering invaluable service in nature reserves, especially bird sanctuaries. I will be more than happy if they find some motivation in my efforts of bringing a new lease of life to this birds' paradise.

Part I

Nature's Playground

Entrance gate to the Keoladeo National Park

OVERVIEW

Maharaja Suraj Mal (1707–63) or Sujan Singh, ruler of Bharatpur, known for his intellect and vision

The Keoladeo National Park (KNP), popularly known as the Keoladeo Ghana Bird Sanctuary, Bharatpur, located at 27°7′6″– 27°12′2″N and 77°29′5″– 77°33′9″E, with an area of about 29 sq km, is a world-famous water bird park. It supports about 380 flowering plants and over 388 bird species, including 42 species of raptors. Out of these, several are migratory, which visit this park every winter from the Palearctic region. The park is located in the south of the Bharatpur township on National Highway 11, 56 km from Agra, 180 km from Jaipur and 190 km south of Delhi. The main Delhi–Sawai Madhopur (Ranthambore Tiger Reserve)–Mumbai rail route passes through the Bharatpur township.

Major vegetation at the Keoladeo National Park

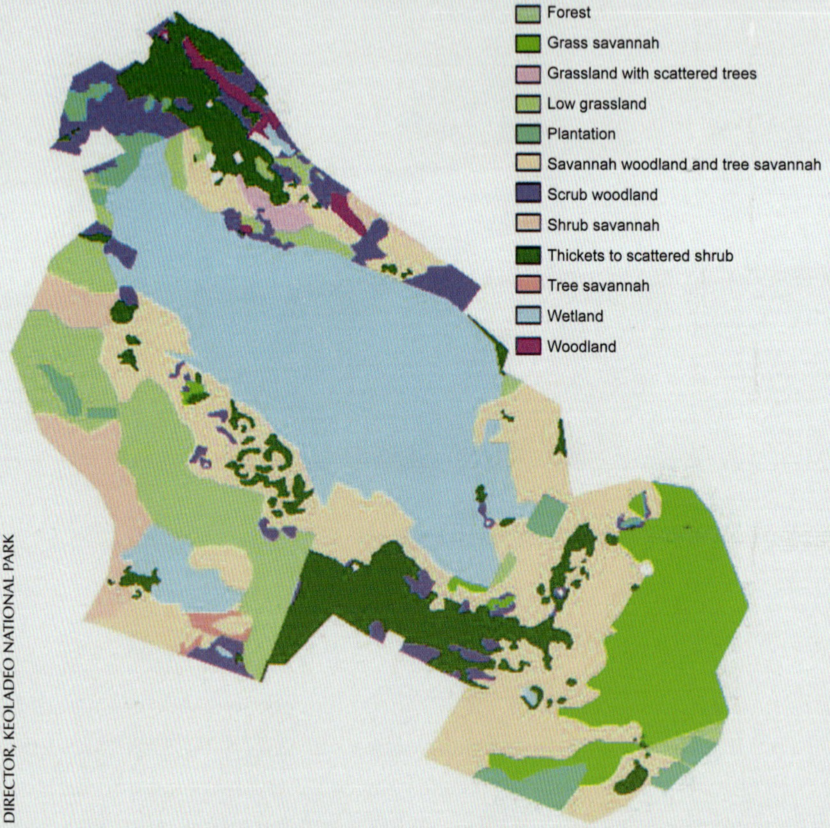

DIRECTOR, KEOLADEO NATIONAL PARK

Shaped like a saucer, with about one-third of its area lying in the centre, the Keoladeo National Park converts into rich marshes or lakes when filled with fresh rainwater during the monsoon season. These wetlands produce a huge biomass of aquatic vegetation, which supports innumerable micro-macro fauna. The southern flank of the park has unique grassland stretched across over 5 sq km. It may be classified as forest, woodland, scrub woodland, savannah woodland, tree savannah, shrub savannah, low grassland with scattered trees and shrubs, plantations and wetlands.

This delightful mosaic of habitats attracts and supports 27 species of mammals, 13 reptiles, seven amphibians, 58 fish, 75 butterflies, over 30 dragonflies and more than 30 species of spiders. An occasional presence of large cats in Keoladeo is on record; the Maharaja of Bharatpur even shot a leopard here in 1965. A tigress strayed into the park at the advent of this century and stayed for five years, till her last breath. Half-a-decade later, a male tiger walked in here as well, but was soon shifted to Sariska.

The Jatoli-Bhainsamori track, which is full of matured kadam trees

Nevertheless, primarily, Keoladeo is a bird sanctuary and certainly a unique one. More than 200 research publications on this park make it a paradise for avian biologists.

The park is a part of the Yamuna floodplains/depressions of Bharatpur, which geologically are believed to be the result of the clash between the Gondwana and Northern plates. An in-depth study of the soil profile has revealed the presence of river gravel and clay in several layers; this confirms the presence of river and standing waters (marsh) in the area in prehistoric times, when it was navigable. Satellite imageries also attest that this entire depression, stretched over huge areas, was underwater till the Yamuna river changed its course. A village named Malah or Mallah, situated on the northwestern border of the park, establishes the habitation of a boatman community in that time, as *mallah* means boatman in the local dialect. The existence of artesian wells in Malah and Ghasola villages further strengthens the theory that advocates the presence of a river flowing from the northwestern to eastern direction, across the present Keoladeo National Park area, in prehistoric times. This entire area is also called 'Matsya Pradesh', which means a Province of Fish.

Flamingos and spoonbills feeding together in the marshes

It is believed that Lord Krishna, an incarnation of the Hindu deity Vishnu, was born in Mathura and passed his childhood in the adjoining village of Vrindavan. Presently, the Yamuna river flows by these habitations. In the Indian mythological stories there is a vivid description of kadam (*Anthocephalus cadamba*) groves in the Yamuna floodplains, where Lord Krishna used to play. These sacred groves persist even today in certain patches in the park, close to the Jatauli and Ghasola areas. Silviculturally, kadam is regarded as a climax species (a riverine succession stage). Therefore, on one hand, these groves indicate the presence of some river system here and, on the other, their Krishna connection adds considerable value to the park.

During archaeological excavations, shards of 3,000-year-old ochre-coloured pottery have been found in Malah, Rampur, Aghapur and Darapur villages, all situated on the northwestern to southern boundary of the park. Weapons comprising swords, long spears and large harpoons made of copper, dating back to 1000 BC, the Copper Age in the Indian subcontinent, have been

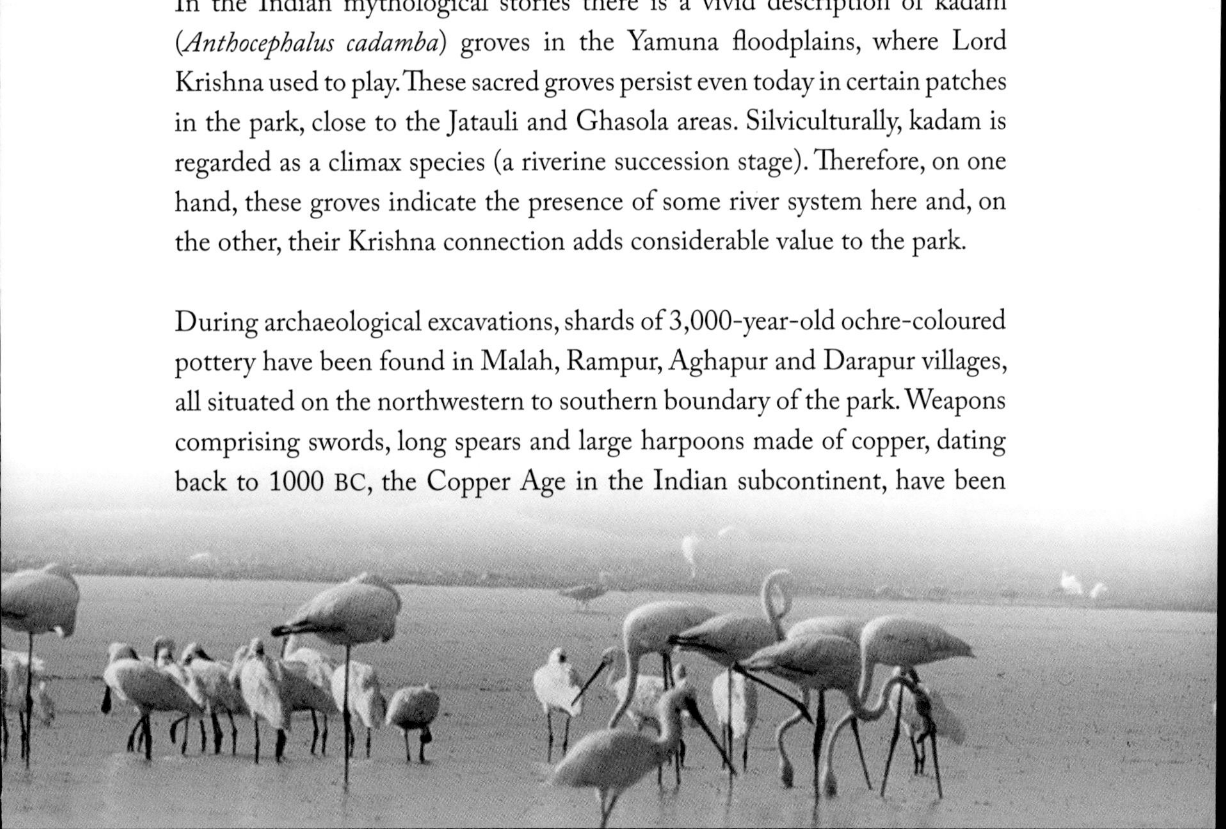

NAVIN SHARMA

found in the vicinity of the park. Figurines of elephants and seals with several incisions, recovered from these sites, indicate the presence of huge marine creatures and other large mammals, even elephants and rhinos.

The marshes at the Keoladeo National Park are a product of these geographical as well as biological events.

Post-monsoon salt production in the dried shallow depressions was the main source of economy of the people of this area. This continued till 1930 when the British forced a ban on salt production. Till date almost the entire Bharatpur suffers from salinity of water. Defaced buildings due to heavy salt deposits on the outer walls are a common sight in the town. Here, during the monsoon, floods were almost a regular annual feature. Therefore, in the mid-eighteenth century, Maharaja Suraj Mal, one of the most powerful Jat rulers in the country, created the huge Ajan Dam, close to the present park boundary, to save the town and adjoining villages. Who could have imagined that this would, one day, give birth to this splendid park?

In local dialect, *ghana* means dense. The name Ghana Keoladeo suggests that this part of the floodplains must have borne dense forests. Centuries ago these forests

Bluebull feeding on aquatic vegetation in the lakes

Majestic Siberian cranes. **Facing page:** *Remnants of the heritage building 'Kadam Kunj', camouflaged by huge kadam trees with a moat all around it. A favourite camping site of the then Maharaja of Bharatpur*

were connected to the open scrubs of Kanua, a place situated close to the park, where, in 1527, Babur defeated the mighty Rajput king Rana Sanga of Mewar in a historic war and established the Mughal empire in India. Later, a Jat kingdom was established in Bharatpur, which prospered under the leadership of the brave king Suraj Mal who fortified the city by raising a massive earthen wall all around it. He captured Delhi by inflicting a crushing defeat on the Mughal emperor and expanded his empire to include Agra, Dholpur, Mainpuri, Hathras, Aligarh, Etah, Meerut, Rohtak, Farooqnagar, Mewat, Rewari, Gurgaon and Mathura.

In 1825, the British won the impregnable Lohagarh (iron) fort of Bharatpur. It was only after this victory that they took over the entire Rajputana. They did not, however, remove the royals from the throne but for all practical purposes held the reigns in their hands. Delhi and Agra were important cantonments of the British forces. Therefore, taking advantage of the forests and huge grassland of these floodplains, spread on the lower side of the Ajan Dam, in 1850, the Maharaja of Bharatpur reserved a large area of the Ghana forests as a deer hunting site to facilitate British officers and the royals. Close to the end of the nineteenth century, during the reign of the minor king Ratan Singh, the British appointed Prince Harbhanji of Morvi (Gujarat) as regent to look after the state affairs of Bharatpur. During this period (1896), the Ghana/Jatoli Canal was dug to take in surplus water from the Ajan Dam and store it in the depressions of Ghana, located between the Ajan Dam and Jatoli and Ghasola villages. The dam

water brought a lot of fish, micro/macro flora and fauna along with it, which started attracting a variety of water birds, especially ducks and geese. The Ghana saucer, spread over almost 29 sq km has about 1.5 m high edges towards its western side and about 1 m on its eastern side (Ghasola village). Its central part (Sapan Mori area), with a depth of approximately 2 m, is the deepest part of these marshes. To cater to the feeding requirements of the diverse water fowl, Prince Harbhanji paid due attention towards regulating the water levels. He divided this huge depression area into several lakes by erecting a number of earthen bunds. These bunds also worked as fair weather roads/tracks that helped the management personnel as well as the hunting parties in reaching inaccessible areas during the duck shoots. The regulation of the water level through the creation of several additional sluice gates augmented the number of resident as well as migratory birds.

For ages, the floodplains of the Bharatpur district were being used by water birds, especially several species of ducks, during winter for migration from Central Asian regions. In fact, Bharatpur falls in their migration route. Many of these birds use it as a 'staging ground'. They congregate here to disperse

Pelicans feeding in the lake while the late breeders are still on the nests

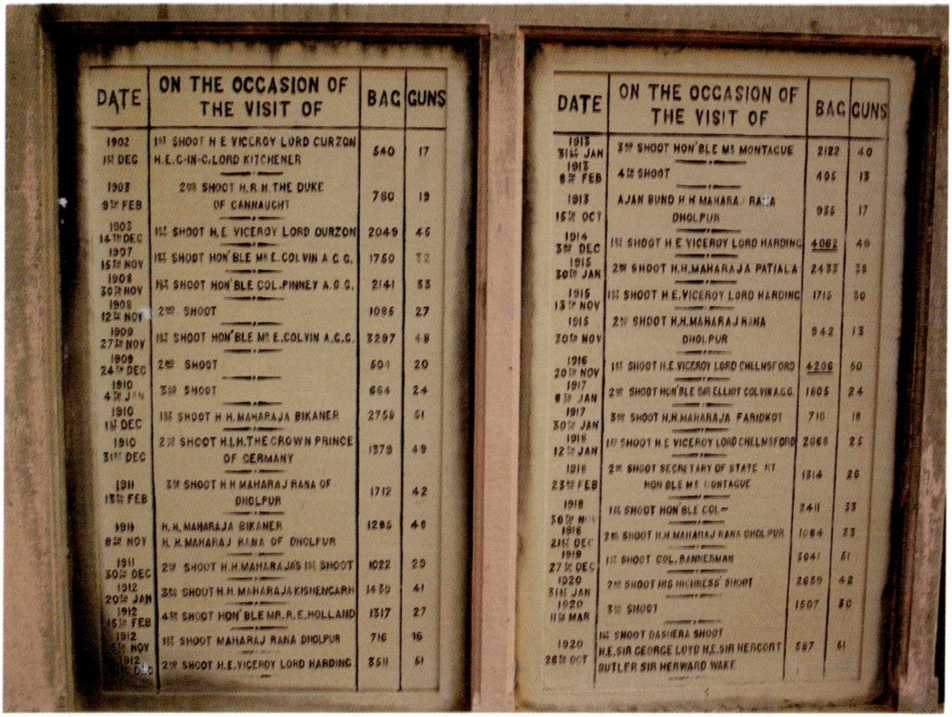

Duck shooting record engraved on sandstone slabs at the Keoladeo complex

further to the south, towards the central and eastern regions in the Indian subcontinent. On return migration, they again congregate here before flying back to their homeland. These managerial interventions worked as a magnet to attract the water birds from all around to the lakes, which soon became a haven for migratory birds.

Bird shoot had always been a preferred sport of the British. In 1902, the first formal duck shoot was organised here for the Viceroy, Lord Curzon. He appointed a qualified English forest officer to prepare a management plan for this duck shooting site. Several additional dykes and bunds were created

PANDIT NATTHAL LAL SHARMA

The Maharaja of Bharatpur with guests after a duck shoot in the park

here. The huge Ajan Dam was thoroughly repaired; the Chiksana Canal was built to the southeast of Ghana to irrigate the adjacent agricultural fields with dam water. This canal, which passes through the Koladahar area, served as a drain to carry the excess water of the dam and the adjacent agricultural fields during the monsoon. Harbhanji also developed a system to utilise this waste water to fill the huge grassland tract of the Koladahar area. Consequently, a lot of water birds who were feeding in the shallow waters developed a special preference for the low-lying patches of the grassland. This motivated the Maharaja to construct a small masonry camping outfit during duck shoots, called Kadam Kunj, for himself and his close friends. Remnants of this small building are visible even today. It is surrounded by a moat for providing safety against wild animals and sudden attack by enemies.

In 1910, a wildlife wing was set up by the state under its *bagar* (forest) department and an impressive gate was built at the entrance of this duck shoot reserve. It can still be seen on the main Agra-Jaipur highway. In 1930–35, *Acacia nilotica* (babool) trees were planted on these dykes and earthen mounds inside the lakes to provide camouflaged shelter to the shooters and perching places to birds. This later gave birth to the famous heronries.

A Lord Shiva temple, named Keoladeo, is situated in the heart of the park. Keoladeo means the only lord, that is, Shiva. The park got its name from this ancient temple. Had it not been for the British overlords, the Jat rulers would never have allowed anyone to shoot birds so close to this place of worship. The birds' shooting record has been engraved on stone slabs close to this temple. Time is the greatest game-changer. With the advent of Independence and the disappearance of the British from Indian soil, things started changing. A new phase of these marshes emerged. The Ghana marshes, earlier known as duck shoot reserves, became famous internationally for not only their huge congregations of migratory waterfowl but also for the spectacular heronries of piscivorous birds.

The Keoladeo temple, from which the park gets its name

Obviously, all this was not achieved in a day. There were dedicated people and it was their incessant persuasion that converted this bird slaughtering sports stadium into a sanctum sanctorum for innumerable winged creatures, mammals, reptiles and insects. Their crusade started right after 1947. Officers such as the late Kailash Sankhala, who was in charge of the Ghana reserve, tried hard to seek protection for this invaluable nature heritage through an appropriate legal instrument. He was supported by Dharam Kumar Singh, a well-known conservationist and Dr Salim Ali, in getting Pandit Jawahar Lal Nehru, the then Prime Minister of India, to declare the Ghana reserve as the Ghana-Keoladeo Bird Sanctuary in 1956. As a result, a ban on any kind of hunting, trapping of birds and animals became effective here. The Maharaja of Bharatpur, however, continued to enjoy the special privilege of duck shoots along with his royal guests, which got extinguished in 1971 when the privy purses of Indian kings were withdrawn by the Government of India. To regulate grazing and to protect the sanctuary from encroachments, a masonry wall was constructed all around it in 1977–80. In 1981, the persistent efforts of Sankhala and Dr Ali led to the sanctuary being named the Keoladeo National Park. A year later, buffalo grazing was closed in the park. In 1985, Keoladeo was declared as the prestigious 'Ramsar Site' and, in the same year itself, the United Nations Educational, Scientific and Cultural Organisation (UNESCO) unanimously declared it a 'World Heritage Site'.

On an average, the Bharatpur subtropical region receives about 662 mm of rain during the three months of the monsoon, that is, from mid-June to mid-September. More than 375 species of angiosperms enrich this small park. The woodland is mostly dominated by kadam, babool and ber trees. Jamun is conspicuous but confined to a few patches on the water fringes. From a management point of view, the entire park is divided into 15 blocks, coded from A to O. The widespread grasslands of Keoladeo, mainly located in the southeastern part (Koladahar), are prone to fires during summer. The Bharatpur wetlands have been of immense importance for ornithologists, being the only wintering home of the Siberian crane in the entire Indian subcontinent. Unfortunately, after 2002, the Siberian crane has not migrated to Keoladeo. Shortage of water in the park and poaching on their migration route seem responsible for their disappearance. A serious effort was made, from 1992 to 1998, to introduce captive Siberian crane here, hoping for their adoption by the wild stock but, unfortunately, this failed.

The construction of dams over the Banganga and Gambhiri rivers has severely affected the water supply to the park from the Ajan Dam, causing serious ecological changes in the last three decades. Consequently, the entire park got engulfed by trees and shrubs of the fast-growing weed tree, *Prosopis juliflora*. Three new water resources were developed between 2007–12 on a war footing and, from 2007 to 2008, a mammoth operation was carried out by the park management with the involvement of the people to get it freed from the menace of *Prosopis juliflora*.

Though these efforts have helped, the danger is not yet over. It is a highly fragile ecosystem; therefore, the park authorities have to keep a strict vigil on getting the required share of water regularly from newly-developed sources as well as the conventional source (Ajan Dam). Alas, if only our politicians could be more sensitive towards nature conservation. I strongly believe that we all need to come together to support this World Heritage Site and make sure that nature's kingdom, this delightful home to an incredible variety of birds, is maintained in its full glory.

NAVIN SHARMA

DYNAMIC WETLANDS

Compared to woodland and other natural habitats, wetlands produce biological matter and forms in greater varieties and larger numbers. The shallow lakes of Keoladeo receive a lot of nutrients through outer water sources and are hence exceptionally fertile. The woody and non-woody parts of the vegetation that grow here add rich nutrients to the water body and soil through their decomposition. This gives birth to new lives. Many of the organisms pass their entire lifecycle in and around these marshes.

Peculiarly, Keoladeo has temporary swamps. Periodic flooding and drying has been going on here since the origin of these depressions and is an integral part of its ecology. Almost on a regular basis, with a gap of a year or so, the catchment areas of the Bharatpur floodplains face drought and, consequently, the Keoladeo lakes dry up. During good monsoon years, the Ajan Dam

The shallow lakes of Keoladeo are rich in nutrients and attract all kinds of birds

supplies enough water to fulfil the optimum requirement (550 mcft) of the park. With this much water, most of the park area, except the high saline areas or bluffs, gets inundated, but water from higher areas recedes fast and it finally gets confined to centrally located deeper areas, shrinking up to around 8.5 sq km. After winter, with the rise in temperature, water evaporation increases. Gradually, the rising temperature soars up to 46 to 49 degrees Centigrade by May–June every year.

The periodic droughts and seasonal drying during summers convert the lakes into dry beds with broken soil. The aquatic biomass disappears altogether. Heavy casualty takes place among small animals especially fish, amphibians and reptiles such as turtles. Except for the summer nesters, most of the birds disperse to the neighbouring areas for their survival. Eagles and Egyptian vultures feeding on the upturned turtles become a common sight in the dried marshes. Reptiles such as lizards and snakes, especially pythons, take shelter under bushes and trees. Pythons also

Vegetation bursts into life during a season of good rainfall.
Facing page: *Turtles trapped in the cracked earth of a dried lake in Block B while moving in search of water. These were rescued and released by the author in the deeper water body of Mansarovar, near the Keoladeo temple, in early July 2008*

aestivate in burrows during the sun scorching day hours. In the process, organic material gets converted into inorganic elements to further enrich the lakes with fresh nutrients, which give birth to new organisms during the monsoon. Thus, the periodic drying prepares the lakes to produce aquatic vegetation in the coming monsoon, by saving these against eutrophication, stagnation of piles of rotting vegetation and silt.

NAVIN SHARMA

ANSAR KHAN

A frustrated Sarus attacking a lapwing (left) and Sarus cranes holding a conference-cum-feast in the rich lakes

The season of the rains is crucial for Keoladeo. Generally, during the second week of June onwards, clouds emerge in the sky. The pre-monsoon showers of June instil hope among the inhabitants—humans and wild animals alike. The dried lake beds get charged and spring back to life. The animals and plants that had managed to survive through the harsh summer burst out and multiply at a fast pace, thus exhibiting their survival instinct. Overnight, several thousand insects emerge from the dried lake beds and stagnant water pools. Nature produces micro and macro organisms in infinity to support the primary and secondary consumers.

Sadly, each year does not bring a good monsoon to this belt. But when the Rain God is merciful, in addition to Karauli hills, the floodplains of the

Bharatpur region also bring a lot of water to feed the Ajan Dam to its full capacity. Keoladeo then receives sufficient water to feed about 65 million fry and an enormous quantity of algae, fungi, zooplankton and phytoplankton. Vegetation bursts into life through the germination of the dormant seeds and sprouting of the plants, which had survived the drought. The zooplankton and phytoplankton feed the lower animals, fish feed higher forms of birds and animals and, in turn, these are consumed by the predators, mostly raptors, including vultures and reptiles such as pythons. The beauty of the system is such that the lakes overflow with desired vegetation to support a huge number of consumers. These marshes, in the true sense, act as supermarkets by producing and supporting such a huge quantum and variety of plants and animals. The fish find enough food in the form of aquatic vegetation and micro fauna. The water, teaming with fish, stimulates the piscivorous birds to mate and breed. Thus the world-famous heronries are formed here.

By August–September, the entire scenario changes. A new sheen on leaves appears everywhere! The lakes with shallow water depths get stocked with grasses and sedges. The babool trees are festooned with bright yellow inflorescence. The water hyacinth, though an undesired water weed, adds great beauty to the landscape through its dark green leaves and maroon-white tiny flowers.

With the progressing monsoon and water intake, several aquatic and non-aquatic herbs, shrubs and trees start flowering throughout the park, which changes the landscape altogether. The real charm, however, surfaces by the end of September when numerous beautiful lilies fill the lakes. The white lily flowers of *Nymphaea pubescens*, erected on hollow cylindrical stems, appear in huge colonies. Their attractive creamy white petals open only after sunset.

Wetland Plants

The entire flowering community of 96 wetland plants growing in these lakes can be classified into six categories: Free Floating (5 species), Rooted with Floating Leaves (5 species), Free Submerged (4 species), Rooted Submerged (7 species), Emergent–Amphibious (18 species) and Marsh Land (57 species). Out of these, the major species in the aquatic blocks are *Algae, Cyperus alopecuroides, Cyperus bulbous/rotundus, Cynodon dacttylon, Eichornia crassipus, Hydrilla verticillata, Ipomea aquatic, Nymphaea nouchali/stellata, Nymphoides cristata, Nymphoides indica, Panicum paludosum, Paspalidium punctatum, Paspalum distichum, Scirpus littoralis, Scirpus tuberosus, Sporobolus helvolus* and *Typha angustata*.

Among the emergent vegetation, grass such as *Pseudoraphis spinescens, Paspalidium punctatum, Panicum paludosum* and *Paspalum distichum* grow rather fast during the monsoon with the intake of water into the lakes, lest they get inundated. Their lush green leaves emerging out of the water level create a wet prairie almost throughout the wetland. A large number of ducks feed on the leaves and seeds of this grass.

Sedges such as *Cyperus littoralis, Scirpus tuberosus* and *Cyperus rotundus* that grow on the water edges also attract several ducks and cranes, especially the most important winter visitors, the Siberian cranes, which are fond of their tubers and rhizomes. Species such as *Hydrilla, Najas, Potamogeton indicus, Potamogeton crispus, Vallisneria* and *Ceratophyllum* are among the main submerged plants that feed a huge number of ducks.

and close by 9am or 10am to avoid the heat. Flowers that have not been fertilised with the help of the insects acting as their pollinating agents open in the night to close back the following morning. This process keeps going on till the end of October.

ANSAR KHAN

Top: *Water lily (*Nymphaea nouchali*) blooms only at night.* **Below:** Azolla, Spirodela polyrhiza *and* Wolfia arrhiza *are important duck weeds. These unanchored free-floating tiny plants keep drifting in the lakes, propelled by the winds*

The community feeding of thousands of piscivorous birds is ample proof of the richness of the Keoladeo marshes

Another lily species, *Nymphaea stellata*, with shorter stalks and smaller flowers of a dull blue shade, also blooms in the lakes. Somewhat bolder, it blooms all day long and bears the sun throughout the monsoon; it also disappears after October. *Nymphoides indicum* dangles freely in the lake as it leaves the soil within a few days of its germination. They float on the water with the help of their beautiful round and broad green leaves. These beautiful white flowers are borne by stalks emerging out of the water from rhizomes. Several plants, webbed and interlaced, produce a mat-like formation on the water surface and form an independent colony that floats freely. This also facilitates these plants to travel towards the desired water depth in search of nourishment. Their rapid movement during windy days produces a magical effect. The legendary forester, Kailash Sankhala, bestowed the title of Gardens of God to Keoladeo because of these lilies.

Nymphoides cristata is the fourth lily and the only one that blooms during summer. It is also a free-floating plant. These white flowers provide immeasurable relaxation to burning eyes during visits to the dry prairies in the intolerably hot summer months. The best specimens can be seen in small ponds close to the Kadam Kunj area.

In this unique aquatic system of Keoladeo, various floral species have different roles in fulfilling the specific food requirements of different faunal species. The reed formed by colonies of *Typha* plays the most important part in completing the eco cycle by providing ample food to primary consumers such as insects, fish and several species of birds. The submerged leaves and stems act as food stores for various fish species. Mosquitoes and several other insects feeding on its leaves, shoots and woody stems breed here to multiply in enormous numbers. The secondary consumer insects such as dragonflies and mantids may be seen flitting around in search of these mosquitoes and other insects. Several species of spiders also prefer to lay traps to catch flying insects. These reeds, full of mosquito larvae, are the preferred feeding grounds of frogs as well. They also provide an excellent roosting habitat for the beautiful purple moorhen, popularly known as lipstick bird for its red beak, as well as for the rosy pastor, wagtail, Spanish sparrow and many other birds. Though powerful raptors such as the ringtail fishing eagle use these reeds as perch, still bittern, purple heron, streaked baya and finch prefer to breed here. Kingfishers may also be seen hunting from these perches.

I carry vivid memories of the moment when I toppled from my seat into the lake while capturing photographic evidence of the nesting activities of a streaked baya in a typha reed, close to the Barso borewell. The best specimen of typha reed can be seen between the Shanti Kutir and Rambandh waters.

Oryza rufipogon and *Oriza sativa* are two wild rice species that are found growing in the lakes along with other emergent grasses. The green leaves of

NAVIN SHARMA

A tranquil moment at the park when spotted deer and cranes look for sustenance, undisturbed

these are eaten by several insects and birds; their raw seeds are consumed by ducks and the ripe seeds that fall into the water are eaten by fish along with other submerged vegetation. These aquatic plants cause a huge biomass in the lakes of which a major portion is consumed by not only birds, insects and fish but also by large animals such as the blue bulls, feral cows and sambars. Still, a sizable quantum of this biomass remains unutilised and keeps drying gradually after October and is almost totally killed during the pinch period of May–June. The plant biomass gets trampled under the hoofs of these animals and gets blown off with dust storms. The lakes are then ready to receive a fresh intake of water to grow fresh vegetation. Thus, this fascinating cycle of nature keeps revolving year after year to feed the ultimate survivors, the larger forms of life.

BEWITCHING HERONRIES

Keoladeo is famous for its spectacular breeding colonies of piscivorous birds. Fifteen species of water birds such as egrets, herons, storks, cormorants, darter, spoonbill and ibis nest here on the waterlogged babool trees to form breeding colonies called heronries. Several thousands of nests are made by them across the entire park. Though these nesting sites are more or less fixed, which they choose for nesting every year, the number of nests may

A grey heron holding a prize for its hard labour

NAVIN SHARMA

differ on particular sites in successive years. This variation is chiefly due to the shift in availability of water to the park, which, in turn, impacts the availability of food for the birds.

These 15 species have different methods of feeding, mainly due to their body structure; therefore, they have preferences for different water depths. The park management has excelled in water management, especially in maintaining several water depths to cater to the feeding requirements of the various bird species. The smaller birds prefer shallow waters whereas others, gifted with long legs, may feed in deeper waters of up to one foot or so. Large egrets, spoonbills and storks, especially painted storks, are happier catching fish from water bodies deeper than a foot. These heronry breeders are categorised into two groups, according to their feeding habits. Cormorants and darters are swimmers while others are waders, which either stand or walk in the water for feeding. The pond heron generally uses perches to catch its feed from deep as well as shallow waters.

Waterlogged trees, especially with spiny creepers wrapped all around them, attract these breeders for they provide them with security against terrestrial predators. Most of these species make their nests in mixed colonies. Small birds such as cormorants and little egrets feel safe in the company of mighty storks and spoonbills. The large birds also have a preference for this kind of combination because one tree cannot bear the burden of many large birds, resulting in a lesser number of nests, which means a lesser number of fighters against the predators. The babool trees not only provide nesting places but their green mini branches, full of elasticity, are also used as nest building material by almost all these piscivorous birds, irrespective of their kind and size. The Keoladeo swamps provide an ideal condition for babool trees to

NAVIN SHARMA

Painted stork adults organise fishing classes for their young ones

grow, especially on dykes, bunds and mounds, waterlogged or standing on the banks of the lakes. Tolerance against water and salinity is an important characteristic of this hardy plant and that is probably why it is flourishing in every part of the reserve.

NAVIN SHARMA

The availability of 58 species of fish in huge quantity is the chief attraction for these breeding birds. The smaller birds need fish fry or fingerlings but the storks and spoonbills or darters and cormorants look for large-sized fish. It is estimated that in good monsoon years, breeding birds make about 10,000 to 15,000 nests in the park. A study conducted by BNHS in 1988 reveals that over 460 tonnes of fish were consumed by the nestlings and adults of the 13 colonial breeders (openbill stork and cattle egret do not consume fish) in the breeding season alone. The Keoladeo lakes are capable of providing a fair share of this enormous quantity. Of course, the balance requirement is met by feeding in the adjacent areas of the park.

The **openbill stork** is the first nester of these colonies. It eats mollusks, water insects and worms picked from muddy puddles and shallow waters with sparse vegetation. For this purpose, nature has gifted it with a special beak that has a slit. Initially, it forms pure colonies, but is later joined by other species. This stork contributes to about nine per cent of the nests in the heronries and ranks fourth highest among the colony breeders here. The **painted stork** is undoubtedly the most beautiful nesting bird of Keoladeo. Nature has decorated it with amazing colours; during the breeding period, its feathers acquire rich, bright shades. It is a profuse breeder and ranks second, with a contribution of about 20 per cent nests of the total colony count. Its style of courtship is unique. The male first occupies a chosen place for nesting on a tree. When a female approaches, he offers her a long, soft tree stick to be used for nest building. Only if the gift is accepted, does she join the male and their declaration of pairing is done by the clattering

There are huge quantities of fishes found in the park, which attract breeding birds such as the oriental darter

An openbill stork bringing nesting material

of huge beaks by both. Parent painted storks are very caring towards their pure white woolly chicks, whom they provide shade against the burning sun by spreading their wings in a kaleidoscopic manner.

The **blacknecked stork**, though not a colony breeder, is a highly picturesque bird. It is rather huge, measuring about four feet in height and has an enormous black bill, coral red legs, a glistening blue-black head and neck, white underparts and pied (black-and-white) wings. The sexes are alike except for the conspicuous yellow eyes of the female. It is usually seen as a solitary bird wading in shallow waters. This stork has a preference for fish but also eats frogs, reptiles, crabs and so on. It always lives in a pair. In the park, it breeds in September–October on high kadam, babool or peepal trees and lays three to five eggs. Four to five pairs of this majestic bird used to breed in Keoladeo almost every year but the water crisis has discouraged them from breeding here. Hopefully, with the resumption in water supply, they may resume their breeding.

Four out of the 13 species of egrets found in India breed in Keoladeo. Large, intermediate and small egrets occupy their berths on the trees along with little and intermediate cormorants (shags). Grey heron and white ibis also join them. They are then joined by larger birds such as spoonbills and painted storks. The **little egret** is more or less a milky white bird with black legs and beak. During breeding period its feet become yellow. The male and female lure each other by bowing with erected plumes. It lays two sea-green eggs. According to the annual nest count done by the park management, this highest breeder among egrets ranks fifth among colony breeders by contributing about eight per cent of the total nests of the colony. The **intermediate egret** male has a darker orange-red colour in its eyes as compared to the female. The couples change nest duties with a display of beautiful plumes. It breeds two to three times in a season to recover the loss of its spoiled nests. It forms five per cent of the nests of the colony to become the seventh largest breeder here. The **large egret**, with its long, supple neck and spear-like yellow beak, is truly an attractive bird, especially with its long breeding plumes. During their courtship, the male and female greet each other by touching bills, bending back and occasionally coming forward to entwine necks. The sight of the male stretching its neck while rising on its tarsal joints and grabbing a tree branch compels you to keep gazing at their activities for hours. Sankhala has mentioned that till 1992, that is prior to the ban imposed on grazing, these birds never made more than 100 nests here but the number increased substantially afterwards. With the reduction in water supply, the number dwindled but, in 2016, with enough water in the park, it made 210 nests.

The **cattle egret** is quite different from the other egrets in its feeding and nesting habits as it is basically a terrestrial bird, whereas the others are water birds. It feeds mainly on grasshoppers, bluebottle flies, insects and so on. This egret occupies the inner portions of the lower branches of trees but is very much a breeding colony bird. From 1991 to 2010, on an average, it made 76 nests but, from 2011 to 2016, the number was substantially higher—912 per year, almost a twelvefold increase. In 2016, cattle egrets made 1,662 nests, which make them the sixth highest among all the heronry breeders in the park. The growing human and traffic disturbance due to urbanisation outside

has compelled the birds to breed here in the safety of the park; this change needs to be studied minutely.

Three species of cormorants, locally known as pan kauvas, also share their breeding colonies. On the basis of their size they have been named as little, intermediate and large cormorants. These are jet black swimming birds that prefer open water, with floating vegetation, trees and mounds. They are all pure fish-eaters and may be called fishing machines. The **large cormorant** is the size of a small duck. Its tree-borne colony looks like a huge vibrating machine as several throats flap together on individual nests. From the nesting point of view, this species occupies the third place from the bottom in the list of the heronry breeders, with a contribution of just 1.6 per cent nests to the colony here. The **intermediate or medium cormorant**, also known as Indian shag, with 31 per cent contribution, occupies the first place among the colony breeders. **Little cormorant** chicks soon learn to cry for food and insert their beaks into the gullets of their parents lest the other siblings snatch it. With 12 per cent contribution, it ranks third from top among the colony breeders.

A purple heron (above) in search of food. **Facing page:** *Painted storks in a conference prior to occupying trees for nesting*

The cormorants are excellent swimmers and divers; they use the technique of fishing together by herding the fish into one corner and then catching them en masse. Egrets, though waders, join them to take advantage of the situation. This scene of community hunting in the early hours of the morning is absolutely fascinating and avid nature photographers can often be found capturing this live drama that takes place in the park.

The **oriental darter** is another fascinating bird of these breeding colonies. It is popularly known as the snake bird because of its huge slender snake-like neck and spear-like strong beak. Its chicks are born snow white, but they gradually change colour. The bird is an excellent swimmer and diver, like a submarine. A voracious fish-eater, it prefers catching fish by piercing through it with its beak; it is indeed an incredible sight when it happens to catch a fish horizontally in its beak. For swallowing, it throws the fish overhead and then catches it back in its beak. The large fish are thrashed on hard surfaces to get them to a proper size to swallow. It is most picturesque in its nest, with three or four white chicks, fighting with each other for food and thrusting beaks deep into the long neck of their parents to reach their gullets for food. No visitor to the park can miss the presence of this bird, which may be seen either providing shade to its chicks in the nest by spreading its huge wings or drying their wings after diving into the water. This charming bird makes 2.2 per cent of the nests in the park, ranking tenth among the heronry breeders.

Facing page: *Cattle egrets getting to know each other in this paradise of birds and (below) intermediate egrets displaying their attractive breeding plumage*

NAVIN SHARMA

Herons are other beautiful birds that add colour to the mesmerising swamps of Keoladeo. Three out of the four herons found in India are colony breeders. The **grey heron** male first occupies the nesting site and then calls for its mates in a short but sharp note. The female, on reaching the site, rattles its beak with the male and they flap their huge grey wings together and also preen each other. They then settle down to mate. This bird lays two to three sea-blue eggs, which are hatched with utmost care by both parents. The **night heron** is a pretty but shy bird. The grove of trees standing on the bund of the deeper water body near the Keoladeo temple in Block D is the best place for its sighting. Pairing is done only after the male offers a nesting twig to the female; it is generally nocturnal.

The **purple heron** possesses a long slender neck with rufus colour on the dorsal side; fish comprises 70 per cent of its diet. Since it also breeds in

Eurasian spoonbill on a nest, protecting its young ones from the scorching sun.
Facing page: *Purple herons, cormorants, egrets and painted storks share the same trees for breeding without any reservations*

Typha angustata reeds, people tend to believe that it is not a colony nester; but I have personally checked its nests in the trees a number of times. It contributes merely about 0.3 per cent to occupy last place whereas the grey heron occupies the second lowest (one per cent) and the night heron the eighth place with a contribution of three per cent nests to the heronry. Unlike other piscivorous birds, the grey and purple herons habitually breed in March as well. In March 1986, I found their post-winter heronries in the Mansarovar lake, near Keoladeo. But the nests, with eggs and hatchlings, were predated upon by the ring-tailed fishing eagle, spotted eagle, booted eagle and marsh harrier. Even adults were injured or killed.

The **spoonbill** is another beautiful huge bird in this heronry, with its black legs and broad yellow tip on a flattened spoon-like black bill. Being a late breeder, it is compelled to make nests as a single species on trees or jal and faras (*Tamarix aphylla*) shrubs in waterlogged areas. Flocks fly in a V-formation or in diagonal single lines. Their young ones seem to be always crying for food and they impatiently thrust their bills into their parents' gullets to take out fish. The **white ibis** is a large white bird with a strikingly naked black head and neck and a long, stout, curlew-like black beak. It is a close relative of the sacred Egyptian ibis. For breeding, it prefers pure colonies and lays about three to four eggs. On an average, it has contributed about three per cent nests to the heronry here so far, thus securing the ninth position.

After the chicks of these colony breeders are born, the jungle resounds with the cacophony of the young ones, crying hard to get their parents to give them food. They are given regurgitated food for quick digestion. The chicks take about two months to fly with their parents and then are taught to feed themselves from the lakes. These classes are spectacular.

It appears that the female grey heron has agreed to mate with the male.
Facing page: *A jet black oriental darter couple on a nest with their snow white chicks*

NAVIN SHARMA

DAULAT SINGH

The habitat and availability of food required for successful breeding wholly depends on the timely intake of water in optimum quantity. This is evident from the fact that till the seventies the nest count in the heronries used to be 10,000–15,000 per year but, with the reduction in water supply, it fell down. From 1991 to 1998, with an average water intake of 433 million cubic feet (mcft) per year, the number of the nests got reduced to an average of 5,800 per year. Again, with further deterioration in the water supply from 2000 to 2010, the average nest count fell to as low as 733 per year. But afterwards, with an added supply from other sources, the water intake rose to 424 mcft per year and the nest count to 4,543 per year. In 2016, Keoladeo received a huge amount of water (630 mcft) and, as a result, the heronries got adorned with 20,778 nests, which is the highest ever in its history.

I have enjoyed this nature's paradise for many years but every monsoon is special for me when the temptation of saying 'hello' to these peace ambassadors becomes irresistible. For this is when they gather in their brightest feather coats, wings, bills and legs to lure their partners.

NAVIN SHARMA

The spot-bill duck is easily recognisable because of the vibrant colours of its beak

Resident Ducks, Rails and Jacanas

Four species of ducks and two of rails breed in and around the park. Of these, the **spot-bill duck** is the most versatile. Though it is also called grey duck because of its grey-brown colour, it is more popular for the bright red, black and yellow colours of its beak, which make it look highly ornamental and distinguished. Summer and autumn are the seasons when it breeds in Keoladeo. Its nests are made on water edges, in grassy patches or mounds. For feeding, it prefers open water with submerged, sparse vegetation. The spot-bill duck shows a special preference for *Paspalum distichum, Chara* species, grass seeds, *Nymphoides* seeds, *Nymphaea* and so on, but it also feeds on mollusks and insects. For roosting it prefers mounds. It is interesting to watch them swimming—these ducks, including the chicks, move in a single file.

The **cotton teal**, which breeds in the hollows of trees, is a sparrow-sized small duck. It prefers 60–80 cm water depth and is generally seen with six to 10 ivory white ducklings, feeding or swimming in open waters with submerged vegetation such as *Hydrilla* and *Spirilla*. Insects and crustaceans such as lobsters, crabs, shrimps, crayfish, water-fleas and woodlice also form part of its diet. This duck does not enjoy socialising with other species. During a good monsoon, the ponds behind the 'Nursery' and in the Sitaram temple complex are the best places to watch it swimming and feeding in flocks.

Comb-ducks roosting in the marshes

The **nakta or comb-duck** is big for a duck. The back of the bird has a peculiar blending of blue, green, brown and black colours. The female is smaller in size and the male bears a knob on the upper side of its bill, which gets conspicuously enlarged after breeding and helps in its identification. Small flocks may be seen feeding in the reeds and open water patches that have floating vegetation. The duck walks and dives well and perches freely on boughs. If disturbed, it emits a low grating croak and a loud honk in the breeding season. During the monsoon season, July to September, it lays eight to 12 pale cream eggs in the natural hollows of trees standing inside the water or on the edge. Brooding is done by the female only and it generally breeds outside the park. It feeds chiefly on wheat, wild and cultivated rice, echinochloa and other vegetable matter, but occasionally on frogs, insects and so on. It feeds mostly outside in agricultural fields but roosts inside the park, preferably on mounds and grassy patches inside lakes.

The **lesser whistling teal** is a chocolate brown bird that cannot go unnoticed because of its long neck and erect posture. In the park, Bakalia is the best place where these may be sighted in large flocks. Their take-off and landing style is peculiar. It breeds in bushes and tree hollows on the water edges; it is also seen breeding in the abandoned nests of the pied myna. For feeding they prefer rooted floating vegetation, especially *Nymphaea, Nymphoides seeds, Najas, Grass seeds, Chara, Eleocharis* and so on. But, for resting, they opt for mounds and islands in the *jheel*s. January counts (2014 to 2017) revealed the presence of 1,572, 1,632, 747 and 685 birds of this species, respectively, in the park. The flock activities of this agile bird make the scenic lakes even more vibrant.

The **purple moorhen**, with its attractive purple-blue body, is a highly charming rail. The blood red colour of its short heavy bill, forehead, long legs with broad toes, especially adapted to walking on reeds, enhances its beauty. In Keoladeo, it is popularly known as the lipstick bird. Like other members of the rail family, it keeps flicking its tail up and down, displaying the white coverts hidden underneath. It is generally seen in large numbers in the reeds and grass close to the Keoladeo-Barso main track. Their feeding and flying behaviour is similar to that of the water hens. The crackling and hoarse calls of the bird, however, do not match its beauty; it is particularly noisy during the breeding season. The male is rather comical in its courtship display, it proposes to the female with loud chuckles and much bowing while holding a twig of grass, weed or reed in the bill. This bird feeds mainly on shoots and vegetable matter of emergent vegetation consisting of grass such as *Paspalum distichum,* reeds such as *Typha angustata, Eleocharis plantaginea* and sedges such as *Cyperus alopecuroides, Scirpus littoralis* and emergent vegetation such as *Ipomea aquatica*. It feeds on insects and mollusks as well. During the

NAVIN SHARMA

The purple moorhen in the swamp. **Facing page:** *The Indian moorhen enjoys swimming*

months of September and October, it makes 50 to 60 nests on small, raised platforms in the lakes with grass/sedges and lays three to seven yellow-reddish buff-coloured eggs that have blotches and spots. Incubation takes 25 to 27 days. It roosts on trees standing on the water edge. Occasionally, it clambers awkwardly up the reed stems. During the pinch period of May to

June, all the birds leave the park and their number starts growing only after July. The shortage of water from 2000 to 2010 had impacted their numbers considerably. As per counts done in January through direct sighting, 318, 214, 318 and 793 birds were found in the park during 2014–17, respectively.

The **Indian moorhen** is a slate grey and brown bird with white edges in its closed wings and conspicuous white undertail coverts. When inside water it gives the appearance of a small duck. The moorhen bears a conspicuous red mark on the forehead and base of its small light green bill. The bird's long legs and prominent toes are green. It is generally seen swimming in lakes with partially submerged vegetation. From June to September, it lays five to 12 eggs in bulky nests made on sedges and grass or in low shrubs near water. The eggs are coloured like those of a purple moorhen. In the park, 1,056, 523, 597 and 706 birds were counted from 2014 to 2017, respectively.

NAVIN SHARMA

Watching the nesting activities of the jacana is a feast for the eyes. It makes nests on water, taking the help of the floating vegetation. This technique not only protects it against terrestrial predators but also against raptors as the grass and sedges all around the nests camouflage them. It exhibits special skills in saving its nest from being drowned or floating away. Both the jacanas—the bronze-winged and pheasant-tailed—are favourites of bird photographers. Prior to 1982, their nests were being trampled by buffaloes. Therefore, the ban on this grazing has increased their population, but, later, the dearth of water in the park affected them adversely. After 2012, with improved water supply, their nesting has again increased. A gradual rise in water level suits these birds for nesting. Hence, in order to facilitate their successful nesting, the park management should regulate their water intake at their favourite breeding sites.

As its name suggests, the **pheasant-tailed jacana** bears a pheasant-like beautiful arched tail and has a highly attractive breeding plumage. It forms shapeless nests on water with the help of floating vegetative material and lays four olive brown eggs in the beginning of August. This open and shallow nest is anchored on all four sides with vegetation lest it topples and inundates or gets dragged away by the wind. Nest building is done very cleverly. The bird does not usually carry the material with itself; instead, it leaves the material close to the nest and then pulls it while sitting on the nest. The colour of the eggs and the nesting material help in camouflaging the young ones. A hide-and-seek modus operandi is adapted by the bird while flying to

The bronze-winged jacana shifting two hatchlings tucked under its wings

ANSAR KHAN

and from the nest to ensure that the nest is not detected by predators. It never reaches the nest in one go. Walking in a slow pace towards the nest, it takes an occasional pause and then suddenly climbs the nest unnoticed. Only the male bird hatches and guards the nest. In a season, the female pairs with two to three males to lay two to three clutches of eggs to be hatched and cared for by the males. Scientists see this as an evolutionary progression in the reproductive process.

The pheasant-tailed jacana is an exceptionally intelligent bird. In case the bird has to leave the eggs unattended in hot hours, it brings water in its breast feathers and wings to spray on them, lest they get overheated. Also, it uses its tail feathers as a fan to cool the clutch and provide shade against the strong sun. Since hatching is done by a single parent, this technique of making nests under the clear sun has evolved in order to enable the eggs to hatch faster. Hatchlings take 28 to 29 days to come out and then take no time in leaving the nest. It is no less than a wonder to see these fledglings swim through metre-deep water in a half-submerged state, in a hurry to reach a safe hideout. The **bronze-winged jacana** derives its name from its olive green and bronze wings. A white band on its eyes, surrounded by jet black feathers, makes it look ornamental. It builds floating nests like those of the pheasant-tailed jacana but prefers sites sheltered by typha reeds to ensure safety against aerial predators. The nest is a piled-up heap of water weeds, enough to hold four eggs. The glossy eggs, with thread-like designs, help in camouflaging against predators. Hatching and caring of eggs/chicks is done by the male only, like the pheasant-tailed birds. Hatching is done during the cool hours of morning and evening. The chicks leave the nest the day the last one comes out of the shell. It is indeed a wondrous sight to catch the male floating with the fledglings tucked neatly under its wings. The

ANSAR KHAN

The male bronze-winged jacana floating with its chicks (some hidden under its wings)

An alert flock of lesser whistling teals

bronze-winged jacana also nests during March. In 1991, in the third week of April, I found three coloured eggs in a bronze-winged jacana's floating nest, in the Sapan Mori area. The marsh harrier has proven to be the chief destroyer of jacana nests in the park. In 1988, when the improved water status in the park had helped in the development of excellent heronries, a large population of marsh harriers was drawn here, from end-August to the second week of September. I personally observed them attacking and spoiling the nests.

Yet, prey and predator both live in these fascinating regions of the Keoladeo National Park, in complete rhythm with nature. Their vibrancy and variety never fail to enchant.

Where do the Birds Come From?

The migration of birds with a definite pattern and large magnitude has always raised curiosity, especially among the serious birdwatchers. Ornithologists are eager to learn more about this phenomenon and also about their breeding places and migration routes. It is believed that a proper study in this direction was started in the beginning of the eighteenth century after the recovery of a garganey teal in Germany, marked sometime ago in Turkey. This incident motivated scientists to think of ways of running systematic

CHHOTE KHAN

Innumerable migratory birds heading for the Keoladeo National Park

studies in this field the world over. Ornithologists devised various methods and, finally, bird ringing was evolved; it earned universal acceptance.

In Keoladeo, this method was initiated by the then Maharaja of Bharatpur in 1939. Various water birds were captured in mist nets and a non-corrosive alloy ring was put on their legs for identification. This ring carries a code and address to which it should be returned if the bird is caught. All important details pertaining to the ringed birds, such as the name of the species, weight, age, sex, plumage, wing spread, body length and so on, with the date, time and place of ringing, are documented with care. Dr Salim Ali was the key person behind this project. Till 1981, more than a hundred thousand birds belonging to most of the migratory species were ringed at Keoladeo. Simultaneously, several birds that had been ringed at their respective breeding grounds and transitory stations were caught in the park.

Many of the birds ringed at Keoladeo were later found in Medak (Andhra Pradesh); Point Calimere (Tamil Nadu); Bengaluru; Shivpuri (Madhya Pradesh); Jhansi, Mathura, Rai Bareilly, Kanpur and Saharanpur (Uttar Pradesh); Haryana, Amritsar, Srinagar and in North Pakistan, Iran, Kabul (Afghanistan), Russian Turkestan, Kazakhstan, Siberia, among others. A complete list of these recoveries has been published by BNHS in its journal (Vol. 47, No. 4, August 1948) and its annual report (Salim Ali, Studies on the Movement and Population Structure of Indian Avifauna, BNHS, 1981).

The large-scale ringing programme divulged invaluable information. It is only due to these exercises that today the breeding areas and the migration routes of most of these birds is no more a mystery. It has been established

Map showing the corridor serving as the grand Central Asian flyway for the migratory birds wintering in Keoladeo

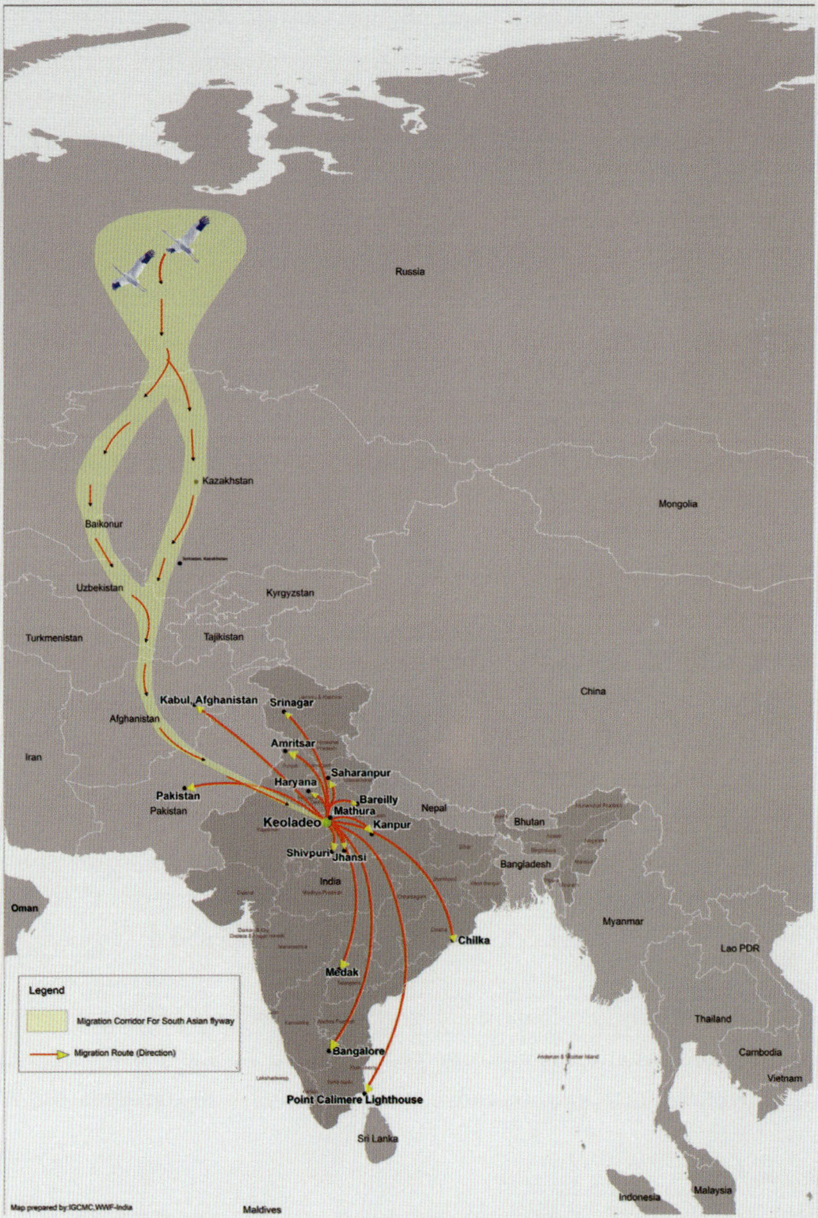

WWF-INDIA

that millions of birds start their journey towards this part of the world when feeding grounds of their homeland (the former USSR territory) get decked under snow heaps, denying them any kind of food. They take the trans-Himalayan journey, which comprises some of the world's toughest hill ranges. The Bharatpur swamps are located on this grand South Asian flyway migration route of the birds. Out of these migrants, several thousand stay in these swamps throughout the winter while a huge number use the Keoladeo lakes as a staging area. They stay here for some days to get rid of their fatigue, having completed an over 5,000 km-long arduous journey and to replenish for another journey towards Chilka and the neighbouring lakes of Odisha and other areas up to Point Calimere, the southern tip of the Indian subcontinent. Thus many of these migratory birds cover a distance of nearly 8,000 km.

Yet, in spite of knowing this, we have not been able to comprehend how birds as small as sandpipers and stints, weighing a few hundred grams, navigate to cover such huge distances crossing the great Himalayas. It is a general belief that the birds take guidance from the moon and stars at night and the sun during day hours. Though birds understand the geography of their migration routes, at times poor light and foggy conditions derail them from their path, resulting in their landing at places where they have never been seen before. A painted snipe (*Rostratula benghalensis*) ringed in Bharatpur was found in Darbhanga (Bihar) and a white stork (*Ciconia ciconia*) ringed in Germany, found in Bikaner, are glaring examples of these accidental deflections.

Many scientists believe in the theory that most of the long-ranging migrations among birds, mammals and insects are guided by the Earth's magnetic field, which is just 30 to 60 millionth of a Tesla. By all standards, this is a very weak field. This can be best understood by the fact that the Magnetic Resonance Imaging (MRI) being done in medical science uses a magnetic field of 1.5 to 3 Tesla. Even these scientists are unable to understand as to what mechanism helps these animals to make the best use of such a weak magnetic field and reach the pinpointed destinations in the desired time. A much-believed theory is that in a bird's retina, photoreceptors absorb light and consequently a photochemical species is produced. This is sensitive to the magnitude and direction of even a weak magnetic field like that of the Earth. This theory is backed by the fact that blue light photoreceptors have been found active in the retinas of migratory birds during the act of magnetic orientation.

However, it has not yet been confirmed that a magnetic field as weak as the Earth's can produce detectable changes within a photochemical molecule; nor has a photochemical molecule been shown to respond to the direction of such a magnetic field. Scientists may be able to solve this mystery in the future but it is for sure a highly strange act of nature. In many species, the juveniles, the first-timers, start on migration earlier than their parents.

It is interesting to observe that most of the migratory waterfowl females reach the park in larger numbers than the males, but they arrive later. Also, the males have a tendency of dispersing freely while the females stick to certain areas only.

NAVIN SHARMA

Bar-headed geese, basically a grazer, arrives late at the park

Migratory Water Birds

The greylag, bar-headed, brahmini, pintail, common teal, gadwall, wigeon, garganey teal, shoveller, red-crested pochard, common pochard, white-eye pochard, tufted pochard, mallard, whistling teal, coot, spot-bill, cotton teal, comb duck, white-breasted waterhen, Indian moorhen and purple moorhen comprise the 22 waterfowl that are commonly found in the Keoladeo National Park. Of these, only the last six are resident; the rest are all migratory.

The **garganey**, also known as the blue-wing teal, is the first winter visitor to this park. The medium-sized bird acts as a flag-bearer and is an indicator of the beginning of the arrival of thousands of migratory water birds. This long-ranging bird uses Keoladeo as a staging ground. It goes to the extreme south from here and then again appears in the park sometime between January and March, before returning to the breeding grounds. Owing to a shortfall in water, in the last two decades its number has declined considerably. With improved conditions now it is likely to increase in the coming years. In September itself, more waterfowl and waders such as sandpipers, snipes, plovers, stilts, avocets and crakes arrive to join these teals. After September, the number of migrants keeps increasing with every passing day. By November, geese and more ducks join the fleet. From the viewpoint of number and species, these ducks are the most prominent, as compared to the other water birds. The dimorphism of sexes is a characteristic feature with ducks. Generally, the males, adorned with brighter colours, also differ in size and other traits from the females. In contrast to geese, polyandry and polygamy is common among ducks.

The greylag, bar-headed, pintail, shoveller, coot, wigeon, gadwall, common teal and ferruginous duck have the main share in the entire population of water birds in Keoladeo. Surface feeding and diving ducks visit the park in the same proportion. Diving ducks such as the pochard depend chiefly on major submerged and floating plants for food. Grass habitat is preferred by the greylag, bar-headed, common teal, garganey and wigeon whereas the pintail, shoveller and coot prefer an *Ipomea* habitat. The gadwall opts for grass blades as well as algae. All these species, except for the pintail, also feed on animal matter. Most of the waterfowl prefer a water depth of about 20 to 60 cm but the common pochard, Indian moorhen and cotton teal prefer 60–80 cm whereas the coot favours a depth of more than a metre.

Of the surface feeding ducks, the **pintail** is the most common. It is a distinctive and elegant duck. Its white chest and white stripes, extending on either side of the chocolate-coloured head, long, thin neck and pin-like pointed tail make the male easily distinguishable from a distance. The pintail is not a vocal bird but occasionally whistles softly. It feeds by preference on grasses, especially their seeds and also on *Nymphoides, Nymphaea, Ipomea* and *Ceratophyllum*. While feeding on the submerged vegetation it gets overturned, submerging its bill and neck in the water, showing only its prominent pointed tail and lower body parts. Its preferred habitat is *Ipomea* with sparse grass.

The **wigeon** visits the park regularly with other ducks but in smaller numbers. It bears a highly distinguishable yellow vertical mark on its chestnut-coloured forehead, almost like a *tilak* (a sacred vertical mark made on the forehead by the Hindus). In flight, the white patch on its upper wing

Pintails (upside down), coots (black), pochards, shovellers and others busy in feeding

is very striking. In the early morning, while in flight by the lakeside, it may be heard emitting a peculiar high-pitched 'whee-o' whistle.

Like the pintail, the **shoveller**, too, is one of the most common ducks found in the park. The shoveller's bold colour patterning is distinct. The male, with its glossy dark green head and neck on a white and chestnut body, is strikingly beautiful. It bears a shovel-like conspicuously broad bill, from which it gets its name. Though it may be found in any part of the park, the shoveller has a marked preference for the open waters of Bakalia and Mansarovar. It may be seen swimming with its bill half in and half out of the water. The large bill helps to sieve small food particles from the water surface, which is why it commonly feeds while swimming. Its feeding behaviour matches that of the gadwall and common teal. During flight it can be easily identified by its orange legs and pale greyish-blue forewings. Waters with rooted floating vegetation and sparse grass are its choice of habitats. It prefers feeding on grass, insects, azolla, mollusks, *Ipomea*, nymphoides and the *Chara* species.

The **common teal** is the smallest wintering waterfowl found in the park. The male, distinguishable by the broad green stripe on its bright chestnut head, looks as if it is wearing green sunglasses. The bird ranks among the most beautiful because of this green stripe. It can be seen feeding in small ponds and ditches or in shallow waters. It is photogenic while foraging, dabbling (paddling, playing or splashing in water) or swimming with its head and neck submerged, like the shoveller and gadwall. These three species have a preference for the same kind of habitats. The common teal feeds by preference on algae, insects, grass, nymphaea, mollusks, nymphoides, hydrilla, ceratophyllum and the *Chara* species. It has been observed regularly going out of the park to forage in the Ajan Dam and nearby fields. Though the gadwall prefers to spend most of its time in water, it is a good walker and may be seen grazing on the ground as well. The conspicuous white on its speculum is a good identifying feature while in flight.

The **ruddy shelduck** is a large bird in comparison to other ducks. It is also called 'brahmini duck' or 'surkhab' for its saffron colour. The male can be differentiated from the female by the narrow black band around the middle of its neck and head. In India, the bird and its attractive feathers have become a symbol of womanly beauty. They pair for a lifetime. These special characteristics have made the bird an important subject of Indian romantic poetry. The destruction of their breeding grounds in Tibet, Ladakh, Mongolia and Central Asia has depleted their number. About 30 to 70 birds spend winter in the park and stay here till late, without bothering about the rising

The ruddy shelduck spends the winter months in the park

temperature. Of course, in the last two decades its number has declined considerably. The **common shelduck**, a link between geese and ducks, is a rare sight here. The male, a little larger in size, bears a typical red knob (lump or bulge) at the base of its bill.

The **coot** is a gregarious black bird with a grey beak. It prefers open water habitats with sparse grass. Though it feeds on algae, mollusks, grass, nymphoides and *Ipomea*, it prefers the hydrilla and ceratophyllum species. It uses adjacent grassy patches for preening and resting. The coot associates mainly with the Indian moorhen, red-crested pochard, shoveller and gadwall, among others. It may be seen in every water body of the park but it prefers water of about a metre's depth.

The **mallard**, though widespread in the world and quite common in Europe, visits Keoladeo in very small numbers. It restricts itself to the northwestern part of the subcontinent. With its purple-brown chest, green head and neck and white neck ring, the mallard ranks among the most beautiful waterfowl in the park. Its neck band makes it easily recognisable. The so-called three-bird flight is frequently observed with two drakes (male ducks) pursuing a female. In 1989, I observed a single mallard staying back in the park and it continued living here for many more years, maybe till it died. Perhaps, it had developed some ailment or weakness that did not allow it to fly back to its distant homeland.

The coot prefers water of about a metre's depth

The **marbled teal**, though a rare winter visitor to Keoladeo, is of particular scientific interest. It is taken to be a link between dabbling and diving ducks. It feeds both ways, that is, by dabbling or upending in shallow water and like true diving ducks.

Four species of pochards visit Keoladeo. The **red-crested pochard** is a rare bird here. It only likes open water bodies and that is probably why it visits the park a little late, when the emerging vegetation is cleared by the other ducks. The male bears a bright orange-red crest on its head, which shines from a distance. It is an accomplished diver and feeds on aquatic plants even located at greater depths. It also feeds upended and occasionally dabbles on the surface or on mud. I have never seen it socialising with the other species. About a hundred birds visit the park but they stay here only if clear water bodies are available. The **common pochard**, another diving duck with a conspicuous broad, black bill, shows a distinct liking for submerged vegetation on which it forages from deeper areas as well. It visits the park in a number even fewer than the red-crested pochard. The **tufted duck**, with its blue bill and bright yellow eye, is an attractive bird but visits here in negligible numbers. In flight, its white wing bar and pale belly is distinctive. It, too, feeds in deep water and eats mainly freshwater mollusks, larvae of invertebrates and plant seeds. The **white-fronted goose** occasionally visits the park. Like the other geese, it stays here during the day, but in the evening leaves to feed in the agricultural fields, adjacent to the Ajan Dam and Bandh Baretha. As its name indicates, the **bar-headed geese** bears two distinguishing black bars on its head. Like the sarus crane, the male and female usually mate for life. It breeds during summer in Tibet and Ladakh, areas of the higher Himalayas and highlands of Central Asia at an elevation of 14,000 feet or more. Nesting is done on islands in marshy lakes and rocky outcrops along the margin of swamps. Dr Salim Ali recognised it as the sacred 'Rajhans', which is found in large numbers in the Kailash mountain in Tibet. Like other geese, it nests in colonies. It reaches Keoladeo in November–December and stays here till late April. The **greylag geese** has two subgroups and it is the eastern one (*Anser anser rubrirostris*) that visits Keoladeo. It breeds west of the Ural mountains in Central Russia, lives in large flocks and comes to the park in good numbers. During flight the greylag may easily be identified by the pale grey colour of its forewings. It, too, pairs for life and occasionally emits distinguishing tri-syllabic long calls with extended notes. It uses almost every part of the park.

The number of all waterfowl visiting Keoladeo, except for the bar-headed geese, is determined chiefly by the preceding year's water intake. In 2014, the park received very little water; consequently, in 2015, the birds' number

fell though the water intake was good. But this improvement attracted more birds in 2016. Fortunately, in 2016, the water supply improved still further and this brought more birds in 2017, though in this year the water intake fell down drastically to only 175 mcft and many birds left the park within a few days of their arrival. Contrary to this phenomenon, the number of visiting bar-headed geese corresponds to the water intake of the current year only.

Flocks of black-tailed godwits add colour and variety to the park

ANSAR KHAN

Greylag geese visit Keoladeo every year and stay here throughout the winter.
Facing page: *Pelicans visit the park late so that they can catch the big fish with ease*

These birds seem to have developed a different system of communication among their groups. Pelicans are huge birds and voracious fish-eaters. For this purpose, nature has gifted them with not only a long beak but also a conspicuously big pouch attached to the throat in which they collect the fish through scooping. There are eight species of pelicans of which three, namely, great white, grey and spot-billed, are winter migrants to Keoladeo. Though not regular visitors, they remain a star attraction throughout their stay. The males are larger than the females. The **great white pelican**, also known as the white, rosy or eastern white pelican, is distinguished from the other pelicans by the pinkish tinge of its white plumage. Generally, they hunt fish in a group of six to eight, in a horseshoe formation. In India it breeds in Kutch (Gujarat). In the recent past, 89 birds visited Keoladeo in 2014 and 107 in 2017; they remained absent in between.

The **dalmatian pelican** is the world's largest freshwater swimming bird. With grey legs and yellow eye patches, it looks more plumy. This bird is globally threatened; only 10 birds reached Keoladeo in 2014 and there were 30 in 2017. The spot-billed pelican, also called the grey pelican, is a globally threatened species. Spots on its upper mandible, dull colours and the greyer plumage are its distinctive features. Its huge breeding colonies in Andhra Pradesh have become popular tourist attractions. From 2014 to 2017, not a single spot-billed pelican visited Keoladeo, probably due to the long spell of droughts here, which persisted for many years till 2011. The pelican species visits the park a little late in winter and leave before it becomes too hot for

NAVIN SHARMA

Beautiful tall flamingos are special guests at the Keoladeo lakes

them in March. By that time the grass and sedges subside and the water pools dry out partially, exposing fish that have grown to a good size. Pelicans seem to prefer the Mansarovar lake, near the Keoladeo temple.

Both, the greater flamingo and the smaller flamingo, visit the park and the Ajan Dam between November and December, but not regularly. Only 14 smaller flamingos came to this area between 2014 and 2017. These are long-legged white-pink birds. Nature has gifted them with not only a long, slender neck but a special yellow-pinkish banana-like bill with a conspicuous black tip. The **smaller flamingo** is shorter by about 40 cm but is more pink in colour than the greater one. The special bill with a slit helps in feeding and sieving out mud and undesirable stuff before swallowing. In India, these beautiful birds are revered as sacred birds and honoured with the title of Rajhans; these breed in the saline/brackish lagoons of the Kutch district in Gujarat. The word, 'flamingo' has been derived from the word, 'flame'. Its scientific name, '*Phoenicopterus*', means 'blood red feathers' in Greek. In flight, it stretches its neck and legs to form a linear shape. It flies either in a 'V' or straight-line formation. The sexes are alike. Feeding flocks emit goose-like honking sounds.

The **greater flamingo** feeds on insects, seeds, mollusks and crustaceans, while the lesser/smaller eats algae and diatoms. The former is found in Europe, Africa, Central Asia, Central and South America but the lesser flamingo can only be seen in Africa and India. They live and migrate in large flocks but do not socialise with the other species. Their large groups, in lakes or in flight, fill the space with an attractive pink colour. Peculiarly, they keep standing on one leg for most of their time in water. They live in huge flocks at breeding sites but, before breeding, split into small groups and perform synchronised ritual displays by stretching their necks upwards and uttering calls with their heads flagging and wings flapping. These displays are not aimed at particular individuals but for the entire group. Loners find their mates here and community nesting takes place.

Flamingos form strong pair bonds. As they have a preference for salty areas, they visit Sambhar lake (about 40 km from Jaipur) in several thousands almost every winter. I have seen them wintering in the small lake of Didwana (Nagaur district) and at Sardar Samand lake (Jodhpur district) in huge numbers. In the Bahamas, the flamingo enjoys the status of a national bird, a position that these colourful, long-legged birds truly deserve.

NAVIN SHARMA

The sarus crane, the tallest flying bird in the world, is the emblem of the park

Majestic Cranes

The Keoladeo swamps support four species of cranes. Of these, the **sarus crane**, about five feet in height, is the tallest flying bird in the world. With a light grey colour on its body, adorned with a red head and grey forehead, this beautiful bird has rightly been chosen as the emblem of the Keoladeo National Park. The most characteristic part of the crane is its fidelity; the pair stays together forever. During their unique courtship dance, the female first points her beak to the sky and trumpets, which is immediately responded to by the male with a more sedate, though shriller trumpet (sonorous cries). Bowing and half-spreading its wings, it continues in a half-cadence, 'preow-preow-preow'. In fact, this unison call is a proclamation of firm possession of territory. Their main breeding season is August to October; they also breed in February–March, though the success rate of this breeding is low.

During the seventies, there were over a thousand of these cranes in the park, but the number kept falling steadily year after year till the 1990s, when it dropped drastically. After 2010, barely 10 to 15 birds have arrived in the park each year. A regular fall has also been noticed in the number of breeding pairs, which is evident from the fact that 27 pairs bred in 1969, which dropped to 16 in 1980, four in 1984, 11 in 1985, seven in 2001 and five in 2003. During 2016–18, only three nests were made each year. Solitary nests are made by the couple on waterlogged, raised platforms with material collected from the vegetation available at the site itself. The couple carefully keeps mending and raising the nest by putting more grass and twigs in order to save it from being drowned in the rising water. Only two

Aggressive display by a sarus crane to defend its eggs from the predator

white eggs are laid within a gap of two to three days. Both parents incubate alternately by changing duties regularly after two or three hours. This duty change is executed quite ceremoniously, with the bird on duty bowing and trumpeting to express its gratitude towards the replacer. Both of them then dance for a while, accompanied by high-pitched trumpeting. This piercing call may be heard from over a kilometre or more. The eggs are so strong that the shells cannot be easily pierced through by crows and others. The first egg hatches in about 32 days; the second egg a day after the first one. The golden hatchlings start walking within hours of birth. During the first week they are fed dragonflies and other insects but afterwards the chicks start picking their food themselves. The weaker of the two is discarded and left behind by the parents to die. Therefore, by November, generally only one golden chick is seen with the parents. The chicks grow rapidly by 2 to 2.5 cm per day to soon attain the height of their parents. They prefer 20–40 cm deep wetlands to enjoy rhizome of the *Nymphaea* species, *Scirpus tuberosus* and *Eleocharis plantaginea*. Occasionally, they feed on mollusk, snake, insect, fish and frog. They also keep moving into the neighbouring agricultural fields to devour the ripening gram and wheat crop. But, towards the end of March, most of the water pools outside the park dry up, forcing the birds to return to the leftover water pools in the park. Their larger congregations can hence be observed in the park during the summer months. Apart from water shortage, the growing use of pesticides in the agricultural fields adjacent to the park is one of the chief reasons responsible for the rapid decline in the population of this celebrity bird.

Promoting organic farming around Keoladeo is the only solution to this serious threat. Also, regular monitoring of its population is very important. From this point of view, the effort of Krishn Kumar Gupta, Founder President of Ghana Keoladeo Natural History Society (a Bharatpur-based NGO), is highly appreciable. Initiating in 1983, this society has conducted the 37th annual count of the sarus crane in February 2019, in and around the Keoladeo National Park.

The number of visiting **common cranes** has also been affected. I had personally counted 21 birds in Keoladeo in February but since then the number has dropped down to zero. Not a single common crane has visited Keoladeo from 2014 to 2017. These birds also share the Kunovat river basin with the Siberian cranes for breeding. Therefore, in order to study their exact migration route, two common cranes (Eurasian cranes) were caught in Keoladeo and released in 1993 after planting a Platform Terminal Transmitter (PTT), a radio telemetry device, on them. Both these birds followed the same route and safely reached the breeding ground within a short span of one month. The PTT worked very well and the information was of immense value. This was the first-ever authentic information received about the route and stopover points of this crane. A.S. Brar and other organisations involved in this project deserve full credit for the successful completion of this important mission.

Sarus cranes doing a courtship dance; they pair for life

NAVIN SHARMA

Map showing the migration routes followed by the two common cranes released from the Keoladeo National Park in April 1993

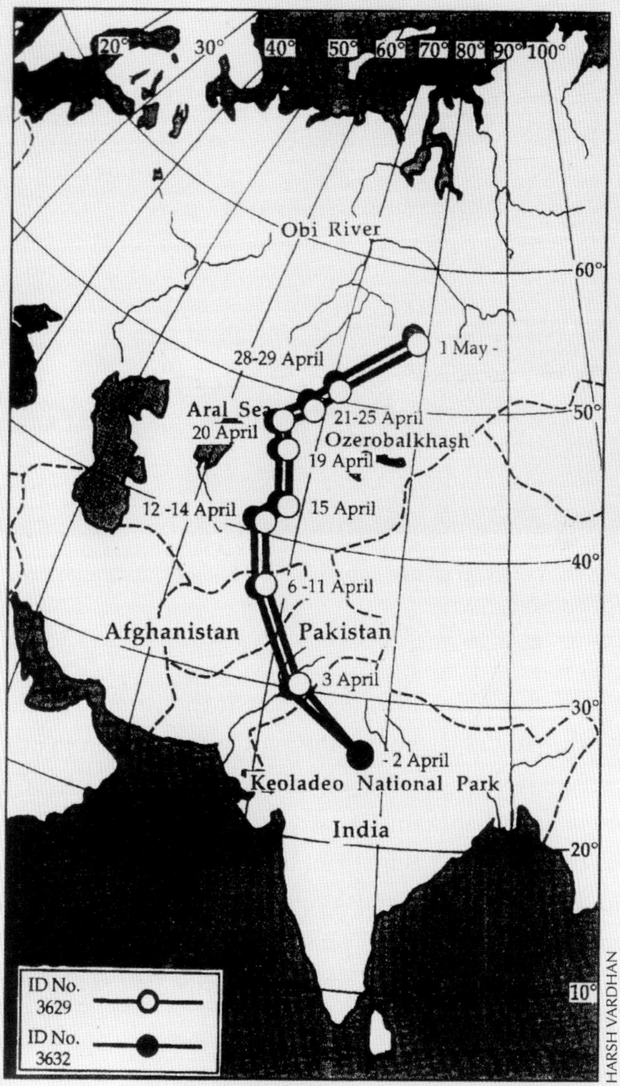

HARSH VARDHAN

Like the Sibes, the common cranes, too, show a preference for the shallow waters of Block E in Keoladeo

The **demoiselle crane** is another beautiful winter visitor to Keoladeo. These birds utilise the park as a stopover during their migration to other parts of India, especially western Rajasthan and Gujarat. Their largest population may be seen in Khinchan, a small town of the Jodhpur district, located in the extreme western deserts of Rajasthan. In these Thar deserts, the demoiselle is regarded as a sacred bird and its visit is taken as an auspicious omen and indicator of good crops and prosperity. While staying in Keoladeo, it will generally forage in the gram and wheat fields that are located adjacent to the park.

The Star Attraction

The Siberian crane (*Grus leucogeranus*) has been heralded as the star attraction in Keoladeo for long. It is a snow white huge bird with pink legs and a red face; its beak's red is mixed with black. The black tips on its wings are clearly visible during flight and preening. These huge birds, with immatures, had been reaching the park every year in October till 2002, making the arduous journey of about 5,500 km from the breeding areas. They prefer a habitat with less than 30 cm of water. The Siberian crane is basically an omnivorous bird but has a preference for plant material. At Keoladeo, it feeds mainly on the rhizomes and tubers of *Scirpus tuberosus*, *Cyperus rotundus*, *Eleocharis dulcis*, *Nymphaea* species, *Scirpus littoralis*, parts of *Hydrilla verticillata*, *Potamogeton* species, *Vallisneria spiralis,* basal parts of the leaves of the *Limnophyton* species and tips of the culms of *Eleocharis*. Occasionally, it feeds on aquatic insects, mollusks, worms and probably fish.

Ornithologists believed that in the 19th century about 2,000 birds used to winter in the marshes of North India. Dr Ali saw some birds in 1937 at the Prayagpur lake, located in the Bahraich district of Uttar Pradesh. A.O. Hume, a British civil service officer and ornithologist of immense repute, had also recorded the sighting of the crane in the Najafgarh lake, which is close to Delhi. Dr Vijayan, who led the BNHS ecological studies at Keoladeo from 1980 to 1990, contended that the ban imposed on grazing by livestock in the park was mainly responsible for the disappearance of the Siberian crane from Bharatpur. He had recommended the reintroduction of buffalo grazing in the park. However, another detailed field study conducted

at the park by US scholars did not agree with what Dr Vijayan had expressed. According to the report (1997) of the International Crane Foundation (ICF), USA, 'The loss of adult and young birds during migration through Pakistan and Afghanistan is thought to be the leading factor behind the decline of the central population of Siberian cranes.'

Poaching along the migration route seems to be the main reason for the disappearance of these birds. As Research Officer at the Keoladeo National Park from 1988 to 1991, I have observed that habitat degradation at the

Siberian cranes (the snow white tall birds in the front). They used to visit Keoladeo in large numbers during the 1990s

park, due to a shortage of water supply, had also contributed to this loss. Reduction in water means a reduction in feeding and roosting areas for the birds. Lack of food at Keoladeo means that the birds, especially the juveniles, do not have the strength to take such an arduous journey. This causes mortality during return migration, thereby resulting in a low rate of breeding among the survivors in the Russian habitats.

Map showing the migration route of Siberian cranes

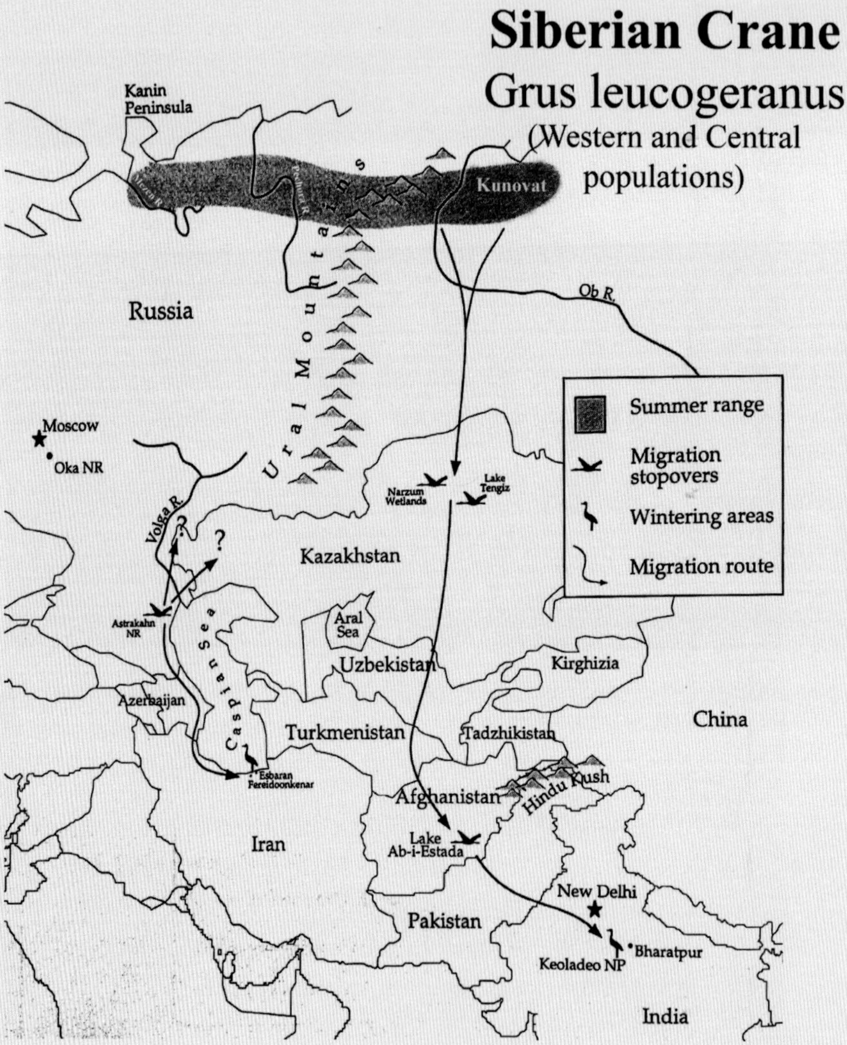

INTERNATIONAL CRANE FOUNDATION, USA

Only 17 cranes came to the park in 1989, which was a drought year. Of these, eight left in mid-winter in search of food. We conducted a ground survey of several important water bodies located in the adjacent Dholpur and Mathura districts to look for them. On 8 January 1990, a search party, consisting of Rakesh Fauzdar and Mool Chand, both employees of the park, succeeded in locating one family of Siberian cranes with a juvenile at Talab-i-Shahi, a scenic water body in the Dholpur district of Rajasthan. It was about 80 km, as the crow flies, from Keoladeo. This was a great achievement and invaluable information on their movement and speed was gathered.

These birds left Talab-i-Shahi at 10.05am on the next day and they were observed landing at Keoladeo at 3pm. On 10 January, they again left the park at 2pm and were seen landing at Talab-i-Shahi at 4.15pm. These birds returned to the park on 12 January at 2.45pm but left the next day at 11.30am and landed at Talab-i-Shahi at 1.20pm. Thus, the birds travelled the distance of about 80 km within a span of about two hours, that is, 40 km per hour.

All of us at the park were pleased with the experiments that were conducted to explore the movement of these birds. This led to an aerial survey to be undertaken of the wetlands of Uttar Pradesh and Rajasthan and a small aircraft was provided by the Government of India for this purpose. Bholu Abrar Khan, who served as the forester at the park and who possessed immense knowledge of birds, accompanied me on this survey. Our first sortie commenced on 4 February 1990 from Jaipur airport and the second was made on 16 February 1990 from Agra airport, which was administered by the Indian Air Force. V.M. Arora, the Divisional Forest Officer (Wildlife) posted at Agra, accompanied me on this expedition. We could not, however,

Siberian cranes displaying their typical feeding behaviour in the Keoladeo swamps

locate a single Siberian crane. The tiny aircraft flew at a height of about 3,000 m; its speed could not be lowered and visibility from its windows was not good enough to identify particular birds with the naked eye as binoculars could not be used due to the speed. This experience taught us that aerial surveys through these kinds of aircraft are impractical.

The Siberian crane breeds in Arctic Russia in Yakutia and West Siberia (Bird Life International 2001). Only three populations of this species are known in the world. These populations not only breed at distances from one another but also migrate to different geographical locations. Hence, they have been recognised as western, central and eastern populations. In 1981, the Russian scientists Alexander Sorokin and Kostyukov discovered the breeding habitat of the central population on the lower reaches of Ob and Kunovat rivers, about 60 km east of the Gorki township. It is this population that we were receiving annually at the park and are trying to understand their local migration. The population flies over dense forests and vast agricultural fields in Russia, Kazakhstan, the deserts of Uzbekistan, Turkmenistan and the high mountains of Afghanistan, then over the well-irrigated plains of Pakistan to finally reach the safe aquatic habitat of the Keoladeo National Park. The birds fly mostly during day hours, taking advantage of the thermals, stop at some shallow lakes to feed and roost for the night and then resume flight the next morning. This long migration through a tough terrain, full of forests, high mountains and cool deserts and the preferred feeding habits of the bird posed indescribable challenges to the species; hazards along the flyover places were numerous and till two decades ago no conservation effort was in sight. Indiscriminate poaching took its toll and the bird number continued to decline annually.

The Keoladeo National Park has not merely been a safe haven for these cranes but also an ideal feeding ground replete with choices in food—aquatic grass, sedges and rooted vegetation. After the seventies, however, the park had been facing recurrent droughts, but the Government did not find a solution. Forest authorities had little or no say in acquiring the optimum quantity of flowing water to the park during the monsoon—nearly 550 mcft. Lack of flooding during the winter months caused an alteration in the vegetation status. This continued unabated. Blocks D, E and L, the usual haunts for the Siberian crane, had acute dry conditions in the peak of winter, exposing the grass cover. Invasive species took over and the staple feed for the Siberian was to remain dormant as well as underground. Deterioration in habitat, a factor responsible for wetlands, had come up as another detrimental feature for the crane.

HARSH VARDHAN

A.S. BRAR

Russian scientist Alexander Sorokin finally releasing the Siberian crane at Keoladeo. **Facing page:** *Experts getting ready to release the Sibe* **(above)** *and* **(below, left to right):** *A.S. Brar, Director, Keoladeo National Park, Minakshi (Mini) Nagendran, International Crane Foundation and Alexander Sorokin with a captive-reared immature white Sibe*

In 1992–93, two juvenile cranes, **White and Bugle**, reared in captivity, were released in the Keoladeo National Park to make friends with the five wild Sibes that had wintered in the park that season. The objective was that the captive bred birds would, hopefully, fly back to the breeding grounds along with the wild Sibes, so as to raise the number of specimens at the grounds. But none of these could fly back to the breeding grounds along with the migrants. The ICF experiments were to add strength to the bird numbers at the park. Though no wild Sibes reached Keoladeo the following year, four additional captive reared juveniles were released here and they got attuned to the park habitat and avian species and were found associating with the sarus crane and the Eurasian common crane. The sarus is a resident species while the common crane is migratory to this park. This raised hopes that the captive bred Sibes would follow the common crane when it flew back to the breeding grounds, but this did not happen.

White and Bugle were kept at Keoladeo for the summer of 1993, to see if they could adapt to this place while the rest of the birds were at the Jaipur zoo. The results were encouraging. The birds adapted superbly to the hot summer conditions of the park but, unfortunately, White was killed by a black-necked stork. As a safety measure, Bugle had to be shifted to the Jaipur zoo. When the next season commenced, in October 1994, the surviving four Sibes (**Boris, Bugle, Gorby and Billy**) were brought back to Keoladeo. Surprisingly, these birds preferred to fly out of the park habitat to live in agricultural fields in a range of 12 to 13 km. Boris, Gorby, Billy and Bugle were last seen in the park on 12 November 1994, 20 November 1995, 20 January 1996 and 15 February 1996, respectively. It was getting difficult for the park authorities to monitor their movements and no one knew where the birds had escaped.

Hope got revived in 1996 when, one fine morning, three wild Sibes landed in Keoladeo. There was another wave of experiments and, in February 1997, four more captive reared birds (Behrami, Anabur and Ayafat, all females and Alkonoft, a male) were released in the park. The wild ones, however, flew back to the breeding grounds that month itself, before the captive birds could mix with them. Ayafat died in September 1997. In June 1998, the other three birds left the park. On 17 July 1998, an injured Anabur was rescued by the police and handed over to the park authorities but it died the next day. Thus, the three attempts made to introduce the captive reared juveniles into the wild population failed. It was disheartening for all of us. But nature is known to spring surprises and, least expectedly, a pair of Sibes turned up in the park in the winter of 2002. Everyone was extremely happy to observe a possible revival of the fading population of these critically endangered birds. They stayed for the winter and after these birds flew back, no Siberian crane has been found in the entire Indian subcontinent.

The ICF is engaged in ceaseless efforts at Crane City in the USA as well as at other places, devoting its expertise on the eastern population, wintering them in China, hoping that these cranes will one day return to India. Keoladeo may well have the opportunity of welcoming them once again.

BIRDS OF PREY

The Keoladeo National Park supports more than 52 species of predatory birds, popularly known as raptors. Here, you can find a sizeable number of eagles, buzzards, harriers, falcons, shikras, osprays, goshawks, besras and owls. Several raptors breed in the park and many other non-breeders also visit regularly, generally pursuing the migratory waterfowl from far-off lands. Eagles are large birds and, of all the eagles visiting Keoladeo, the Pallas' fish eagle is the largest. It is an excellent fish hunter that picks huge fish from the water surface in a single dive. The black-and-white ring on its tail, displayed during flight and its white head make it easy to recognise.

This raptor used to breed in the park regularly till the eighties, but suddenly it stopped appearing here for reasons not known. Though the Keoladeo swamps have lost several important migrants in the recent past due to a shortage of water but, from 1988 to 1996, there was no scarcity of water, therefore habitat degradation does not seem to be the factor responsible for this. Its population the world over is estimated to be just 2,500 and it has been included in the list of endangered species by IUCN. Scientists believe that habitat degradation across its range, in the form of cutting trees (loss of breeding sites), a high level of pollutants in the water bodies caused due to an excessive use of pesticides in their catchment and the mixing of factory affluents, the expansion of water hyacinths as well as increased fishing, both

---

Facing page: *The Pallas' fish eagle, the largest of all the eagles visiting Keoladeo*

legal and illegal, are the basic factors responsible for this drastic fall in its population. Unfortunately, so far no sincere work has been undertaken to protect the main water bodies that are inhabited by these beautiful and powerful birds.

The **short-toed snake eagle** regularly breeds on trees in the park's grasslands. It has a large owl-like head, short toes and white under feathers. This eagle feeds on small mammals, lizards and snakes and it is indeed interesting to watch it struggling with a cobra. During one summer, I got an opportunity to photograph the adult feeding a snake to its young ones on a nest in the Koladahar area. The **lesser-spotted eagle** also regularly breeds in the park. The **greater-spotted eagle**, closely resembling the lesser-spotted, is a winter migrant here as well. These similar-looking birds with white spots on their bodies and short tails can be distinguished from each other by their diverse habitat preferences. The greater-spotted eagle prefers an aquatic habitat and mostly hunts waterfowl while the lesser prefers woods and grasslands to feed on small mammals, lizards, birds and so on.

In May 2007, I observed an adult lesser-spotted eagle charging on a fully-grown snake. The attack was so sudden that the snake could not defend itself and got injured in the fight. The bird tried to lift the snake but failed. In the meantime, the snake managed to sneak into a burrow. The bird kept trying harder, using its strong beak and toes, but it just could not succeed in pulling out the snake and it ultimately left.

The Koladahar grasslands are favourite breeding grounds for this eagle. A month later, I located one nest with a chick on the top of a kadam tree in the Koladahar area, not far from the new watchtower.

A short-toed snake eagle feeding a snake to its chick in the Koladahar area

Tawny and **Steppy** are two eagles that look alike. In fact, these are two sub-species that inhabit the park. The former is a non-breeding resident while the latter is a winter migrant and stays for a short period only. Tawny is an opportunist bird that uses wetlands for waterfowl during winter but, during summer, it switches to grasslands to prey on small mammals and reptiles.

The **crested serpent eagle** is best at preying on snakes. It is a dark brown bird with brown and pale white bands across the tail. It can be easily identified by its dark brown crest, which erects prominently when the bird is alarmed or

NAVIN SHARMA

excited. It may be found perching on dry tree branches in wooded or grassy areas. **Bonelli's eagle** is another non-breeding resident eagle. It is a brown bird with pale markings on its nape and tail. Kadam Kunj is its preferred habitat. **Golden eagles** and **imperial eagles** are other huge birds that visit the park. The imperial stays here for two to three months while the sighting of the former is indeed rare. The imperial may be identified by its black-brown plumage with white feathers on the back.

All six species of **harriers** are found in India of which five are winter migrants to Keoladeo. It is a diurnal carnivorous bird that has long legs, a long tail and long wings. It has an owl-like face but is like a black kite in size. The male and female of this species are quite different in size and colour. The males have black margins on their wings. During migration they sleep in a community, at one place, generally in high grasslands, away from habitation. At times they even roost on *Icornia cresipus* (jal kumbhi) in the water

The crested serpent eagle, a dark brown bird with brown-and-white bands across the tail

areas. Birds feeding even 20 km apart gather a couple of hours prior to sunset at the roosting place and again leave for the feeding grounds before sunrise. This gives them a sense of protection against predators such as the jungle cat, jackal or mongoose.

The **marsh harrier** is a super active predator of the Keoladeo lakes; it keeps waterfowl mobilised throughout the day. It breeds in the Palearctic region. The marsh harrier is smaller than eagles but is nonetheless the largest among all harriers and is a champion among other birds of prey. The male is a brown bird with brown forewings, black wing margins and mid-wings and a grey tail. The females are chocolate brown in colour, with a dull white head, white shoulders and breast. Its magical midway turn and sudden dive to pick the identified bird make it an unparalleled hunter. I have observed dozens of these birds roosting in the grass of Koladahar and they are among the first arrivals in the park. They often prolong their stay in the park up to March in order to feast on the nests of the late heronry breeders.

Four species of buzzards inhabit Keoladeo out of which the **crested honey buzzard** is the most common. This brown bird has long legs and a long tail with a white band but a pigeon-like small head with a short crest and a dark throat stripe. It soars on flat wings. The male has a blue-grey head, while the female's head is brown. It is a specialist feeder, living mainly on the larvae of social bees and wasps, eating bits of comb and honey. It breeds in the Koladahar area but may be easily sighted by the roadside between the Shantikutir barrier and Bakalia.

The **white-eye buzzard** (*Butastur teesta*) is a slim, small-sized hawk that is easily identified by its white irises, white throat and dark mesial stripe. Its name *Butastur* indicates that it is between the *Buteo* buzzards and *Astur*, an old name for the sparrow hawks. It prefers to be in the dry, open forest or cultivation. In Keoladeo it may be seen near Chowki Ramnagar, Bahnera, Ghasola, Aghapur and Naswaria. Its sighting has increased considerably since 2007, after the eradication of *Prosopis juliflora*.

The **shikra** is a small raptor and, like most other *Accipiter* hawks, this species has short rounded wings and a narrow long tail. The adults are whitish on the underside with fine rufous bars and their upper parts are grey. The males have a red iris while the females have a yellowy-orange iris. In flight it emits a short and sharp *kik-ki ... kik-ki* call. The shikra is an expert hunter and its call is mimicked by drongos to steal food from other birds. It breeds in Keoladeo during summer. This bird gets its name from the Urdu word, *shikari* (hunter). It was a favourite among falconers in India and Pakistan and trapping birds through shikra was a popular sport among royalty in the olden times.

Vultures render a very important role in balancing nature by scavenging on the carcasses of dead animals. A group of vultures is called a kettle, committee or wake. The term 'kettle' refers to vultures in flight, while 'committee' refers to vultures resting on the ground or on trees. 'Wake' is reserved for a group of vultures that are feeding. Vultures in South Asia, mainly in India and Nepal, have declined dramatically since the early 1990s chiefly due to the presence of residues of the veterinary drug diclofenac in animal carcasses. Even though the Government of India has now banned the drug for use on animals, it may take decades for vultures to come back to their earlier population level. A study conducted in 2016 reported that of the 22 vulture species, nine are critically endangered, three are endangered and four are near threatened.

An expert hunter, the shikra breeds in the park during the summer months

Keoladeo inhabits five species of vultures of which the Indian white-rumped, long-billed, Egyptian and red-headed have been breeding in the park. The griffon vulture, too, visits the park, but rarely. In 1991, I had photographed more than 200 vultures on a carcass in Block F1, near Barso. I have witnessed their rapid decline over the years and it is now encouraging that vultures such as the Egyptian vulture have started visiting the reserve.

The number of vultures found in the park has dwindled since the early1990s

Owls are masters of mimicry. They can produce the exact sound of a crying baby, the musical sound of a lady's anklet or even the typical 'churr-chu-churr-chu' of a traditional water-lifting machine. It is indeed a pity that the 'owl' is being used as a derogatory word for fools. Owls, feeding mainly on rodents, are true friends of farmers but superstitions popular among rural people are taking a heavy toll on India's owl population. Tantriks and pseudo doctors of witchcraft fool people by performing rituals in the name of fighting evil spirits, curing critical illnesses, gaining wealth or power or fulfilling the long-cherished desires of their illiterate clients. For these rituals they use the flesh, bones or claws of live or dead owls. The owl has

A barn owl being sold illegally in Coimbatore

been bestowed a place of honour in Hindu religion as it is the vehicle of Lakshmi, the powerful goddess of wealth. But, unfortunately, illiterate and greedy people are killing these precious birds. Governments must enforce the law with strictness and wildlife lovers and NGOs should run campaigns to educate people, especially rural folk, about the positive role this bird plays. Keoladeo is enriched with 10 species of owls of which five breed here. These are nocturnal birds; therefore, humans get little opportunity to watch them.

The **spotted owlet**, a small, beautifully spotted bird with an oval face, is the most common raptor found in the park. These can be easily sighted sitting on a tree branch just outside their holes, especially during winter, while basking in the sun. All the rickshaw-pullers of the park know their hideouts. The peculiar habit of popping their heads up and down is rather typical of this owlet.

The **dusky-horned owl**, also called the dusky eagle, is a huge, grey, long-eared owl with yellow irises. Its thick vertical ear tufts look like horns. This owl inhabits wooded and watered areas and usually breeds in the abandoned nests of raptors. Every year, two to three pairs breed in the Bhainsamori and Kadam Kunj areas of Keoladeo. In January 2007, I observed it incubating eggs on a kadam tree in the Jamun area (Block L). During the next month itself, I found another pair on a nest with their young ones in the Koladahar area. The **collared scops owl** is a common owl of the park and can be seen roosting by the roadside on a tree branch near the entrance to the Keoladeo temple. Rickshaw-pullers and naturalists show these nocturnals to the tourists. It is a stocky owl of brown-grey colour and even though it is named after the pale collar around the back of its neck, that feature is not diagnostic of the bird. In fact, the V-like shape formed by the tufts of hair that join both the ears to its beak is peculiar of this owl alone and should be used as an identifying feature. Like the owlets, these also use the hollows of tree trunks for nesting.

The **barn owl** is a medium-sized gold-and-white owl. It has black eyes on a heart-shaped innocent bare face. Its upper parts are golden-brown with black-and-white speckles; all these put together make it one of the most beautiful raptors. It is a romantic bird. Before pairing, the female is offered food such as a mouse, lizard or frog. The female occupies the nest only if it accepts the gift. The male owl also shares parental duties. It is a hardy

Spotted owlet young ones coming out of the nest for basking in the sun

bird, unlike its appearance. In April 2007, a person from village Gilgitiya of Uchain (about 20 km from the park) brought one female and a young one of this species to my office. The birds had got trapped in their nest when the tree fell almost two months ago. They probably survived on moisture from the air and the meat of the other two chicks and the male bird.

The **eagle owl** is the largest owl in the park. Yellowish-brown in colour, with streaks, its long ear tufts and orange irises are its identifying features. Its wings are huge. During dark nights, its deep, booming, 'to-whoot-to-whoot'

A black-winged kite feeding mice to its chicks in a nest

call is quite frightening. The **brown fish owl** is a large, flat-headed streaked brown bird with horizontally-held ear tufts and yellow irises. It can be found perching on tree branches near water. It has a short tail and barred wings. The owl's deep 'whoom-whoom' during the night hours is rather scary.

Though five species of kites inhabit the park, the **black-winged** or **black-shouldered kite** (*Elanus caeruleus*) is most attractive by appearance as well as by behaviour. It is a small grey-white bird with black shoulders. It is a summer nester and prefers sparse wooded areas. This kite breeds mostly in the Koladahar area of the park and feeds on small rodents, which it searches out during an aerial survey. After spotting its prey, it hovers like a helicopter in the air and then suddenly dives to lift reptiles or small mammals from the ground.

TERRESTRIAL AND ARBOREAL BIRDS

There is little doubt that the Keoladeo National Park is famous for its spectacular heronries and migratory as well as resident waterfowl, but that is not all. In fact, this 29 sq km park is home to more than 380 species of birds, of which water birds are but a small fraction. A great many terrestrial and arboreal birds of all sizes inhabit this park. Several of them breed in grass and woodland. Though grass intermixed with open and dense wooded areas are preferred by some species for roosting, feeding and breeding,

A small blue kingfisher scaring away a predator

NAVIN SHARMA

NAVIN SHARMA

the great expanse of the Koladahar grassland also attracts these birds. In December–January, these dry prairies are inhabited by a huge population of doves, including migratory Spanish sparrows, which arrive in November to feed in the dry prairie and roost in the reeds.

After January, water starts shrinking in the lakes and that induces the waterfowl to fly back to their homeland. By the end of February or possibly the beginning of March, spring starts knocking at the park's door. This season is the favourite of the terrestrial and arboreal birds as it is mating time for them. The males of a number of species regain their singing skills and suddenly become exceptionally vocal in order to attract a partner. Their mating and nesting activities keep growing with each passing day. Passerine and non-passerine birds, displaying their beautiful colours and designs, not only attract their partners but also human onlookers. By March, most of these guest birds depart and the rising summer temperature reduces the number of visitors. It is now time for the serious bird lovers to roam freely in various areas of the park. In fact, April is the peak time for the breeding of the terrestrial and arboreal birds. Though nests are made almost throughout the park, the mixed forests attract the maximum birds in number and diversity. The grassland of Koladahar, with their tall grass of Vetiveria and Dab (*Desmostachya bipinnata*), stand second in attracting nesting birds.

The mornings and evenings of March are quite pleasant in Keoladeo. Birds become active from early morning itself and the **koel** (*Eudynamys scolopacea*) starts its sweet song. The male, with glossy black colour on its body and ruby

---

Facing page: *The female koel (above), unlike the male of its species, is not a melodious singer and (below) a white-cheeked bulbul feeding its chicks*

red eyes, resembles a house crow but the female koel, with printed brown feathers, looks really attractive. The male emits a highly melodious 'kooh-kooh', whereas the female responds with 'cra-cra', a piercing harsh sound. What a contrast! It seems that this is how nature has balanced virtues in both the sexes. Those staying overnight in the jungle have the special privilege of enjoying the highly melodious calls of the koel, right from early in the morning when it is most vocal. It is, indeed, the perfect way to start the day in such a blissful atmosphere.

The koel is a clever bird; it neither makes its nests nor takes the pain of incubating eggs or raising the hatchlings! It simply lays its eggs in the nests of crows. Though crows are known for their cleverness, they are surely second to the koel. The crow is unable to differentiate between its own and the koel's eggs and, thus, not only does it hatch the eggs but also nurses the young ones for some weeks. One day, the koel suddenly emerges and carries away its young ones.

With growing summer, the shrinking water bodies give way to palatable grass and many other herbs in the vacated moist soil. These, in turn, support numerous insect species. Several invertebrates also get exposed during this drying process; they act as great food stores for birds. Thus, the fringe areas of the water bodies, especially the strips formed between the woods and waterline, host the maximum species of birds to feed and breed. The sighting of shrikes, sparrows, minivets, chats, partridges, quails, bulbuls, among others, is common in such ecotones.

The grassland of Keoladeo are special. A study conducted by BNHS showed the presence of more than 130 species of birds belonging to 40 families

NAYAN KHANOLKAR

The long-tailed minivet (left) and a rosy pastor (right) enjoying nectar from the flowers

in the grassland habitat. Out of these, 11 families of water birds enjoy the advantage of the ecotone between the aquatic areas and the adjoining grassland. Families of doves, warblers, thrushes, chats, babblers and larks are found here throughout the year whereas mynas, drongos, munias, sparrows, kites, eagles, vultures, shrikes and crows keep away from the grassland during the monsoon period. Red-wattled and yellow-wattled lapwings, stone curlews, grey francolins, jungle bush quails and rock bush quails are summer breeders that lay eggs on the ground, in a natural depression or in dense grass. Though breeding among terrestrial birds is an all-season activity, most of the species breed during summer, from March to July. Birds such as the pitta, lark, iora, bulbul, tailorbird, warbler, magpie robin and white eye are known for their charming songs and become more vocal during the breeding period. Their songs provide a relief from the harshness of the hot summer in this part of the globe. Like seed-eaters, a noticeably large population of insectivorous birds such as bee-eaters, rollers, woodpeckers, shrikes, drongos, golden orioles, flycatchers and multi-coloured warblers keep the park vibrant throughout the year by their action-filled activities, especially during breeding time. Some terrestrial birds are highly charming and interesting.

NAVIN SHARMA

The baya weaver male acquires a bright yellow colour during the breeding season.
Facing page: *A pair of ring doves in flight*

In Keoladeo, the red-vented and white-eared bulbuls are the most common. The red-vented has a conspicuous red vent, which becomes dark red during the breeding period of summer. Though it does not sing, its blissful, low-pitched sound and spirited twittering fill the atmosphere with joy. It makes beautiful small basket-like nests on shrubs and small trees. The white-eared is also known as white-cheeked because of its white cheeks. It is fond of peeloo (*Salvadora persica*) and *Capparis aphylla* berries.

Three species of weaver birds inhabit Keoladeo, of which the **baya weaver** and the **streaked weavers** are more popular for their breeding plumage and nesting behaviour. During the breeding period, the baya weaver male acquires a bright yellow colour on its crown, nape and breast. They prefer open areas close to water points and build breeding colonies on scaly high trees, preferably khajur (*Phoenix sylvestris*) or babool. They make beautiful single- and double-storeyed nests by weaving straws. These are a work of art and many people use these abandoned nests as table lampshades. The baya female is fond of the colour yellow; therefore, the male often uses yellow paper and rags inside the nests to lure it. Before pairing, the female inspects the colony with half-built nests and settles in the choicest nest. The male completes the nest and mates with the female, who lays eggs here. Then the male goes on to make a new nest nearby and mates with another female. Several times the angry males cut away the nests if they are not approved by the females.

Four species of **mynas** inhabit the park in large numbers. These are summer nesters and even though they are not very spectacular in colours and habits, these omnipresent birds keep the park vibrant throughout the year. They feed on anything so never leave your breakfast plate unguarded in their areas!

Though Keoladeo is inhabited by five species of doves, the Eurasian collared (ring dove), red collared (red turtle) and laughing dove (little brown) are found in large numbers here. The **Eurasian collared dove** emits a typical deep, tri-syllabic 'kuk-koo-kuk-koo' sound, which is repeated several times in succession. It is because of this sound that it is called 'ghughi' in North India. During the day hours of summer, this local flour mill-like typical call resonates in the jungle, breaking the monotony.

Facing page: *The peacock, India's national bird and green bee-eaters (left), the latter are known to be highly sociable birds*

The **Asian paradise flycatcher**, an extraordinarily beautiful, medium-sized passerine bird, is a favourite of nature photographers. Babblers are highly gregarious birds. Four species of babblers are breeding residents in Keoladeo. Of these, the **jungle babblers** are also known as the seven sisters. The **large grey babblers** live in flocks as large as 40 birds and are the most vocal; at times, they are a nuisance for they tend to bully everyone out of their way. The **common babbler** is, however, a bit different. First of all, it is not a common bird anywhere and also, its call is pleasant to the ears, unlike that of the other babblers. The hoopoe is adorned with an attractive, conspicuous crest, which gets erected as and when the bird requires. For its huge curved beak and heavy crest, people confuse it with a woodpecker. During summer, the entire jungle echoes with its typical penetrating sound, which is repeated in runs, often intermittently for 10 minutes at a stretch. It nests in tree cavities as well as in holes of walls and ceilings.

Keoladeo is inhabited by two species of parakeets of which the **rose-ringed** is the most common. The **plum-headed** is not seen frequently as it remains

NAYAN KHANOLKAR

NAYAN KHANOLKAR

ANSAR KHAN

NAYAN KHANOLKAR

A black-rumped flameback woodpecker (left) on a nest with its young ones and a couple of Indian rollers (blue jays) perched on the branch of a tree

away from the marshes. Parakeets hold a very special place in Indian society and seeing them in the wild is an exciting sight for all.

The **peacock** (*Pavo cristatus*) is the most beautiful bird of the Indian subcontinent and, therefore, deserves the title of the country's national bird. However, the ever-increasing use of pesticides in agricultural fields is taking a heavy toll on these birds. Pairing is done through selection by the female after viewing the courtship dance of several males. Eggs are laid in a shallow pit under the dense scrub and incubation is done by the female only. The hidden nests remain invisible to people and though peacock dances are commonly seen in jungles and gardens, their mating remains unnoticed by people because it is momentary and the action is concealed by the long, huge train feathers of peacocks. Therefore, there are several misconceptions; many believe that their eggs are the product of peacock tears, which it sheds on its legs and feet as these are ugly as compared to its beautiful body and tail feathers.

The **black-rumped flame-backed (golden-backed) woodpecker** is a strikingly colourful bird. Onlookers are spellbound by its glittering bright golden back and prominent red crest. It nests in tree holes. The chicks are born adorned with colours similar to their parents.

The **blue jay or Indian roller** is another common bird here. In many parts of India, it is regarded as a sacred bird and called Neelkanth (a name of Lord

NAYAN KHANOLKAR

NAYAN KHANOLKAR

White-eyes (left) are small passerine birds, a resident breeder in open woodland. Golden orioles (right) make beautiful hammock-like nests on treetops

Shiva) after its blue throat. The grey hornbill is the only one from this genera in the park. This enormous brownish-grey bird has a huge, curved, blackish bill and a long tail. Another characteristic feature is a pointed casque on its black bill. Its nesting is most peculiar; the female lays eggs in a hole in the branch of a tree or in its trunk. This hole is sealed by the male from outside with wet mud and a slit is created to feed the female and the young ones. Excreta and other waste are transferred to the male by the female through her beak. After the chicks are a week old, the female bird breaks open the seal and comes out; both parents then feed the chicks. Photographing the male feeding coloured figs from the peepal tree to the female and the chicks is a real treat.

The **coppersmith barbet** is another beautiful nester found in the park. Though the sighting of this bird, camouflaged in the green foliage of trees, is rather difficult, its distinctive 'tuk-tuk-tuk-tuk' sound makes its presence felt from a distance. During the mating period, the male barbet woos the female by offering figs from banyan and peepal trees. The **magpie robin** is a long-tailed black-and-white bird. At times it emits a rich piping song-like sound because of which it enjoys the status of Bangladesh's national bird. It feeds on insects and invertebrates and nests in tree holes or buildings, even in human habitations. Among shrikes, only the **great grey, bay-backed and long-tailed** breed in the park from April to August; however, the red-backed, brown and grey-backed varieties can also be found here. **Treepie**, a long-tailed bird, is quite noisy, bold and inquisitive. It cleans undesired meat from a tiger's teeth by sitting on its face and is thus rightly titled the 'toothpick of a tiger'. It is a treat to watch the pendant-like nests of **sun birds**. The nest is a vertical oblong pouch suspended from the tip of a thin out-hanging twig, usually not too high above the ground. The **flowerpecker**'s nest, too,

The omnivorous rufous treepie eating a huge fruit and a rose-ringed parakeet (below) enjoying ficus berries

NAVIN SHARMA

NAYAN KHANOLKAR

is a hanging pouch but made entirely of seeds and vegetation worked into a felt-like fibre. The **white eye**, a light green bird, merges with the leaves of shrubs. Its eyes are not actually white but it has a conspicuous white circle around them. Its nest, a tiny hanging cup placed like a hammock between two twigs, remains concealed in foliage. Shanti Kutir, the forest resthouse area where a few pairs invariably breed in a shrub, is a good place to watch its nest. The **golden oriole** is a summer nester here. The male, with a bright golden yellow body, black wings and a pink bill, is an attractive bird. It emits a fluting sound. Nest photography is difficult owing to its location, which they build high on the trees. Though four cuckoo species breed here from April to September the most conspicuous are the **pied and common hawks**. The latter resembles a shikra from a distance. It is highly vocal during April to June when it makes a repetitive call in a high pitch, 'Brain Fever-Brain

ANSAR KHAN

Fever-Brain Fever'; it is rightly recognised as the brain fever bird. Thirteen species of minivets inhabit the park. The **scarlet minivet** may be easily found in the dense foliage of the large trees near Kadam Kunj. It has a loud penetrating musical whistle.

By early October, swarms of **rosy pastors** may be seen landing in Keoladeo. After a few days, most of these head towards the south. By March, they are here again for back migration to their homeland. They are joined by **starlings** (*Sturnus vulgaris*) and a large number of **wagtails** (*Motacilla spp*); together, they enjoy themselves in the reeds till is time to go back. The

Another beautiful nester in the park, the coppersmith barbet **(left)** *carrying peepal figs to feed its chicks and a black partridge* **(right)**

ANSAR KHAN

green, blue-cheeked and blue-tailed bee-eaters are commonly found in the park. These highly sociable birds perch on wires, bare branches and open ground in a single file. They feed in air, mainly on dragonflies, and nest in self-excavated burrows in banks. Once, I found their nests covered by labourers working on the peripheral road near Gulupura. The management has to, therefore, be cautious while constructing or repairing earthen tracks, bunds, mounds and so on.

The **white-breasted kingfisher** is an attractive multi-coloured bird. It is interesting to watch the pair digging a two to three feet-long upward inclined tunnel in an earthen bank, using their strong bills and dragging the dust out with their toes while leaning on their wings. It is a really labourious task. The **lesser pied kingfisher**, a black-and-white bird, is predominantly a fisher bird that may be seen hovering over waters. It can stay in the air like

NAVIN SHARMA

Stone curlew eggs camouflaged in the surroundings (**above**) *and a pied kingfisher* (**below**) *who has succeeded in catching fish from the lake.* **Facing page:** *Crow pheasants can be seen all over the park*

NAYAN KHANOLKAR

A white-breasted kingfisher with a mouse it has just caught

a helicopter and dives into the water with folded wings and emerges out with a fish in its beak. It is a magical bird and a great entertainer in lakes and ponds. The nest of the **stone curlew** is just a few scratches on bare open ground. I have on many occasions found its nests next to the vehicle track, highly susceptible to damage, probably built to save eggs and hatchlings from reptiles, which avoid movements in open areas. This clever bird misleads the predator by aerial attacks and a broken wing display. Its eggs also merge with the bleached pallets of the nilgai. The female hatches the eggs but the male guards and warns of any imminent danger. When the first chick is hatched, the male takes over. It is interesting to watch the parents carrying water in their feathers to feed the young ones. The **grey partridge** (grey francolin) and **quails** breed on the ground in camouflaged nests. These common birds in open forests are most susceptible to poaching.

NON-AVIAN FAUNA

Keoladeo is a small park with about one-third of its area remaining underwater for a substantial period of the year. It is, therefore, not possible to have a huge population of non-avian fauna. Still, its habitat diversity helps in supporting a fairly large number of mammals, reptiles, fish, butterflies, insects and so on. Undoubtedly, water is a critical factor in all the wildlife reserves falling under the dry-deciduous category. From the viewpoint of ecological requirement, the huge Keoladeo lakes are the chief source of attraction and multiplication of numerous wildlife species.

Turtles during courtship; seven species of turtle can be found in Keoladeo

NAVIN SHARMA

Much before the development of the canal system here, the grassland and woodland spread all around the natural depression were developed as important deer hunting grounds by the British. A masonry wall was erected for the protection of the reserve. This resulted in the protection of the animals from poaching but, at the same time, their movements got restricted. It also impacted their foraging area and adversely affected their population. The spotted deer and blackbuck population were probably the worst affected. During the unusual flood of 1972, almost the entire population of spotted deer got washed away from the park, of which only a small fraction could be rescued. Presently, about 500 spotted deer (chital) inhabit the park and are easily sighted. According to George Schaller, a scientist who had worked in Keoladeo in 1965–66, the blackbuck population then was 70, which went down to just 19 after the flood. Later, some blackbucks were added from the Tal Chhapar Sanctuary but the original population could not be revived.

Till the 1980s, the park had a sustainable population of blackbucks. Scarcity of water and habitat loss owing to the invasion of P. juliflora *has led to their extinction from here*

The **sambar**, with its beautiful antlers, can be seen feeding on grass and other vegetation in the wet prairie. It is the largest Indian deer and is basically a browser who chiefly depends on palatable shrubs. The rapid increase in *Prosopis juliflora* caused a huge loss to its habitat. Therefore, its population remained static at around 20. Inbreeding in such a small population may have caused further loss. To counter this, in 1998–99, a few sambar deer were added here from the Jaipur zoo. Unfortunately, this, too, could not improve its progeny. The **hog deer** is a small deer that feeds on low grass. It also loves a cool climate and Keoladeo is certainly not a suitable habitat to support this deer. There were three hog deer here but, unfortunately, they got flushed out of the park during the 1972 flood. Somehow, one hog deer has again arrived here and is sometimes sighted by the lakeside. The **blue bull**, also called nilgai, is the country's largest antelope. It is present here in significant numbers owing to Keoladeo's huge grassland. Though it generally does not prefer to graze in water, it has adapted to grazing on aquatic vegetation such as *Paspalum distichum*. It is a winter breeder.

The **wild boar** is an omnivorous animal but loves grass root. The grassland of Keoladeo are very tempting for them. According to V.S. Saxena, the Divisional Forest Officer of Bharatpur in 1973, after the flood the wild boar population was reduced to 191. The infestation of *Prosopis juliflora* in the grassland had seriously affected its feeding grounds but the overall population of this profuse breeder has not been much affected. They may be seen roaming in the entire park, except for the wetlands.

In 1982, after Keoladeo became a national park, cattle grazing was put to a halt. The reserve was fortified by strengthening its masonry wall that was erected on the periphery. Consequently, some **unproductive cows**, unclaimed by villagers, got trapped here. Efforts are on to evict them from the park; several of these have been transported to far-off places but due to the vested interests of the local people, their total eradication could not be accomplished. Presently, the park is burdened with about 1,500 cows.

The **porcupine** has soft hair but sharp quills on its back, sides and tail. These quills typically lie flat but on a threat these stand erect in an attention mode and function as a persuasive deterrent. The porcupine cannot shoot them at predators, as people generally believe, but the quills detach easily and penetrate the invader. It is a nocturnal and basically herbivorous animal that eats bark, wood, leaves, buds, twigs, nuts, seeds, fruits as well as tubers and grass but it also occasionally feeds on insects, small reptiles and eggs. It is typically a solitary animal. A mother and her young are considered a family group called a prickle. It breeds in winter and during this period it develops a conspicuous bunch of hair on the tail and becomes very vocal. The porcupine lives in deep burrows made in the soil and prefers upland saline patches with soft soil. It is thrilling to watch this animal in the jungle during night hours. Tourists residing at Shanti Kutir or the Forest Lodge (the RTDC hotel inside the park) have the opportunity of seeing this nocturnal animal displaying its beautiful quill umbrella. Quills provide protection to the porcupine against carnivores, but not against poachers.

ANSAR KHAN

The **pangolin** is another important and rare rodent that used to inhabit Keoladeo. V.S. Saxena's report of 1975 is the last documentary evidence available on the

ANSAR KHAN

Hyenas mating. **Facing page:** *The pangolin, said to be the most poached animal in the world*

presence of its original population. In 2011, one pangolin appeared in a village of the Deeg area (about 30 km, as the crow flies, from Keoladeo). The villagers handed over this strange animal to the park authorities. K.R. Anoop, the then Director of the park, sensibly released the animal near the fire watchtower of Koladahar. It gradually shifted from the watchtower area towards the park's Naswaria protection post where it was frequently observed feeding on the staff's food waste from the garbage pit. Two years later, one more pangolin was brought to the park authorities from a village near Beawar (about 30 km, as the crow flies, from the park). It was also released in the Koladahar area.

The **jackal** is an important omnivore of Keoladeo, which no one staying here can fail to notice. These brown-coated dog-like animals are highly social and live in packs. They mate in winter and breed during summer in burrows dug by them or under culverts and even inside large-size cement pipes. The best places to watch them on these burrows with puppies are Block N and close to the Malah boring. During dusk, just before night spreads its darkness over the jungle, they communicate to their group through a unison call. This call closely resembles that of humans. They seemed to have synchronised their unison call with the ringing of the bell of the Sitaram temple, located inside the park on the eastern periphery. With the disappearance of vultures,

ANSAR KHAN

the burden of cleaning carcasses has increased upon jackals so it fortunate that the park is blessed with large numbers of jackals.

The **hyena** is a scavenger that inhabits here in an adequate number. Though it feeds in the adjoining villages it prefers to breed in the safety of the park. In the absence of vultures its responsibility of maintaining hygiene by cleaning off the carcasses of animals and birds has increased multifold in the last three decades. Several small cats, namely, the jungle cat, palm civet and fishing cat, have also enriched the fauna of the park. During the early night hours, the Sitaram temple is the best place to watch **palm civets**, which have formed a niche here. They feed and roost on the tall trees. The **jungle cat**, though not common here, may be sighted in any part of the park even during day hours. The **fishing cat**, however, is the star attraction of Keoladeo. Water

ABRAR KHAN

ANSAR KHAN

A fishing cat (left) on a hunt after dusk and an alert jungle cat, who appears non-friendly. **Facing page:** *A small Indian civet shifting its cub to a safer place*

ABRAR KHAN

NAVIN SHARMA

scarcity, persisting from 1997 to 2007, compelled this nocturnal-specialist fish-eater to remain away from the park for many years but the increased water intake has now drawn it back. During summer, it normally migrates to the canal called 'Sujan Ganga' located in Bharatpur town and the adjoining agricultural fields that have small water bodies. The deeper water bodies of the Keoladeo and Sitaram temples are the best places to see the cat in action.

The **otter**, a specialist fish-eater, is another star attraction at the park. In March 1990, I saw otters taking a dust bath and regularly devouring fish from the deeper water body of Block D, near the Keoladeo temple, between 3pm and 5pm. It was a real sight to watch them chopping off the fish's head before eating; this discarded portion is utilised by black-necked storks who follow the otters for this purpose. Unfortunately, repeated droughts compelled the animal to migrate from the Keoladeo lakes. Improved water conditions in the park may bring it back. I feel that it must be reintroduced here as early as possible in the interest of the park and the species. Keoladeo is a safe haven for this rare animal.

After 1965, when the last **leopard** was shot, no large mammalian predator has inhabited the park on a permanent basis. Though the masonry boundary wall cannot stop the movement of leopards it can certainly hinder their free movement. By nature, the leopard is a long-ranging animal; hide and attack is the modus operandi of this clever carnivore.

Disturbance in the form of tourists and the field officials posted at different outposts spread over the entire park makes Keoladeo inhospitable to leopards. Therefore, leopards have started using the park only for short intervals. In 2017, a male leopard started frequenting the park but did not make many

---

Facing page: *The otter* **(above)***, a rare animal, is found in the park and is said to be a star attraction here. Jackals in a pack* **(below)** *can be highly aggressive while they are feeding*

kills here. Evidently, it was using the park chiefly as a safe hideout. Keoladeo is a park where even the tourists move on foot or cycles on interior trails. The movement of ferocious animals is dangerous.

In 2000, a stray **tigress** reached here unnoticed; no one had any clue as to how and from where it had come. It remained confined to the park's southern zone, mostly Block F3. In those days this entire area was full of thick shrubs and trees of spiny *Prosopis juliflora*. Certainly, such a habitat is the last choice for a tiger but it appears it preferred this block because of the impregnable thickets of this thorny jungle. This shows how frightened

---

Tiger T-7, who had fled from the Ranthambore Tiger Reserve, captured in a trap camera at Keoladeo on March 10, 2010

DIRECTOR, KEOLADEO NATIONAL PARK

the animal was! It lived here for about half-a-decade but was rarely sighted by the park personnel. This behaviour is an indicator of one factor only and that was its old age. In all likelihood, this tigress was driven away by the powerful ones from its home, which was probably at Ranthambore or Kuno (a wildlife reserve in Madhya Pradesh). Keoladeo is certainly not the right kind of habitat for large carnivores and it could not lead a normal life and ultimately died here unceremoniously.

In 2010, a **tiger** once again chose Keoladeo as its refuge, this time it was a male. It was later identified as tiger T-7 of Ranthambore. This was the infamous tiger that had, in August 2010, seriously hurt Daulat Singh, the then Range Officer of the Ranthambore Tiger Reserve. Daulat Singh was trying to tranquillise the animal in the agricultural fields for shifting it back to the safety of the reserve. The panicked tiger fled from the scene and roamed through Agra and Mathura, finally finding refuge in the forests of Keoladeo. Though the animal was safe here, it could not contain itself in the grassland area alone. Moreover, the habitat conditions had also changed drastically since the time the tigress died here as the *Prosopis juliflora* thickets used by the tigress for its secret hideout had been removed during 2007–08. More than once the tiger, marching on the main road (the central spine of the tourism zone), leisurely walked into a residential colony of Bharatpur town, passing through the main entrance gate of the park. Fortunately, it happened in the night hours and the tiger returned back to the safety of the park after a short stroll. Alarmed, the park management soon shifted it to the Sariska Tiger Reserve where it has not only established itself but has already fathered five surviving cubs and has thus become the flagbearer in establishing a sustainable tiger population in Sariska.

ANSAR KHAN

These two experiences and ecological reasons suggest that Keoladeo is certainly not the right kind of home for big cats. The park administration must keep constant vigil over the movements of leopards as well and if the animal extends its stay at Keoladeo it would be advisable to shift it to some suitable tiger reserve.

Fish play a key role in an aquatic system. The success of the world famous Keoladeo heronries mainly depends upon the availability of fish fry and

Catfish being driven out of water by volunteers of Life Line Nature Society. They pose a serious threat to the fish fauna at the park and are caught and killed right on the spot

fingerlings. 'Fry' is the first stage in the development of a fish. When it grows scales and working fins, its transition to a juvenile fish is complete. At that stage, this finger-sized fish is called a fingerling. Up until 2008, the only source of fish into the Keoladeo lakes was the Ajan Dam and, according to a study conducted by BNHS (1980–90), 50 species of fish used to inhabit Keoladeo. New sources such as Chambal (Dholpur) and the Govardhan drain, collecting flood water from Dholpur, Haryana, Bharatpur and Mathura, were added later. This has resulted in a few more species. A bibliographic review report by the Wildlife Institute of India reveals that 57 species of fish have been recorded in the Keoladeo National Park; seven are new and reported after 1995. Of these, **African catfish** (*Clarias gariepinus),* also known as the African magur, exotic magur or sharptooth catfish, is one of the most dangerous invasive aquatic species of the park which, though an omnivore, feeds mainly on other fish. This common African fish was introduced in the fifties to the Indo-China region by the French. In Keoladeo, it was seen for the first time in 2005 (B. Anjan Kumar Prusty et al. 2007). Probably it was introduced in the catchment of the Ajan Dam from where it reached the Keoladeo lakes along with the water. It proved to be a serious threat to the fish fauna here. The park management prepared a plan (2006–16) to eradicate this fish from the Keoladeo lakes. I have seen Bijoy, the then Director of the park, physically working in the lakes, along with staff members, to catch the fish. An NGO, Life Line Nature Society, under its captain Ansar Khan, also took part in this crusade with great enthusiasm. It is owing to their combined and dedicated efforts that most of the catfish were caught and killed on the spot. Though only a small population remains in the park but, with the inflow of Ajan water, fresh influx is bound to infest the Keoladeo lakes; therefore, the park management has to be extra vigilant.

Of the entire fish population, only six species, namely *Channa punctatus*, *Channa striatus*, *Channa marulius*, *Notopterus notopterus*, *Heteropneustes fossils* and *Clarias batrachus*, breed in the park. During the dry period, these fish move to the deeper water bodies of Blocks D, L and K as well as the Sitaram temple. Though, in general, fish breed with the onset of the monsoon, the *Channa* species starts spawning in April. They could well have adapted this mechanism to survive through their next generations. This phenomenon is seen in several annual plant species as well. They produce seeds before dying out and the seed lies dormant till the conditions are favourable. A study conducted by BNHS in 1988 reveals that over 460 tonnes of fish were consumed by the nestlings and adults of the colonial breeders (excluding the open-bill stork and cattle egret, which do not consume fish), in the breeding season. By this fact itself, the annual requirement of all the 22 piscivorous birds may easily be estimated to go beyond 650 tonnes per year when enough water is received in the park. Though the adjoining water bodies contribute significantly, the major requirement comes from Keoladeo's fish stock, which is partly fulfilled by the *in situ* breeding of the six species; outer sources such as the Ajan Dam also contribute significantly.

Fish may be grouped as **air breathers** and **non-air breathers**. Since waters with dense, decomposed vegetation have low oxygen, therefore, non-air breathers, who depend upon oxygen from water only, avoid such habitats and prefer waters with sparse vegetation. But the air breathers such as *Channa punctatus, C. striatus, Clarias batrachus* and *Heteropneustes fossilis* can be seen inhabiting all kinds of waters. The *Channa punctatus* also show a preference for thick *Paspalum distichum* dominated areas. Fish feed on plant material, insects, larvae, algae and microbes; they become tertiary consumers when they feed on other fish. The catfish is the best example of this. Large, fresh shoots, leaves and submerged portions of plants act as home as well as food for fish. The *Typha angustata* reeds, with rotting vegetation and several organisms that thrive on plant life, act as a genuine food store for fish and shoals of fish may be seen feasting and swimming here.

Pythons are huge snakes, but most of them are non-poisonous. Though they are found in most forests in the Indian subcontinent, Keoladeo supports these in exceptionally large numbers. This is mainly due to the easy availability of loose saline soil and the presence of jackals and porcupines throughout the park. Interestingly, pythons live in the burrows dug by these mammals, generally in loose saline soil patches spread across almost the entire park, especially in the southern and southeastern flanks. In marshy areas, pythons prefer hollow trees and termite mounds. The reticulated python (*Python reticulates*) and rock python (*Python molurus*) are the two species found in the Indian subcontinent. Keoladeo is inhabited by the Indian rock python (*P. m. molorus*), one of the two races of the rock python. Another race, *P. m. bivittatus*, is popularly known as the Burmese python. The Indian python has a long life and can survive for over 20 years in zoo conditions. So far, the largest size found in Keoladeo is 11.8 feet.

Python is a non-poisonous snake but it can swallow a big prey such as a deer

ANSAR KHAN

The python breeds once it has reached the age of five. Mating takes place during December to February and around 8 to 100 eggs are laid in March–June. Incubation and protection to the eggs are provided by the female only. Individual pythons can be identified by the size and pattern of the blotches on their body, from neck to tail.

Winter is quite cool in Keoladeo and this compels most of the pythons to hibernate in the burrows and bask under the sun on the surface of these holes. The sighting of many pythons at designated places attracts park visitors but this causes disturbance to the snakes, depriving them of an opportunity to heat their bodies. It will be advisable to erect see-through fencing around these burrows and provide some elevated platforms at a respectable distance from the burrows. This will facilitate tourists and researchers to have a risk- and nuisance-free sighting and they can take photographs of these pythons in leisure. In Keoladeo, birds and mammals form the main part of the food of pythons who have been observed eating spot-bill, purple moorhen, coucal, teal, grey partridge, redstart, hare, chital, porcupine and so on. Pythons have two rows of very sharp teeth angled toward the throat, capable of executing a painful bite. They use their saw-like teeth during the first phase of their attack, which is sudden and then immediately tighten their hold upon the lungs of the prey by coiling around its body. The prey, unable to breathe, soon succumbs and is swallowed head first. Nature has gifted pythons with special jaws. The animal is swallowed inch by inch alternately by its lower jaws. A regular supply of saliva helps in smooth swallowing. In spite of this killing ability, their burrows are shared by porcupines (*Hystrix indica*) and bi-coloured leaf-nosed bats (*Hipposideros fulvus*). White-breasted kingfishers (*Halcyon smyrnensis*) are also seen nesting at the entrance of the python holes.

This python nest was found on Ghana Canal near the park

Surprisingly, these mighty pythons also suffer predation. The common monitor lizard (*Varanus bengalensis*) is observed pilfering hatched and unhatched python eggs. Though their shining skin seems quite delicate, pythons are actually quite tough, yet they fall victim in sizeable numbers to trampling by nilgai and the feral cattle inhabiting the park. During winter, poachers from adjacent villages become more active and they look for wild meat, especially a porcupine's. They destroy the burrows to catch porcupines and thus the disturbed pythons are compelled to leave these holes in search of new burrows. It is noticed that during this season pythons become extremely weak for want of nourishment. Also, during February–March, their frequency of mating and inter-hole movement gets accelerated, enhancing trampling cases. At the end of winter and the onset of summer the gravid females, ready to lay eggs, are susceptible to trampling while moving around in search of safe breeding places.

I have also observed that pythons sloughing (about to shed their skin) become easy victims of trampling as snakes become sluggish and partially blind during such times. Therefore, it is advisable to cordon the zones that have clusters of python holes to save them from being trampled by hoofed animals. Night patrolling should be done in upland areas with porcupine burrows to stop their poaching by adjacent villagers and hunters, such as the Banjaras.

ANSAR KHAN

NAVIN SHARMA

A common monitor lizard (**above**) *eating a snake and* (**below**) *a mongoose catching a snake*

Apart from pythons, many other species of snakes inhabit the park. Of these, **cobra** and **vipers** are quite poisonous. It is interesting to watch a duel between the arch rivals, the snake and the **mongoose**. At times, **monitor lizards** attack snakes but the python takes revenge for the killings. I have observed pythons swallowing these huge lizards at Keoladeo.

A crowned river turtle posing for a photograph

Though **turtles** and **tortoises** seem alike they are totally different from the viewpoint of their habits and habitats. The turtle is an aquatic animal whereas the tortoise is a land animal. Only three species of tortoise and 22 species of turtle are found in India. Of these, one species of tortoise, namely, Star Tortoise and 10 species of turtle are found in Rajasthan. Keoladeo is inhabited by seven species of turtle but no tortoises dwell here. The lakes are blessed with four species of the hard-shell and three of the soft-shell turtle. Compared to the hard-shell, the latter bears a relatively thinner and flatter shell, which also lacks scutes. It has three toes in each limb as against the hard-shell, which has four to five toes.

The **crowned river turtle** (*Hardella thurjii*), known as kala dhond in Hindi, falls under the 'Vulnerable' category as per IUCN classification. It bears four yellow-orange stripes on each side of its head. The male grows up to 21 cm while the female goes up to 60 cm. This shy animal is quite common in Keoladeo and feeds largely on aquatic vegetation. The **Indian roofed turtle** (*Kachuga tecta*), also known as chandan kachhua, is a low risk, near threatened species, according to IUCN classification. Its neck is distinctively striped and bears red or orange crescent marking near the eyes. The carapace is elevated with flat sides and a strong median keel (spiked). So far, no specimen larger than 25 cm in size has been found in Keoladeo.

The **spotted pond turtle** (*Geoclemys hamiltonii*) has been listed as 'Vulnerable' by IUCN and also included in Schedule I of the Wildlife (Protection) Act. It can be differentiated from the other species by the presence of three keels on its upper shell (carapace), downward curved upper jaw and yellow radiating streaks in each scute. It bears several yellow/orange spots on its head and soft parts. The male has a concave plastron and a longer tail that extends beyond the shell. The turtle grows up to 50 cm. It is a specialist feeder on mollusks and is gifted with strong jaws capable of crushing and breaking open hard mollusk shells.

The **three-striped roofed turtle** (*Kachuga dhongoka*) is a Schedule I species as per the Wildlife (Protection) Act and figures in IUCN's 'Vulnerable' category. This brown or olive turtle bears three black stripes along the length of its shell. Its carapace is depressed but the median keel (ridge) is prominent. It attains a maximum length of 50 cm and breeds in March–April. The **Indian flapshell turtle** (*Lissemys punctata*) is a Schedule I species as per the Wildlife (Protection) Act and figures as 'Near Threatened' in IUCN's

NAVIN SHARMA

The Keoladeo National Park is home to 75 species of butterflies such as **(clockwise from top right)** *the butterfly plain tiger (*Danaus plexxipus*), the pioneer butterfly (*Benois aurota*) in tail-to-tail mating and the common cerulean (*Jamides celeno*)*

---

classification. It is the smallest of all the soft-shelled turtles found in India and grows only up to 37 cm. Its shell and soft parts are largely olive green. This turtle is an opportunistic omnivore that feeds on live and dead matters of plants and animals. It nests from June to November and lays four to 15 eggs. During a drought, it may aestivate for months. It suffers continued and widespread exploitation throughout the country.

The **Indian peacock soft-shell turtle** (*Aspideretus hurum*) is a Schedule I species as per the Wildlife (Protection) Act. Juveniles have four to six eye-like markings, called 'ocelli', on the carapace, which resemble the ocelli found in peacock feathers; these markings keep disappearing with age. It grows up to 60 cm. The **Indian soft-shell turtle** (*Aspideretus gangeticus*) is a Schedule I species as per the Wildlife (Protection) Act and figures in the 'Vulnerable' category of IUCN classification. This omnivorous animal is the largest in the park and may grow up to 100 cm. It breeds in the monsoon and can lay up to 50 eggs.

Butterflies are the most beautiful of all insects. Their existence in nature is well established through some of their 56 million-year-old fossils. They have a four-stage life cycle (holometabolous). Courtship is often aerial and involves pheromones; they then mate on the ground or a perch. Copulation takes place tail-to-tail and may last from minutes to hours. Nature has blessed them with a special glue for fixing their eggs to leaves. These eggs develop into larvae called caterpillars. Scientists believe that the larvae of some species belonging to the Lycaenidae family form an association with ants and use vibrations and chemical signals as a medium for mutual communication. The larvae enjoy some kind of protection from ants in lieu of secretions. In the third stage, the caterpillar grows into a pupa, which ultimately transforms in the fourth stage into an adult butterfly by tearing off its pupa skin. Butterflies are often polymorphic and many are sexually dimorphic. Generally they are diurnal, unlike moths. Wasps, protozoans, flies and other invertebrates and organisms are their natural predators. Several butterfly species make use of camouflage, mimicry and aposematism techniques for protection against the predators.

Butterflies, totalling some 18,500 species, are distributed all over the world except for Antarctica. Of these, 1,641 are found in the Indian region (Varshney, 2006) and Keoladeo inhabits 75 species (Trigunayat, M.M.). Many butterflies are long distance migrants; some species take generations to complete migration as no single individual completes the whole trip. There is a reverse migration in the spring. Spectacular large-scale migrations associated with the monsoon are seen in peninsular India. Some scientists believe that butterflies use a time-compensated sun compass and polarised light to navigate even in cloudy conditions. In Keoladeo, though many species are common, there are others that keep migrating to and fro. The large cabbage white butterfly stays in the park during March and April; the glossy tiger is seen during the monsoon; the blue tiger in December and then again in February and March; and the painted lady visits the park in October–November and again from February to April. Butterflies feed primarily on nectar from flowers. Some also derive nourishment from pollen, tree sap, rotting fruit, dung, decaying flesh and dissolved minerals in wet sand or dirt. Many species of butterflies maintain territories and actively chase away other species or individuals that may stray into them. Basking is an activity that is more common in the cool hours of the morning. Butterflies are threatened in their early stages by parasitoids and in all stages by predators, diseases and environmental factors. The study of the structural colouration of the wing scales of swallowtail butterflies has led to the development of more efficient light-emitting diodes. This is inspiring nanotechnology researchers to produce paints that do not use toxic pigments and develop new display technologies.

Keoladeo is an important habitat for butterflies. Its diverse vegetation, which includes a variety of grass and flowers, deserves credit for its rich assortment of butterflies. Butterfly larvae thrive on the herbs, shrubs, bushes and trees found in the park. The invasion of *P. juliflora*, however, should be checked in order to save their habitats. Birth, growth and decomposition are the three stages through which plants and animals pass to complete nature's cycle. Insects have an important role to play in all three stages. Seed-bearing plants owe their germination largely to insects. Honey bees and butterflies are the best example. In their absence, the plant kingdom would have been reduced to an insignificant level as these are the principal transporters of pollen and are responsible for the production of fruits and seeds that give birth to innumerable plants.

Insects also form a major part of food for the animal kingdom and thus help them to grow and reproduce through breeding. It is insects and fungi that largely take part in the recycling of nutrients in the system through the decomposition of dead organisms. Beetles and their larvae, flies, maggots, worms and bacteria are known decomposers. Of course, moulds and fungi (not an insect) also act as active converters.

Keoladeo, with its unique diversity, provides habitat to numerous species of **aquatic as well as terrestrial and arboreal insects**. Almost all the birds, reptiles and amphibians feed on insects. Thus, insects form a huge part of food for the animal kingdom here. They also play an important role as converters by cleaning off carcasses of organisms and dead or rotting vegetable matter and excretal wastes. They convert the complex organic material into simple inorganic elements that enrich the soil and help in the germination of new plants and feed several others to grow, mature and produce flowers and fruits. Indeed, they play an important role in running the food chain in every ecosystem. In the park, macro invertebrates such as worms, insects and mollusks are present in more abundance in variety and numbers than any other group of organisms. They are food for many fish, birds and some mammals. Aquatic insects mainly include bugs, beetles, striders, swimmers, chironomid larvae and the nymphs of dragonflies and damselflies. The tortoise beetle (*Cassida circumdata*), along with its larvae, devours the leaves of the weed *Ipomea aquatica* and checks its growth to a certain extent in autumn and winter.

In the Keoladeo National Park, land insects are in abundance and have a positive effect on the breeding of land birds. Two species and one sub-species of wild rice grow in the lush green wet prairie habitats. Several grasshoppers and other insects thrive on these plants, which further feed many spiders and mantises. The *Typha angustata* reeds are an excellent host to organisms that survive on this plant. Dragonflies and frogs may be seen most active on their prey, that is, gnats and mosquitoes.

*A grand parade by dragonflies (*Ditch jewel*).* **Facing page:** *A carpenter bee enjoying pollen from the flowers of a shrub*

NAVIN SHARMA

Dragonflies and **damselflies** (*Insecta: Odonata*) are among the most fascinating insects of this aquatic habitat. In Keoladeo, deeper lake areas, with open water and loose mud at the bottom, are occupied chiefly by freely submerged *Hydrilla verticillata* and *Najas minor* in association with other important species such as *Potamogeton nodosus, Nymphoides indicum, Nymphoides cristatum* and *Nymphaea pubescens.* These areas provide an excellent breeding habitat to several odonate species, which prefer to lay eggs in the plant tissues of submerged plants. In shallow waters, *Paspalum-Ipomoea*'s association with species such as *Paspalum distichum, Ipomoea aquatica, Scirpus littoralis, Scirpus tuberosus* and *Utricularia* attract several varieties of dragonflies and damselflies. The extensive patches of *Paspalum distichum* offer a perfect hiding and roosting place for smaller damselflies such as *Agriocnemis pygmaea, Ceriagrion coromandelianum, Ischnura aurora* and *Ischnura senegalensis.*

An exhaustive study was conducted by Dheerendra Singh, Brijendra Singh and J.T. Hermans in Keoladeo from 2010 to 2015; the findings were published in 2017 in the *Journal of Threatened Taxa* 9 (7): 10445–10452. According to this study, the park inhabits 37 species of odonata order, belonging to 25 genera of four families—Lestidae, Coenagrionidae, Aeshnidae and Libellulidae. The study also showed that, among these, Libellulidae, with 22 species, is the most dominant family here. It was observed that the suborder Zygoptera is dominated by the family Coenagrionidae. The species from both these families are characteristically found in stagnant, mesotrophic waters with well-developed aquatic vegetation that has a mixture of submerged and emerged plant species.

The Keoladeo National Park, a World Heritage Site, attracts visitors from all parts of the world

THE PARK AND ITS PEOPLE

The Keoladeo National Park is certainly a godsend for many people belonging to various classes and sections of society. As an important aquifer, it has been helping the nearby villagers by providing water for drinking as well as irrigation even during drought years by maintaining an underground water level. And, as a World Heritage Site, its contribution to tourism and the growth of the town's economy is huge.

Many important industries such as the SIMCO Railway Wagon Factory and General Engineering Works were set up in Bharatpur city but, unfortunately, they were shut down, chiefly due to labour unrest, depriving people of employment. In such a hostile atmosphere for the growth of industries, tourism started flourishing here owing to the World Heritage status of this unique park. Several hotels, resorts and restaurants have come up in the town. From the ecological point of view, any additional growth in close vicinity to the park is bound to be counterproductive, but there is enough scope for planned development. This growth in the hotel industry has not only generated employment opportunities but has also helped grow the business of other general merchants and transporters.

Keoladeo is probably the only wildlife reserve in India where some 40 years ago a practice of preparing qualified nature guides from locals was started by none other than Kailash Sankhala. Science graduates were selected for the purpose and one month's rigorous training was imparted to them in order to prepare nature guides well versed with the ecology of the park and its flora and fauna. Only successful candidates were provided licences. Also, periodically, during the lean period of summer, refresher courses are organised for these nature guides. Later on, this prerequisite of science graduation was dropped but the practice of selecting new nature guides through appropriate interviews still continues. Several nature guides of Keoladeo have earned national and international level recognition. Their valuable services are availed by important dignitaries and serious wildlifers, especially birders, from across the world. Raj Singh, Dinesh Verma Durrani, Manohar, Pravin Sharma, Krashn Kumar Gupta, Vijay Chansoria, Dharmendra, Vijay Pal Singh, Laxmi Narayan Mudgal, Pradeep Jain, Udai Singh, Hemal Dey, Brijendra Singh, Randhir Singh and Soran are a few names that come to mind in this context. Recently, the legendary birder Abrar Khan, alias Bholu and Sohan Lal have joined this club of eminence, after retirement from a long and invaluable service at Keoladeo.

The concept of allowing the use of non-motorable vehicles such as cycles, tricycle rickshaws and horse-driven tongas in the park was introduced over four decades ago. This has proved to be a visionary step as the eco-friendly transport has freed Keoladeo from petrochemical-generated gases as well as noise pollution. It provides a quiet, undisturbed and totally safe environment to the casual as well as professional birdwatchers and nature photographers. This arrangement gave impetus to visits of groups of students from Jaipur, Delhi, Agra, Mathura and several other cities.

The wise managers organised short but crisp training sessions for these rickshaw pullers; licences were issued for those who qualified to operate inside the park. Over a period of time, most of these pullers have improvised their knowledge about the birds and ecology. They are quick to spot birds and are capable of guiding the general tourists for a small fee. Some of these rickshaw pullers, such as Ratan Singh and Bane Singh, have even procured proper 'Nature Guide' licences from the park authorities. They are now not only guiding tourists but also accompanying serious birdwatchers in Keoladeo and other nature reserves throughout the country. Most of the rickshaw pullers working here are fairly good at bird identification. Of these, Hari Singh, Raju (Sikh) and Devendra need special mention.

It is also worth recounting that many of these pullers were earlier engaged in illicit activities such as the cutting and smuggling of wood from the park. They were a huge challenge to the park authorities who had to put a check on this menace that was causing serious damage to the habitat. Now, they are leading a life of dignity, commanding respect in their villages. Seeing them with binoculars around their necks and guiding Indians as well as foreigners gives me utmost satisfaction and pleasure. As a manager, I have always solicited their valuable contribution in keeping the park clean. It is my strong belief that if approached properly and respectfully they can prove to be important informers—excellent instruments in keeping a vigil over undesirable activities in the park. Apart from rickshaws, bicycles, too, are quite popular among all kinds of visitors here. Most of the hoteliers provide cycles to their guests for a reasonable fee. The park management also supplies cycles to tourists but there have been complaints of poor upkeep; the management must ensure the proper maintenance of these cycles. Golf carts to ferry the tourists between the main gate and the Keoladeo temple have also been introduced. This battery-operated noiseless, slow speed vehicle has proved to be a wonderful eco-friendly carriage. But, looking at the high number of visitors, more carts should be added to the existing thin fleet.

It is sad to see school children marching on foot from the main gate towards the Shanti Kutir barrier and beyond. For such students and most of the other general tourists there is hardly any object of interest between the main gate and Bakalia. Therefore, such a long march is boring for them. Students are our future ambassadors and we should not miss this opportunity of ingraining in them an appreciation of nature with its colourful inhabitants and the wilderness. It is also the duty of the schools to keep their students briefed about the dos and don'ts—not to make any noise, cause disturbance to other tourists, harm any animal or litter the place during their visits. As Director, I had made it compulsory to take at least one guide per group not exceeding 20 students. The management is expected to strictly adhere to it in the interests of the park as well as the people who visit it.

The necessity of a nature interpretation centre was a long-felt need for this World Heritage Site. Fortunately, World Wide Fund for Nature (WWF)-India took the lead and brought in D. Swarovski & Co (Austria) as an important partner who not only financed the entire project but took a genuine interest in developing it into a real treasure. WWF-India and

Rickshaws and cycles are popular modes of transport here

the then Director of the park, Shruti Sharma, deserve special mention for their dedication. The centre was appropriately named after the great ornithologist, Salim Ali, who has been decorated with the Padma Bhushan and Padma Vibhushan by the Government of India. The Salim Ali Visitor Interpretation Centre was inaugurated by Pratibha Patil, the then Governor of Rajasthan, in 2006. The aim is to reach out to a wide range of people and provide information on the wetland and its unique characteristics through exhibits, nature trails, trainings and other resource material. This centre was conferred the Best Asian Wetland Centre Award 2010 on 23 November 2010 by Wetlands Links International (WLI) at its third international conference in Malaysia. A team from WWF-India received this award.

The state government of Rajasthan, through its Chief Wildlife Warden (CWLW), is maintaining this asset but there is a paucity of funds. As per available data, the number of visitors to the Keoladeo National Park has risen from 50,000 in 1995–96 to 147,000 by 2016–17. Accordingly, the revenue to the state government through entry fee here has risen substantially—from ₹10.18 lakh in 1995–96 to ₹205 lakh in 2016–2017. Sixty per cent of this revenue is charged from tourists as eco-surcharge, which should be spent on the ecological development of the park alone, but not a penny has been spent for the development of this park. Regular programmes must be organised to educate school and college students. These would not only provide them with ecological knowledge but also prepare them as crusaders of nature conservation. It will be advisable to organise 10- to 15-minute audio-visual orientation programmes for the visitors at the interpretation centre. For student groups seeking concessions in entry fee, such a mandatory orientation tour, which could be followed by a quick, 10-minute visit to the interpretation centre, can be educative and fun.

K.L. SAINI, EX-DIRECTOR, KEOLADEO NATIONAL PARK

The Salim Ali Visitor Interpretation Centre (**left**) *and Shanti Kutir, the forest rest house*

The residents of Bharatpur always complain of not being given any privilege over the general tourists. No park can flourish without the support of the locals and, therefore, in the interest of the park, it will be desirable to provide appropriate concession to the local people, similar to what is offered to the students on the entry fee.

The Keoladeo National Park showcases nature in all its glory; this is an amazing place where scenes of paradise unfold before our eyes. Tourism is an important tool in the hands of the park management and should be used intelligently and with the utmost care to maximise its benefits. The aim should be to inculcate a deep love and respect for nature and its wild inhabitants in the visitors, while providing them with an absolutely unforgettable experience.

Challenging Nature

Every protected area in the country, at some time or the other, has faced problems of varying magnitudes. Some succeed in overcoming them; others, sadly, succumb to them. Over the years, the Keoladeo National Park has had its fair share of setbacks, of which the most threatening has been, no doubt, after 1996, when a water crisis posed a serious threat to its very survival. Though interruption in the water supply to the park lakes has been its greatest challenge, nature's kingdom is really fragile and there are several other factors that are threatening the existence of this World Heritage Site. Weeds to wildfires, poaching and pollution have together played havoc here. So, before we turn to the disastrous water crisis in the next chapter, let us take a look at the other elements that disturb the harmony of this park.

Eradication of fast-growing weeds, with the help of a non-government organisation

ABRAR KHAN

Swamps are a dynamic system where grass and woodland species keep encroaching upon the marshes; this phenomenon gets a boost when water scarcity develops in the lakes. Invasion by khus grass is so obvious in the lakes, especially in Blocks F1, F4 and E. After the stoppage of the grazing of buffaloes in the park, *Paspalum distichum* grass and *Cyperus alopecuroides* (motha) sedge have been trying to dominate other important aquatic species and open water bodies. The management has been using several techniques to control the unrestricted spread of these species as they are posing a threat to the aquatic habitat. During winter these are cut and pulled out from the lakes. After winter, the villagers are allowed to take away *Paspalum* under controlled conditions. In summer the infested lake areas are scrapped using bulldozers and then burnt.

Water hyacinth *(Eichhornia crassipes)* also poses a perpetual threat to the water bodies. Every year, it drifts into the park along with the water supplied from the Ajan Dam and other sources. It is the fastest multiplying plant and takes over the open water bodies within a few days. This weed has to be pulled out manually almost throughout the year; the least laxity can prove hazardous to the ecosystem.

Wood collection in the reserve is very common by the residents of adjacent villages as this park has no buffer area. These villages depend chiefly on Keoladeo for their day-to-day requirement of firewood and timber. Another major problem is the removal of firewood as headload by city women. In fact, many people in the Bharatpur township use firewood as the main energy source for cooking and heating and thus, this group of headloaders keeps thriving. Though masonry fencing has been built all around the park, it is often breached. Only regular patrolling and stringent exemplary punishment

Water scarcity has given a boost to the invasion by khus grass in the wetlands

can put a check on this illicit activity. Providing cooking gas (LPG) in these villages and to selected poor families on a subsidy basis may prove to be an effective measure towards minimising this problem.

Most of the people inhabiting the peripheral villages live in grass thatched houses where the grass needs replacement after every two to three years. Fortunately, Keoladeo has enough grass for this purpose, provided it is

The use of bulldozers is an effective way of managing the growing weed menace

removed in a systematic manner. Grassland are home to several bird species and mammals. Many of these, including rare eagles and vultures, breed here; these may be disturbed and forced to leave their nests. The ground nests of terrestrial birds may get spoiled; there could even be a fire hazard. Poaching of animals and birds and theft of other produce may take place. Therefore, I have always been of the opinion that grass should be provided to the villagers in a regulated and transparent manner. During my last tenure, I divided the entire grassland into several compartments and allowed the removal of grass free of cost by the villagers from the designated compartments. In order to provide a year's replenishing time, grass from each compartment should be harvested bi-annually only but strictly after the fall of their seed. For the sake of transparency, properly framed full-scale maps of the park, showing the compartments with a clear note to indicate which year which compartment is to be cut, were hung at all the concerned outposts falling under the various *naka*s (checkposts). These are still hanging there; the faded ones need to be replaced. No system will deliver the desired results unless the park management functions in a dedicated manner. After all, it is a sensitive matter pertaining to people who are our immediate neighbours.

Grazing has been a serious nuisance in Keoladeo for long; even the masonry wall around the park cannot curb this problem. In 1981, after Keoladeo was declared a national park, serious efforts were made by the management to completely stop this grazing. People confronted the park personnel, which led to firing by the state police, in which seven villagers died. This tragedy shook everybody and became instrumental in spoiling relations between the park authorities and the villagers. After this incident, the villagers removed their productive cattle from the park, but several hundred unproductive cows were left feral here. Efforts were made to trap these cows and release them outside the park, but only a few could be caught due to their wild behaviour. Taking advantage of the situation, the villagers started pushing their non-milking cows inside the park through breaches in the masonry wall. They used to take out these cows when they started lactating.

In 1989, a serious attempt was carried out to castrate the feral bulls to stop the breeding of these cows. Also, an experiment was conducted to sterilise them through an injectable chemical. This injection was named 'Talsur' after its inventors, Dr Suri and Dr Talwar of the National Institute of Immunology, Delhi. Maneka Gandhi, the then Forest Minister, Government of India and a known animal lover, was extremely keen on this operation because Talsur could sterilise the bulls without depriving them of the pleasure of mating with cows. Some bulls were injected with Talsur but this could not go ahead for two reasons. First, experts failed to revive some bulls after the process (including tranquillising) and, second, the results were unpredictable as it was only at the experimental stage. So the park management went back to the traditional practice of transporting the cows out, but due to the aggressive nature of those cows and the violent opposition of the local farmers at the places where they were being released, they could not get rid of this problem. Consequently, at present, more than 1,000 feral cows are grazing in the park. Further, the park is fighting a water crisis and these cattle have raised the problem multifold. Effective patrolling and punitive legal action by park personnel against miscreants involved in this illicit grazing is the only solution.

Fire, they say, is a double-edged sword. If used under controlled conditions, it is a boon otherwise, it is a proven killer. In the jungle, this principle is highly relevant. In Keoladeo, the Koladahar area, with more than 5 sq km expanse of grassland dominated by khus and dab, is most susceptible to fire. In fact, prior to 1981, the area used to be given on contract to a trader of scents from Ujjain (Madhya Pradesh), the capital of scent production in India. He used to extract high quality scent from khus grass (*V. zizanioides*) by installing a portable mechanised unit adjacent to the park. Though the contractor used to burn the area in order to ensure a new luxuriant growth of khus in the coming season, accidents through such controlled fires were negligible.

After the notification of national park, things changed drastically and the extraction of any produce from the park became illegal. Within a few years, a huge debris of decomposed khus and other grass got piled on the forest floor. In 1985–86, there were several fires in the Koladahar area. One such incident, which happened on 15 October 1985, got bad publicity and became

Watchtower of Koladahar Chowki

international news. The authorities constituted a committee under Bharat Singh, IFS and another under R. Ramakrishna, IAS, to investigate into the reason of the fire. These committees recommended that the entire grassland should be divided into 40–50 hectare compartments by constructing 20–30 m wide fire lines, which should be maintained properly. Many other recommendations were made to ensure the prevention of incidences of fire and the park management has worked on these; as a result, though fire incidences were still happening every year, they were controlled, allowing little loss to the ecosystem.

I vividly remember one such incident. It was a hot May night in 1989, when a fire broke out in the Ghasola grassland. In the absence of the park Director, the entire responsibility lay on me. We had two jeeps, one petrol and one diesel. I got busy coordinating with the staff members, providing

EDITOR, RASHTRADOOT

Rare eagle owls for sale in the Indian market, Lucknow

them with necessary support such as drinking water, fire beaters, fire tenders and so on. We were using counter-fire techniques as well, to check the spread of the fire in wind-favoured areas. I was using both the jeeps, mostly driving myself as the drivers were busy in actual fire fighting and had no time for the District Collector, Bharatpur and his junior officers who had also reached the spot. They had no idea of the complexity of wildfires in this season in such grassland. By 2am, we heaved a sigh of relief when the entire fire was extinguished; yet, several staff personnel could not be taken off duty lest the fire broke out again. The entire staff of the park, including non-field personnel as well as many rickshaw pullers and guides, helped during this operation. The increasing water shortage is responsible for shrinking wetlands in the grass areas and this has aggravated the fire problem. In 2006, I found the fire lines choked with the tree/shrub growth of *Prosopis juliflora*. This was dangerous and we got it cleared on priority. Several openings were created by chopping branches and removing trees to create view lines in order to facilitate keeping an eye over the vast grass expanse from the watchtower of Koladahar Chowki. An additional triple-storeyed watchtower-cum-guard outpost was constructed in the midst of this grassland. Deep borewells, one right here and the other at Kadam Kunj, were dug.

Poaching of large mammals such as the chital, sambar and wild boar is carried out by the *Nut*, *Kanjar* and *Sansi* communities living not very far from the park. They enter mostly during the moonlit nights of winter through the Bhainsamori or Kishori nakka areas located in the eastern flank (Agra roadside) of the park. Active night patrolling can save animals from them. The neighbouring villagers are involved in poaching of porcupines for meat. Generally, they target porcupine burrows situated closer to the fencing. The poachers have evolved a peculiar technique of ousting the animal from its burrow by filling it with water. Once, during a routine patrol, I discovered a water channel feeding a porcupine burrow close to the reserve boundary at Aghapur. Regular patrolling was enforced from that day onwards to check such poaching traps. During the summer, when water levels go down and the surviving fish acquire a good size, they become prone to poaching by some professionals who mainly belong to the traditional fisherman families located in close proximity of the Govardhan Gate of the Bharatpur township. They target fish such as rohu (*Labeo rohita*), mrigal (*Cirrhinus mrigala*) and katla (*Katla katla*) and smuggle them out to the market in Agra, taking advantage of the national highway. Though rarely, but these poachers have also smuggled Indian monitor lizards (*Varanus bengalensis*) and Indian flap-shell turtles (*Lissemys punctata*) from the park.

Under the leadership of L.K. Sharma, the then Director of Keoladeo, we had constructed a peripheral patrolling track along the boundary wall in 1989–90 and also initiated round-the-clock patrolling, on the basis of the system in practice at the Ammunition Depot, Bharatpur. Though no longer implemented at Keoladeo, I feel it should be re-introduced at the earliest to keep the park well protected.

The location of the park, in the southern flank of the Bharatpur township, has proved a boon for tourism due to its easy accessibility and availability of required facilities, yet the absence of a buffer zone has started posing a threat to the habitation. The park is surrounded by residential colonies and commercial ventures on its north and by farming communities on the other three sides. The V.D. Sharma Committee of 1983 had recommended the creation of a green belt all around the park but, unfortunately, the Government has not acted upon it. Consequently, several new constructions have come up. Any new addition of buildings in the 500 m vicinity of the park has dire ecological consequences. In 1982, when the Mathura oil refinery started its operations, some conservationists raised a hue and cry; active media reports indicated a threat of possible acid rains in Bharatpur. However, the V.D. Sharma Committee gave a clean chit to the refinery on the basis of the scientific data available but cautioned against the use of pesticides and chemical fertilisers in the adjacent areas of the park. BNHS included this aspect in its ecology study (1980–90) and found residues of heavy metal (lead) in the dead fish and birds. The increasing use of chemical fertilisers and pesticides by the farmers in the catchment of the Ajan Dam or Govardhan drain poses a threat to the marine life. Regular scientific monitoring of the water quality of the park lakes by credible institutes is, therefore, essential.

Part II

Debacle in Keoladeo

The Ajan Dam, built in the mid-eighteenth century by Maharaja Suraj Mal

Where Has All the Water Gone?

The ideal annual requirement of this wetland is 550 mcft of water. The Ajan Dam, located adjacent to the southwestern boundary of the park, had been the chief source of fulfilling this requirement and it was working out fine till the seventies. During the next decade, however, a new problem surfaced. The Banganga river, which had been contributing an important share to the Ajan Dam since its inception, started reducing its flow. This important river originates from Manoharpur, a town located on the Jaipur-Delhi highway, at about 40 km north of Jaipur. The river passes through the Jamwa Ramgarh lake (where the boat races during the Asian Games of 1982 were held), and then reaches the Ajan Dam via the township of Mekhpur, covering a huge distance.

Gambhiri, another river that contributes to the Ajan Dam, originates from the hills of the Karauli district, located to the south of Bharatpur. In 1979, the state government started building an irrigation dam (Panchana) on this river at village Kashirampura, on the Hindaun-Karauli route, about 12 km north of the Karauli township. The river travels around 50 km before reaching the Panchana Dam to collect water from the approximately 622 sq km catchment area. Though initially this dam did not seem to cause any problem for Keoladeo but, with the drying of the Banganga, the situation became even worse.

The management of the Ajan Dam is such that after September the entire dam is emptied by supplying water to the farmers located on the lower side of the dam to irrigate their agricultural fields through the Chiksana Canal. The bed of the dam is used by the farmers to raise their crops in this rich moist soil. This method of farming is called 'Tank Bed Farming' or 'Peta Casht' in the local language. Therefore, those farmers with land on the upper fringes of the dam insist that the water level in this dam be kept high so that their fields may absorb enough moisture before the dam is emptied. This is contrary to the interest of the park, which needs the first monsoon waters in order to attract the 15 species of piscivorous birds that come to breed here and make the most spectacular breeding colonies. Denial of adequate water till July does not allow the formation of these colonies. Yet, a late water supply, in an adequate amount, can attract and hold winter migrants but the problem gets aggravated if the shortage of water at the Ajan Dam leads to denial or a very short supply of water to the park, possibly till September. This compels the winter avian visitors to bypass this important wintering and migration staging park.

In fact, the post-monsoon supply of water from Ajan, too, plays an important role in the Keoladeo National Park but, in the changed scenario, the farmers have caused an obstruction to this supply as well. These conflicting interests have become a source of regular dispute between the farmers and the park management. I vividly remember the night of 4 October 1989, when the villagers of Aghapur, under the leadership of their Sarpanch, had forcefully diverted the Ghana Canal water towards their agricultural fields. These miscreants attacked us with sticks when we tried to recover our water supply and succeeded in stealing the entire water, even in the presence of the police.

It is also worth noting that the Gambhiri river traverses a distance of 240 km before it reaches the Sewla head, about 22 km ahead of the Ajan Dam. At Sewla, it crosses towards Uttar Pradesh and then finally discharges into the Yamuna river. It is known as Utangan river in Uttar Pradesh. Thus, it covers a long distance and is a lifeline to several hundred villages of Rajasthan and Uttar Pradesh. From Sewla, the water of this river is drawn into the Ajan Dam with the help of the 22 km-long earthen Pichun Canal. Between the Sewla head and the park, water losses are enormous. Percolation, evaporation, breech in the canal, ineffective sluice gates, more than a dozen earthen dams between the Sewla head and the Ajan Dam, illegal lifting of water from the canal by the farmers, are the factors responsible for these losses.

Hence, post-1996, the water intake into the park had dropped considerably (from 180.41 mcft in 1987 to nil in 2002). This scarcity was killing Keoladeo. Concerned officials and wildlife lovers raised an uproar, demanding that the Government ensure the release of sufficient water for the Sewla head in the Gambhiri river. Unfortunately, the Government went the other way, allowing the height of the Panchana Dam to be raised still further; it could now store 2,100 mcft of water, five times its earlier storage capacity. This was done a few months prior to the general assembly elections (2003) in the state. Obviously, this decision was taken in haste in order to appease the voters.

In the backdrop of irregular and scanty rainfall and an already dried Banganga river, this decision was bound to check almost the entire supply to the Keoladeo National Park. Consequently, 2004 went totally dry, creating havoc. The birds fled, leaving their nests, eggs and even hatchlings in the heronry.

After its height was raised in 2003, the Panchana Dam swallowed the entire Gambhiri river

On strong persuasion from the authorities and wildlife lovers, on 12 August 2004, in an emergency meeting, the Chief Secretary of the state ordered the release of ample water from the Panchana Dam for the park and 320 mcft of water was released. Of this, 20 mcft reached the Ajan Dam due to percolation and evaporation losses in the 240 km-long dry river course. Finally, only 18 mcft reached the park, and hence, after the failure of the breeding of the piscivorous birds, the winged winter visitors, too, bypassed Keoladeo. This drought of 2004 was hazardous; the park simply died. The survival of mammals including sambar, chital, blue bull and feral cattle as well as reptiles such as snakes, lizards, pythons, terrapins and fish brooders, surfaced as a huge challenge before the park administration. Though the floods of 2005 automatically brought enough water to the park, there was no water again in 2006. Adding to the woes, 2007 also went dry and the park did not receive any water. This was a serious blow to the vibrant wetlands. This continuous decline and denial of water supply had brought the park to a standstill. Tonnes of fish brooders died in the dry lakes. It was hard for the terrapins to aestivate in the dried earthen cakes in the lakes. Upside down turtles being eaten by predators became a common sight. Indeed, this marvellous World Heritage Site, a paradise for all who visit it, was dying for want of water! And no hope was left for its revival in the absence of alternate water resources.

HABITAT DEVASTATION

The evergreen and exotic plant, *Prosopis juliflora*, was introduced in Keoladeo during the seventies to provide a green cover to the barren patches located in the park's western and northwestern sides. It is a hardy plant that can grow easily in saline conditions and has a high level of tolerance against water deficiency. The species covered the blank saline patches quickly and looked attractive but the problem began when the plant started spreading into other important woodland. Its vigorous seeding and easy seed dispersal with the high-speed summer winds accelerated the process. Ungulates eating its pods also became a huge source of seed dispersal in far-flung areas. Thus, it started entering not only the woodland but the grassland as well, including Koladahar.

This plant has no food, roosting or nesting value for birds and is hence undesirable in the park. Its acidic nature does not permit other vegetation, including grass, to germinate and flourish. Additionally, at a fast pace, it started replacing other important species such as kadam, ber and pilu (*Salvadora* species). Within a short span of time it had engulfed most of the area. The worried park management had to get rid of this menace even though the eradication of its several thousand plants, including huge trees, was a herculean task. The *Prosopis juliflora* could not be allowed to swallow the park. As a first step, the seed-bearing huge trees were targetted and their stumps were cut but, with their enormous coppicing power, they sprouted back in no time. Now, as a second initiative, the stumps were

Map Showing Status of *Prosopis Juliflora* Menace in the Keoladeo National Park, January 2007

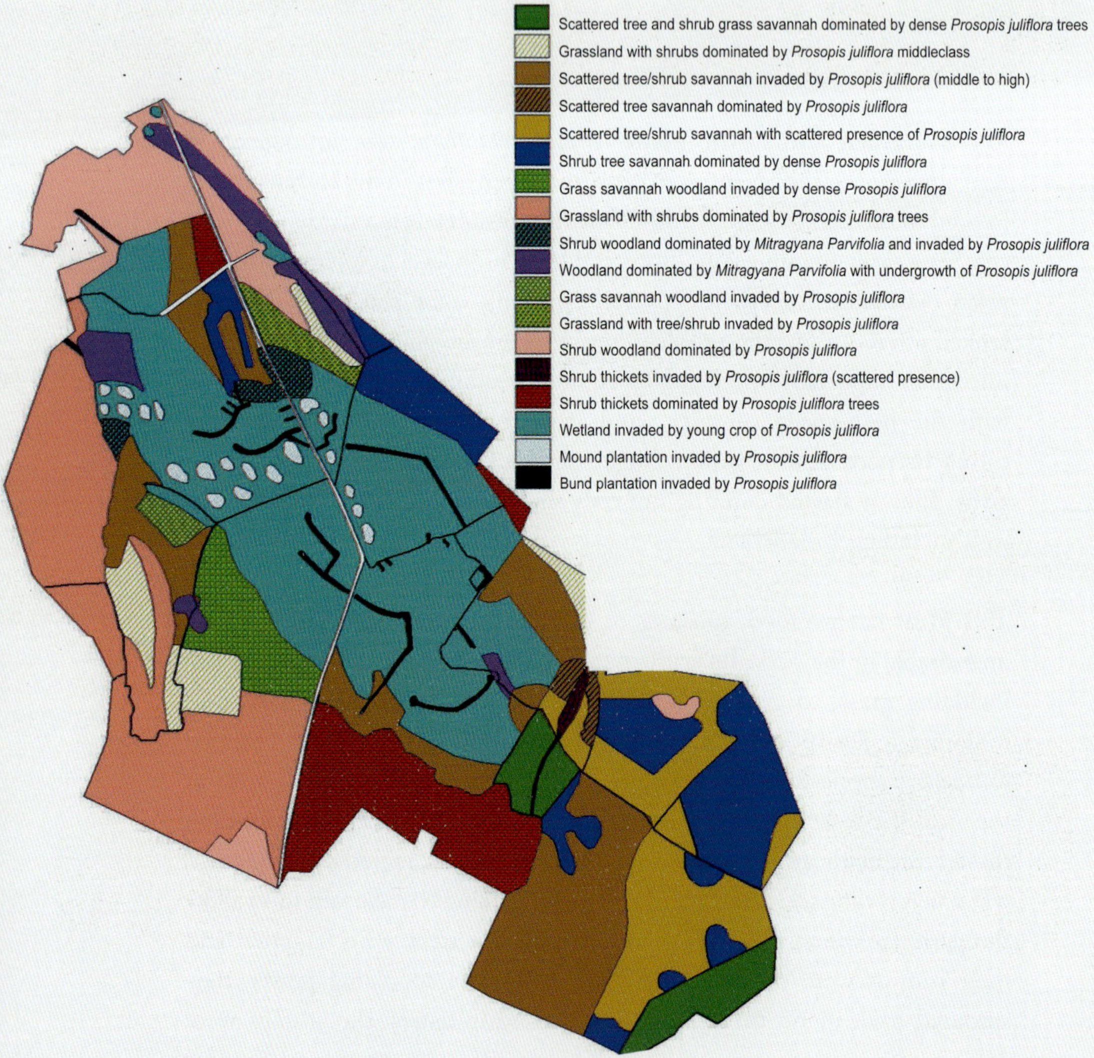

Map prepared by: IGCMC, WWF-India, January 2007

Clockwise from top left: P. juliflora *had spread behind the Director's residence and in lakes. The plant had surrounded the Salim Ali Visitor Interpretation Centre and the Chorkolu area was also totally taken over by* P. juliflora *trees and shrubs*

burned. This technique was repeatedly tried by Fateh Singh Rathore, the then Warden of Keoladeo and his successors but it, too, failed in putting a check on the vigorous sprouting power of this plant. Consequently, the situation worsened in a few years. The only saving factor was that till then the lakes were free from its presence as the *P. juliflora* seed does not tolerate inundation for a long time. This safety cover, however, got shattered in the eighties with a reduction in the water supply to these lakes from the Ajan Dam. Gradually, *Prosopis* started entering the fringe areas of lakes. In spite of the management's best efforts, the water supply could not be improved and the plant succeeded in colonising the lakes as well.

It was a fire-fighting kind of exercise as neither were sufficient funds made available by the Government to pull out all the saplings from the lakes nor could the trees be killed or uprooted from the park. Simultaneously, the fast-spreading *P. juliflora* was able to change crop composition in the woodland by consuming a large share of the scanty water available in the park, resulting in the drying of the invaluable ber and kadam trees. By 2000, it had engulfed the entire park, including most of the water bodies and the vast expanse of the grassland.

This was posing a real threat to the survival of the unique ecosystem of the park. The gravity of the problem may be best understood by the fact that, by 2004, UNESCO's World Heritage Centre had started threatening to delist the Keoladeo National Park if not freed from this menace immediately. The park was slowly dying.

Part III

Rebuilding Keoladeo

Managing a Growing Menace

Apart from finding a solution to the water crisis, another priority was to get rid of the menace of *Prosopis juliflora*, which had engulfed the entire park; billions of plants, including huge trees, could be seen everywhere. Even shrubs were laden with seeds to further aggravate the problem. Considering its vigorous coppicing power, control on this growing nuisance meant the uprooting of every single plant. This was a mammoth task that required a huge amount of money, which the Government was not providing. Selling the trees to contractors could have been an option, but this was prohibited by the Wildlife (Protection) Act.

I was desperate to find a way out. One day, while on an inspection tour of the Malah and Ramnagar areas, an idea struck me: Why not get these trees uprooted by the needy people inhabiting the villages located around the park in exchange of the wood procured in the process? The success of the scheme would, no doubt, depend largely upon the cooperation of the villagers. I discussed this idea with Dharam Singh, a dedicated Forest Guard posted at the Ramnagar beat. He is a Gujjar by caste and belongs to the Ramnagar village, located on the northwestern border of the park. This village is inhabited by people belonging to various castes but the Gujjar community is in a majority here. He had cordial relations with the villagers,

---

Facing page: *The Salim Ali Visitor Interpretation Centre, engulfed by* P. juliflora *trees here, is now surrounded by beautiful groves of glabrous karanj and other shady trees*

Inspection of the eradication work

especially within his community. Though Dharam Singh was doubtful about the result of this scheme, he was keen to find a solution to the growing menace of *Prosopis juliflora*. He is an avid birdwatcher and was extremely worried about the present plight of this World Heritage Site. That very day itself I chalked out a plan to allot a sizeable area to every individual family willing to uproot all the small and big plants/trees standing in that specific plot in exchange of the wood procured from the uprooted trees. In order not to antagonise the village head and other elected public representatives, I decided to form Eco Development Committees in the villages and register all those who were interested in this scheme. I discussed this idea with my Assistant Conservator, Range Officers and Foresters/Head Guards. Though they were equally keen to see the park freed from this nuisance but, unfortunately, not one of them was hopeful of the success of this experiment. Their response was quite disheartening but I really had no other option. I motivated the staff personnel and we unanimously decided to start the project from Ramnagar. On 15 February 2007, an Eco Development Committee was formed by registering almost all the villagers; plots of 1,000 sq m were marked for each family. It began with a single family of four members but soon, after constant persuasion and motivation from our side, others started joining this operation. The wood procured was weighed on the spot and a record was maintained in a permanent register. There was complete transparency and all these entries were verified by the Range Officers. I personally supervised the activities.

I replicated this experiment in other villages where we obtained highly encouraging results as well. Fortnightly reports were dispatched to the senior officers and though most of them were satisfied with this endeavour, some declared that it was a gross violation of the Wildlife (Protection) Act as well as the ruling of the Supreme Court of India. One officer cautioned me that I was inviting the wrath of the Supreme Court and may even land in jail. But, I kept accelerating the pace of the eradication work. It was possible with the active support of Mr Mehrotra, the Chief Wildlife Warden of the state. Bharatpur is a typical town with a complex political atmosphere. On the one hand, Dr Digamber Singh, belonging to the Bharatiya Janata Party, was a Cabinet Minister from Bharatpur and, on the other, his arch rival, Maharaj Kumar Vishwendra Singh, Member of Parliament from the Congress party, was a regular visitor to this park. This fact itself could have generated a lot of problems for the park administration but I had equally good relations at a personal level with both these political stalwarts and neither of them caused any difficulty. On the contrary, one day, after inspecting the *Prosopis* eradication work under progress during the sun-scorching heat of summer,

Dr Singh expressed his approval. Being a senior medico, he could appreciate the importance of this work. The regular visits of Maharaj Kumar, who is highly knowledgeable about birds and their ecological requirement, provided me immense support.

On 25 July 2007, the 15th and the last village located on the periphery of the park joined this uprooting operation. I did occasionally receive complaints from the villagers about the theft of wood and undue favour shown by the field staff members for personal gains; these were quickly resolved. There was no major hurdle, though a number of times I had to stop the work of certain villagers as a punishment for not uprooting the plants or removing the overburden from the plots. In such cases, after a gap of a few days, they were allowed back after they completed the task in the desired manner. Once, during a round of Block B, which is close to Jatoli village, I found a huge log of old wood of babool (*Acacia nilotica*) being carried by four persons in a hand-driven trolley. They were the brothers of Ranno, my favourite driver. I seized the wood and placed a fine of ₹4,000 on them for this offence; this was all done in the presence of Ranno. This discouraged the others from engaging in any kind of illegal activity.

In this operation, 4,485 people, belonging to 15 villages located on the periphery of the park, worked for 216,648 man days and 1,019.87 hectares of area spread over the entire park was freed from all sizes of *Prosopis juliflora* plants, including several thousand huge trees. In lieu of this labour, the people earned 230,841 quintals of wood. Seeds of ber (*Ziziphus species*) and babool (*Acacia nilotica*) were sown in all the pits created during this operation. The uprooting of seedlings/saplings from the entire lake system

The eradication work was first started in the Ramnagar forest through the Eco Development Committee **(above)**. *Involving the villagers in the eradication of* Prosopis juliflora *has proved to be a great success*

Above: *In 2007, Jim Leape, Director General, WWF International* **(extreme right)** *and Ravi Singh, Secretary General, WWF-India* **(to his right)** *visited the* Prosopis juliflora *eradication work in progress at the park and interacted with villagers and the author (wearing cap).* **Below:** *After the eradication of* Prosopis juliflora*, the native Salvadora species was freed and the exposed grounds have lured white-eye buzzards*

was also done simultaneously. These non-woody plants had to be extracted by employing paid labourers. Looking at the quantum of work, we needed a lot of money, which was provided by WWF-India; I am grateful to its Secretary General and CEO, Ravi Singh, for this timely help. WWF also saved the details of this entire *Prosopis* eradication operation through digital documentation and videography. At this juncture, I got transferred to the

Extract from the report of the joint World Heritage Centre/IUCN mission that visited this park from 10 to 14 March 2008

There had been little or no supply of water to feed wetland habitats in the property during 2006 and 2007. These dry conditions were conducive for the continued invasion of the property by the thorny scrub *Prosopis* which covered 11,000 hectares (40% of the total surface area of the property) of wetland and grassland areas of the property by 2007, rendering extensive areas inaccessible for water birds and grazing mammals, and out-competing indigenous vegetation. Given the very poor conditions over recent years, there is serious concern that the property may be a candidate for inscription onto the List of World Heritage in Danger.

[During this visit we observed that] the threat from invasive *Prosopis* scrub is being managed by involving local villagers, to remove trees and to use the timber for personal consumption (firewood and fence posts). The work involved is significant and is carefully supervised, ensuring that the entire root systems of the trees are also removed, preventing regeneration through coppicing.

The mission welcomes the increasingly close relations between the KNP authorities and the local communities, as manifested by the establishment of eco-development committees and by their participation in *Prosopis* control programmes.

Delegates of the IUCN mission in discussion with the villagers

Sariska Tiger Reserve during the third week of July 2008. My successor, Rajesh Gupta, completed the remaining task.

Though everyone was greatly pleased with this operation, yet initially some hoteliers had showed their disapproval on the removal of greenery (*P. juliflora* trees) from the arterial road of the park but we succeeded in convincing them. I had anticipated criticism from the media as several thousand green trees were removed and their timber was also not kept by the department but, to our utmost surprise, the media never raised a voice. On the contrary, they showed their utmost displeasure on my transfer before the Additional Chief Secretary, Rajasthan, in a press conference held during his visit to the park. I was, however, elated when the ACS appreciated my work and declared that it was not just a transfer, but the selection of an outstanding officer to undertake the prestigious project of tiger rehabilitation at the Sariska Tiger Reserve, which had lost its entire tiger population at the hands of poachers.

The native vegetation, overpowered and suffocated by *Prosopis juliflora*, was now free. With the first monsoon showers, ber, babool, precious kadam (*M. parvifolia*) and several other species started germinating. The lost biodiversity was returning to rejuvenate this birds' paradise, bringing wide smiles on the faces of all Keoladeo lovers. I would, however, like to conclude with a word of caution. Nature is dynamic and, therefore, aftercare is extremely important. The park management is now quite conscious about uprooting new saplings from the water bodies and the work carried out by volunteers of the Life Line Nature Society is certainly commendable. But, shockingly, within a span of nine to 10 years from my departure, several thousand new seed bearers have come up in various parts of the woods and grassland. If these are not stopped, the day is not far when once again the park will be taken over by *P. juliflora*.

THE HINDU • SATURDAY, OCTOBER 27, 2007

Ghana park witnesses a major weeding operation

A vast area now free from Prosopis juliflora, a tree species

Sunny Sebastian

- Operation carried out with help from villagers
- Authorities took advantage of lack of water

BHARATPUR: The authorities are making hay while the sun shines at the world famous Keoladeo Ghana National Park near here. There is very little bird life this season in the absence of water for the second consecutive year in the wetland, yet the birders are chirping merrily as, making the most of an adversarial situation, the park management has carried out a massive weeding operation here with active support from the local villagers.

Over 6 sq km area of the 29 sq km park -- a World Heritage site and Ramsar Convention wetland -- is now free from Prosopis juliflora, a tree species which had spread not only in the 11 sq km wooded area but also to the grasslands, taking advantage of the changes in the eco system in the wake of recurrent droughts. The inhabitants of as many as 15 villages in the park neighbourhood are happy.

"This kind of removal of Prosopis juliflora has been unparalleled anywhere in the country. The activity has brought incredible goodwill to the park from the local villagers besides helping the native vegetation to come up," said seasoned conservationist and Keoladeo-watcher Harsh Vardhan after a recent visit to the sanctuary.

There was nothing the park management could have done about missing water which was to come either from good rains during the monsoon or from the Panchana dam situated in the neighbouring Karauli district. As the State Government, afraid of the reaction from the farmers in the downstream area of the Panchana, refused to listen to the desperate appeals for release of water from the environmentalists and the park officials, there was nothing much to do -- or so it seemed.

"In the 1980s, the water supply to the park started getting reduced. Taking advantage of the dry conditions, Prosopis juliflora started spreading. Within a span of a few years it not only took over the entire woodland but also infiltrated the unique grassland.

Even the wetland, spread over 11 sq km, got engulfed with this weed," says P. S. Somashekhar, Conservator, Forests.

Prosopis juliflora has vigorous coppicing power. The park authorities had made several attempts in the past to kill the mother trees but could not succeed as even the burnt stumps sprouted with great vigour. The mammal population in the park such as Blue bulls, chital, wild boar and feral cows, which consumed the ripe seeds, helped its propagation. The only option seemed to be uprooting each individual tree.

"By 2006, the situation got very critical. Then we formed an Eco Development Committee in February this year and registered all the villagers. Strategically Ram Nagar was selected as the first village to start this experiment," notes Sunayan Sharma, Field Director, Keoladeo Ghana.

The Ram Nagar experiment, carried out under strict supervision of the forest personnel, proved successful. The villagers, grouped family-wise, were allocated plots of 10x100 metres area each from where they removed the mother trees, new seedlings and saplings, plucking them by root.

The villagers—men, women, children, once shooed away by the park authorities for attempts at cutting grass—were allowed to take away the wood so procured.

CREATING NEW WATER RESOURCES

It was the first week of November 2006 and no water had been given to the Keoladeo National Park. The management was trying its best to save the fish brooders, hiding in the deep water bodies of Block D, next to the Keoladeo temple and opposite the duck shooting record stones.

At that time, five shallow borewells were under operation at Bakalia, Sapanmori, Keoladeo and Dabri; one open well with an electric motor at the nursery located in Block A was also under operation. A deep borewell was being commissioned at Aghapur *naka*, the point from where the Dakan/Ghana Canal enters the park with water from the Ajan Dam. It was at this critical juncture of the park's history that I got posted to Keoladeo. Fortunately, the Aghapur borewell dug out sweet water, which was taken by us into the main (Ghana) canal. I now got a shallow borewell dug at Kadam Kunj and, against all speculations, this, too, delivered sweet water in ample quantity. A diesel pump was fitted here and it started feeding the small and big mammals, birds and reptiles of this area. Two silent but powerful generator sets were purchased on top priority; one was used to run, day and night, the Aghapur boring and the other was used at the Dabri well, enhancing its discharge capacity by three times. This was an emergency and we did not have enough time to observe the required formalities pertaining

---

Facing page: *The eradication of* P. juliflora *and the development of new water resources have brought the heydays back to the Keoladeo National Park*

to the purchase of these sets. The top bureaucracy did not like the idea and was critical of my move but the Chief Wildlife Warden supported me.

The borewell at Koladahar *naka*, located at the southern border of the park, was also exhausted due to repeated droughts. It was the only source of water for the wildlife of the area (the entire grassland falling under Block G), as well as for those posted at this important forest checkpost. In a quick decision, a shallow borewell was dug at about 700 m from the existing point, on the main track between Koladahar and Kadam Kunj (within Block G). Fortunately, this proved to be a success. A diesel engine was fitted here and a large earthen waterhole was dug to feed the entire wildlife of this prairie that stretched over a huge area.

These temporary measures gave us little relief but were not enough to save the park. We needed to have some proper alternate water resources, otherwise it was merely a matter of years before Keoladeo would have turned into a dense forest of *P. juliflora*. It was such a complex puzzle and no one had any clue of what to do next. Like Keoladeo, about 300 villages located all along the 240 km-long water course of Gambhiri were facing a drought-like situation due to the stoppage of its flow at the Panchana Dam. I also tried to motivate these villagers to persuade the Government to earmark enough water for release from Panchana so that Keoladeo, located at about 200 km from the dam, may also receive its due share every year. The villagers shared their agony with us but were helpless against the political power of the community that was deriving all the benefit from the Panchana Dam. The case of the victim villagers looked totally hopeless as the message was loud and clear that it was very difficult to reverse the Government's decision. The enhanced water-holding capacity of Panchana could not be reduced.

ANSAR KHAN

The borewell at the Koladahar fire watchtower proved a boon in this fire-prone grassland and for the wildlife inhabiting the dry prairie

The only solution now lay in developing some other water resource and for this I held marathon meetings with the concerned irrigation officers. Meanwhile, to meet the immediate requirement, two additional deep borewells were dug at Ghasola (to feed Blocks D and E) and Malah (for Blocks L and N). Undoubtedly, these wells could save the park's vegetation and non-aquatic wildlife to some extent but the vibrant wetland ecosystem was dying before our eyes.

In 2003, the Government of Rajasthan had prepared a drinking water scheme to feed 23 lakh people inhabiting the five towns and 999 villages of

A borewell at Bakalia

the Dholpur and Bharatpur districts. It was named the Chambal-Dholpur-Bharatpur Drinking Water Supply Project. As per the project, an intake well with a base of 40 m diameter was to be dug in the Chambal river (at Dholpur). Since the water was to be drawn from the Chambal river falling under the National Chambal Gharial Sanctuary, therefore, the Government, through its Public Health Engineering Department (PHED), went to the Central Empowered Committee (a committee of the Supreme Court of India) to seek its sanction. On the recommendations of this committee, the Court permitted the state government to execute this drinking water project on the condition that till 2010 (the first four years of the project), 310 mcft and thereafter 62.5 mcft of water would be released to Keoladeo, free of cost, from this project. It gives me great satisfaction to note that I, as a representative of the Forest Department (Technical Assistant to the

Chief Wildlife Warden, Rajasthan) had a significant role to play behind this momentous decision.

Under the prevailing conditions, it was a welcome decision but we were aware that, from the biological point of view, this Chambal water, brought in a closed pipe covering a distance of about 100 km, was bound to be less oxygenated or partially dead. Also, it was not expected to bring vegetation or micro/macro life to the park and, therefore, it could not replace the Ajan water. But it could certainly help as a supplement to the borewells of the park. Everyone was eagerly waiting for this water to reach the Keoladeo lakes but, unfortunately, the project got delayed due to a dispute and litigation between the contractor and the irrigation department at the state level. This development was heartbreaking for us.

In the meantime, I learnt that, in 2005, a proposal was sent by the then Director of the park to the Government for diverting rainwater from the Chiksana Canal to the park. The project was expected to deliver about 50–100 mcft of water to the park during the monsoon and could be of great help in supporting the successful formation of heronries here. Sadly, this proposal got turned down by the then Principal Secretary of Forests in the Government of Rajasthan.

The Chiksana Canal passes through the southern part of Keoladeo, it enters at Nasvaria and exits at Darapur, flowing about two km inside the park. It starts from the lower side of the Ajan Dam and was basically meant to irrigate the agricultural land located between the Ajan Dam and the park (Naswaria side) after 15 September, when the dam is emptied to allow cropping in the tank (Ajan) bed. Most of the land being irrigated by this

New Canal, a 10 m (width) and 3.66 km (length) open canal

canal falls under the Punjabi Ka Nagla and Naswaria villages. During floods, this canal acts as a control device to save these villages and their agricultural crops. Apart from seepage from the Ajan Dam, this canal also receives rain water from a local catchment of about 7.5 sq km.

I was convinced that, as a short-term strategy, it was worthwhile to tap this water. We badly needed water for the survival of the aquatic system and so I decided to push this project once again with all the possible arguments readied. I had to play a little trick to bypass the office of the Principal Secretary, Forest. I succeeded in persuading S.N. Thanvi, the then Principal Secretary, Water Resources, Government of Rajasthan. The project got sanctioned yet the budgetary provisions worth ₹41 lakh were still to be made. Days were running out. I wanted breeding colonies established in the ensuing monsoon of 2007 at any cost. Harsh Vardhan, Founder Secretary,

Tourism and Wildlife Society of India, an internationally renowned wildlifer, extended a helping hand. He held several meetings with S.N. Thanvi and the Chief Minister. Ultimately, we succeeded in getting the budget sanctioned from the Water Resources department.

Though the Chiksana Canal project could assist in supporting the heronries during their making, especially during July, it certainly could not support a system that requires 550 mcft of water every year. Therefore, it was imperative to have adequate alternate resources to meet this requirement. This question was baffling us day and night. One afternoon, while reading the irrigation map of Bharatpur for the hundredth time, suddenly the Govardhan drain, under-passing the main Bharatpur-Mathura highway, caught my attention. I could see a blue line, representing this drain, meeting the Yamuna river after traversing a long distance in Rajasthan and Uttar Pradesh. An urgent meeting with the concerned irrigation officers revealed that this drain receives water from the KP drain, which stretches between the Kama and Pahadi areas of the Bharatpur district. The drain collects flood water from the plains of the Kama and Pahadi areas but it also gathers a huge quantity of water from several floodplains falling under the Sohna district and other adjacent areas of Haryana state, discharging into the KP drain at the Khalluka regulator located at the Pahadi-Haryana border. After travelling a distance of about 20 km, the KP drain discharges into the Govardhan drain, which also collects water from the floodplains of the Mathura district, close to Radha Nagari and the low-lying areas of Bharatpur that get flooded almost every year during the monsoon. Thus, the Govardhan drain receives a lot of flood water to finally discharge into the Yamuna river, under-passing the Bharatpur–Mathura highway at Rara, about 12 km from Bharatpur.

Available data showed that during normal rainfall years this drain could contribute about 400 mcft water to Keoladeo if tapped before it discharges into the Yamuna. A plan was hurriedly drawn to tap this water at a point called Santruk, located at about 7 km from Rara and was submitted to the Collector, Bharatpur, in the last days of 2007. He was to forward it to the state government on top priority. But, in the absence of the Collector, who had gone abroad, the officiating Collector, Tripathi, kept it lying with him, in spite of several reminders from me. In a chance meeting, I briefed Rajasthan's Forest Minister about this; he rebuked Tripathi and, finally, the project reached the Minister and the other concerned officers.

This ₹2,000 lakh project was prepared to initially transport water to Keoladeo from the Govardhan drain through an open canal of about 20 km length, passing through agricultural fields.

In 2005, after the annihilation of tigers from the Sariska Tiger Reserve, the state government had formed a State Empowered Committee under the chairmanship of V.P. Singh, Member of Parliament from Bhilwara

A project was initiated to transport water from this Govardhan drain to the park

(Rajasthan) and a noted conservationist. He showed keen interest in the revival of Keoladeo and during one of his visits to the park, I briefed him about this Govardhan drain proposal. He was ready to take up the matter on a priority basis and, on his insistence, I prepared a PowerPoint presentation and showed it to Yashwant Thorat, Chairman, National Bank for Agriculture and Rural Development (NABARD), in Ranthambore. His wife was also a Member of NABARD and is an enthusiastic birdwatcher. They were concerned about the water problem that Keoladeo had been facing and, understanding the urgency of the matter, Yashwant Thorat sent his team of experts to Keoladeo within three days. They inspected the drain and were quite convinced about the feasibility of this project. With a view to avoid any conflict of interest with the farmers, they suggested that we replace the open water channel with an underground pipeline. Undoubtedly, this change would ensure uninterrupted water supply to the park but the project cost was expected to go up by three times.

In the meantime, another important development took place. Dr Digamber Singh, the then Cabinet Minister of the Government of Rajasthan, visited Keoladeo and he showed great interest in the project. Those days, luckily, the state assembly was in session. He took no time in convincing the Chief Minister, who declared her commitment towards the implementation of this project at the earliest. This announcement proved vital in seeking the cooperation of the concerned bureaucrats at the state level in expediting the matter. At a high-level meeting, the irrigation department was instructed to prepare a detailed project report for the supply of 400 mcft of water to Keoladeo every year. It was also decided that the project would be executed by the irrigation department as a deposit work of the forest department, but maintenance was to be done by the park administration.

Since Keoladeo is a World Heritage Site and any intervention of this magnitude could not be possible without seeking the consent of experts of national and international repute, we had to seek their advice at the earliest. Ravi Singh and Dr Parikshit Gautam, Director, Fresh Water Bodies, WWF, extended their full cooperation. A consultative workshop was organised by us at the park on 26–27 April 2007 to deliberate on future options for water for Keoladeo. It was attended by 31 participants including renowned scientists and subject specialists such as Professor Brij Gopal (School of Environment Sciences, Jawaharlal Nehru University, New Delhi), Dr V.S. Vijayan, Dr Vibhu Prakash, Dr B.C. Choudhary (Professor, Wildlife Institute of India, Dehradun), Professor K.K. Sharma (Head of Zoology Department, Maharshi Dayanand Saraswati University, Ajmer) and Dr Parikshit Gautam. Arun Prasad, former Director of the park, also actively participated in the deliberations. Field visits were arranged for the participants. The group endorsed the Chiksana Canal and Govardhan drain projects and recommended immediate action for their implementation. The experts also laid emphasis on the revival of the supply of the biologically enriched water from the traditional water source of the Gambhiri river and recommended that an urgent macro-level assessment of the restoration of the Gambhiri basin be initiated.

These recommendations cleared the path for the Government to go ahead with the implementation of these projects. We did not want to lose Chiksana Canal water in the ensuing monsoon but the irrigation officers were moving distressingly slowly. Again, Dr Digamber Singh came to our rescue. He instructed the officers to start the Chiksana Canal work immediately. The next morning, in the presence of the district administration, he laid the foundation stone and digging commenced on the same day.

The Santruk station, which pumps Govardhan drain water to Keoladeo

This 10 m-wide and 3.66 km-long open canal, 'New Canal', connecting the Chiksana Canal (near Koladahar) to Sankhala Hide (Block E) got completed before the monsoon arrived. And, in the first monsoon (2007) it contributed about 70 mcft of free-flowing water full of zoo/phytoplanktons and lots of fish. It rendered great support in maintaining the breeding colonies in making. This was a great moment for all Keoladeo lovers and I am sure that, apart from supporting breeding colonies, the New Canal will prove to be a boon to the entire wildlife inhabiting this dry prairie. It was now time to focus on the Govardhan drain project. Constant persuasion led to the completion of the detailed project report through the irrigation department. The report recommended intercepting the Govardhan drain at Santruk and then lifting the water to be supplied to Keoladeo through a 17.1 km-long underground pipeline passing mainly through fallow government land. The project cost was estimated to be about ₹6,000 lakh. The state government sent the project to the forest ministry of the central government, which further forwarded it to the Planning Commission of India. This committee, headed by Dr Indrani Chandrasekharan, Advisor to the Planning Commission on Forest & Environment, was sensitive enough to plan a site visit without any delay. Their dates (second week of August 2008), however, coincided with the tiger rehabilitation programme that I was looking into at the

Tiger Reserve, which I had just joined in July. Since the Govardhan drain project was my baby, therefore, rightly, the Chief Wildlife Warden assigned me the task of interacting with the committee during the site inspection. I rushed to Keoladeo and briefed the committee about the water ecology of the birds' paradise and its deterioration after the stoppage of river water from the Gambhiri at Panchana. Luckily, the committee members could appreciate the crisis and were convinced about the feasibility of the project. The Chairperson promised quick sanction of the desired grant from the Government of India.

Keoladeo lovers were now eagerly looking forward to the early execution of the Govardhan drain project. As promised, the grant reached Rajasthan state from the central government without any delay. But, unfortunately, in the meantime, the elections in the state brought a new government of a different political party. Everything got changed and the powerful V.P. Singh committee was scrapped. No one in the new government was ready to give priority to this project. Infighting was going on among the concerned officers and the irrigation department to give the lucrative contract to the person of their choice. Still, there were officers like Mr Mehrotra, who by now had become Head of the Forest Department and Keoladeo lovers such as Harsh Vardhan who were very vocal on such matters. Constant persuasion ultimately led to the execution of the work on the ground. The project that I had prepared in 2008 was completed in 2012, a delay of four precious years. In Keoladeo, this drain water entered through the Jatoli village, located on the eastern side of the park. The intake tank was constructed at the Jatoli forest *chowki*. From here the water is channelised into the existing distribution system of the park. In 2012, as a test case, only eight mcft of water was drawn from the Govardhan drain but, in 2013, the drain made a significant contribution to the ecosystem of Keoladeo by providing 186 mcft water, full of fish fry, micro organisms and aquatic vegetation. As a result, the heronry supported 5,870 successful nests.

Piscivorous birds gathered in still larger numbers here during the next year, but the park did not receive a drop of water from the Ajan Dam, owing to denial from Panchana. By now the birds had formed a huge heronry close to the Sapanmori area. This denial posed a serious threat to the survival of the newly-born chicks. In such a crisis, when the nesting birds were about to fly away, leaving behind their nests, the Govardhan drain contributed 290 mcft water in many bursts and this helped in not only saving the heronry, with 7,926 successful nests of all the 15 species of heronry birds, but also in holding the migratory waterfowl here till late February and early March. Again, in July 2016, when the heronry was about to be abandoned for want of water, the Govardhan drain supplied 137 mcft water. In late July and August–September, a flood-like situation occurred in the catchment of the Gambhiri, leading to an overflow of the Ajan Dam and consequently 457 mcft water was released from the dam for Keoladeo. These brought back the glorious days of the Keoladeo National Park; the heronry gave a record number of 20,778 successful nests of all the 15 colony breeders. Again, in 2018, in the total absence of Ajan water, the Govardhan drain contributed 690 mcft water to support the establishment of huge heronries in Blocks B and D. I was greeted by broad smiles on the faces of the naturalists, rickshaw pullers and the park personnel when I visited the park in mid-January. The hug of gratitude they gave me was my true reward.

Since 2011, as per the apex court's verdict, the Chambal-Bharatpur-Dholpur water scheme has also started contributing water to Keoladeo. Though this

Intake point (at protection post, Jatoli) where the biologically rich Govardhan drain water enters the park

water supply is erratic for want of strict orders from the Government, it has nonetheless been a considerable help, especially in the years when the Govardhan drain could not contribute enough water due to the failure of the monsoon in its catchment. Thus, new water resources have been generated to supplement the deficit in Keoladeo. Their success may be best adjudged by the fact that, from 1991 to 1998, 5,800 nests, on an average, were made in the heronries with a water intake of 433 mcft per year. Between 1999 and 2010, with an average supply of 171 mcft per year, the nests' number fell down to as low as 733 each year. Now, with the addition of these three new water resources, between 2011 and 2016, the average water supply has got raised to 459 mcft per year, resulting in an average of 7,249 nests each year, which is even higher than the 1991–98 period. The birds are in paradise, once again!

DEBATABLE ISSUES

The Keoladeo National Park is very different now from what it was before 1982 when its legal status was that of just a sanctuary. During those days, buffaloes and other cattle could be seen grazing and trampling all over the place; in fact, the entire area used to be full of buffalo dung. It was difficult for the tourists as well as serious birdwatchers to roam freely here because of these animals; they were even seen on the main arterial road stretching between the main gate and the Keoladeo temple. The safety of the camera equipment of the nature photographers was a serious issue as well. Kailash Sankhala in his book, *Gardens of God*, writes about the pulling down of the nests of the heronry birds by the buffaloes.

The sanctuary managers and birders wanted this grazing to be stopped in order to revive the wilderness in the true sense but this could not be possible without strong government support. The status of a national park, it was felt, could provide the required legal instrument to extinguish all kinds of

Blue bulls in the wet prairie

rights from this land of birds. Therefore, birders, under the captaincy of Sankhala, worked hard for this and, ultimately, in 1981, succeeded in getting it declared as a national park. Now, the motivated nature lovers doubled their efforts to stop the entry of cattle inside the park. On 16 March 1981, Dr Salim Ali wrote, 'I am told that measures have been taken to eliminate cattle from the park completely within a fortnight. If this can be done, this will be the most laudable achievement of the management and it should make all the difference to the improvement of the park. I wish Mr Sankhala and Mr Panney Singh success in this attempt.'

Other important associates and great ornithologists such as Zafar Fateh Ali and Humayun Abdul Ali had also been strongly demanding the stoppage of grazing. Sankhala, then Chief Wildlife Warden of the state, sitting at the helm of affairs, was already in action. Since the interest of several thousand villagers was at stake, such a bold step could not be taken by the park authorities without the active support of the political bosses.

The Government was hesitant to annoy its voters. Sankhala, who was quite close to nature lover Indira Gandhi, the then Prime Minister of India, succeeded in convincing her to put a halt to this illicit act. A nod from the iron lady geared the Government to provide police assistance to the park personnel to stop grazing forever. On a stipulated day in 1982, the park management closed all the gates through which cattle used to enter here but the violent villagers broke open the gates and forcefully entered with their cattle. The resisting park personnel and police were pelted with stones by the violent crowd. In self-defence the police had to open fire in which seven villagers died.

Though the gates were again sealed and a permanent halt to grazing was ensured, the harmony between the park personnel and the villagers was spoilt forever. The Government appointed a commission to conduct a detailed enquiry into this tragic episode. This went on for several years and though no official was found responsible for the mishap, the gulf between the park authorities and the park's neighbours could not be bridged, even though various steps were taken by the park management to improve the relationship. Several villagers were recruited in government jobs. Licences to operate cycle rickshaws and guide tourists inside the park were liberally provided to these villagers. These sincere efforts did help somewhat but deep wounds tend to take a long time to heal.

The stoppage of this grazing, especially of buffaloes, which are fond of entering water and feeding voraciously on *Paspalum distichum*, locally known as *Aincha*, was bound to give impetus to the unfettered growth of this grass.

Facing page: *A sarus crane nests in the midst of the* Paspalum-*dominated wetland*

Within a couple of years, the grass emerged as the dominant species in all the lakes. The growth of some floral species also got hindered due to the interference of the fast growing *Paspalum*. Undoubtedly, these changed habitat conditions could not be conducive to all the animals. In 1980, a 10-year project for the study of the ecology of the park was taken up by BNHS with Dr Salim Ali as its Principal Investigator. Dr Vijayan was made the Project Scientist with his headquarters at Bharatpur. In a quick reaction, he held *Paspalum distichum* responsible for spoiling the habitat and ecology of the park and recommended reopening the gates of the park to revive buffalo grazing.

In the summary report of 1980–85 (KNP Ecology Study) Dr Vijayan wrote, 'Two hundred buffaloes may be introduced in one of the blocks preferably in the Kadam Kunj area.' And, in every following annual report not only was this recommendation repeated but it was also emphasised that Siberian cranes are avoiding visiting Keoladeo due to the *Paspalum* nuisance. The 10-year concluding report (1990) of this project stressed, 'When grazing on park land was prohibited in 1982, *Paspalum distichum*, an amphibious, perennial grass, grew unfettered and just within the space of a year started engulfing water bodies…Siberian cranes lost out because the tubers of the sedges they fed on were stifled and became almost inaccessible. This is an important reason that Keoladeo lost its Siberian visitors.'

In 1990, on the conclusion of this study, a seminar was organised by the project authorities, with funding from the Government of India. Being a Research Officer of the park, I was also a participant and had presented a paper jointly with V.D. Sharma, the then Chief Wildlife Warden, Rajasthan, on Siberian cranes. Unfortunately, this platform was also used by

Siberian cranes feeding in the wetlands

these project authorities largely to hold the stoppage of buffalo grazing as the main culprit for the declining number of Siberian cranes in Keoladeo. Most of the delegates were unaware of the fact that grazing was stopped chiefly on the demand of Dr Salim Ali himself. The seminar organisers left no stone unturned in feeding the misinformation to the delegates that the park officials, including the Chief Wildlife Warden, have stubbornly stopped buffalo grazing, which has spoiled the habitat; and that, if buffalo grazing is not opened immediately, the park is bound to die. This was sheer exaggeration. This kind of negative publicity with bias against the state's wildlife management was uncalled for. The park authorities were not even given an opportunity to clarify and apprise the delegates of the facts during the three-day seminar.

Though I am in agreement with Dr Vijayan that, post-1982, excessive growth of *Paspalum* had emerged as a problem, it was well anticipated and, therefore, measures were being taken to curb its growth. Villagers were being allowed to pull out the grass manually and carry it for their cattle, under supervision. Also, periodic bulldozing, followed by burning, was being done in selected areas. All these actions had proved effective.

Paspalum distichum is not a weed and has important food and habitat value for many waterfowl and other wild animals. A detailed and systematic ecological study of the Keoladeo wetlands was conducted by the School of Natural Resources, Ohio University, Columbus, USA, from 1984–87 and, contrary to the recommendations of Dr Vijayan, the investigators have not opined in favour of grazing. The study report (September 1988) reads, 'Most of the wetland areas of the park are now dominated by *Paspalum distichum*. We consider this to be the result of the release of *Paspalum* from over-grazing since 1981 and consider the wetland areas of the park generally to be in no better or worse condition than they had been prior to 1981. *Paspalum* has altered the structure and composition of the wetlands, but it has not ruined them.' The report further states, 'An important, but narrow band of seasonally flooded vegetation between *Vetiveria* savannah and *Paspalum*-dominated wetlands also attracts wildlife, particularly ducks, geese and Siberian cranes in wet years.'

Dr Vijayan has also accepted the ecological values of *P. distichum*. In the summary report (1980–85) he writes, 'All the egret species show preference to *Paspalum distichum* patches against other habitats. During the monsoon, when water comes into the park, they apparently experience difficulty in catching fish. As the grass mat is not thick enough they cannot settle on it and feed. Hence they resort to scooping fish while flying. But as the grass settle on the water surface like a mat, they spend most of the time on this for feeding.' He also states, 'Most of the species (water fowl) showed definite preference for grass habitat during 1987–88 and 1988–89. However, in the winter of 1988–89, the species, which preferred this habitat, decreased mainly because of the changes in the grass composition. *P. distichum*, the most common grass, was replaced in most places by *Pseudoraphis spinescens*, which was not preferred by most of the waterfowl.'

Paspalum distichum is the preferred food of the sambar, nilgai and feral cattle, among others. Seeds of this grass that are found in their dung during most of the year bear evidence of this fact, as quoted by the Wildlife Institute of India in its bibliographic review report of 2009. The loss of the visiting population of Siberian cranes in Keoladeo in this part of the world is a huge loss, but holding the stoppage of grazing responsible for this seems misleading and baseless.

According to a 1997 report of the International Crane Foundation, USA, 'Hunting pressure during migration has likely been a significant factor behind the steady decline of the central population, which winters in Keoladeo. Crane hunting is a traditional sport in areas of

---

Facing page: *Bar-headed geese feeding on* Paspalum distichum

Afghanistan and Pakistan where the population passes during migration.' Ronald J. Sauey (1985) concluded that the losses of central population are almost certainly attributable to hunting, while George Archibald (1992) noted that uncontrolled hunting in the region is, 'The weakest link in this chain of...survival for the central population.'

The conclusion drawn by Archibald and Sauey is supported by the data available regarding the dwindling number of Siberian cranes visiting Keoladeo—in 1964–65, more than 200 birds visited Keoladeo but in 1970 it got reduced to 76. Further, in 1979, it fell to 33. In 1981, that is, just before the closure of grazing, the number was 38; but, in 1984, that is, after the closure of grazing, it rose to 41. In 1988 it fell to 23, then to 17 in 1989 and only 10 in 1990. The last two birds visited the park in 2002. It is evident from the data that the main problem was in the migration route and not in the increased richness of *Paspalum*, as clearly mentioned by the International Crane Foundation in its report.

The Ohio University's report states that *Paspalum* is beneficial to many ungulates and waterfowl and no effort should be done to eradicate it from the park: 'The primary objective of vegetation management, however, should be to re-establish a variety of plant communities, not to eradicate *P. distichum*. *Paspalum* seems to be a preferred food for many of the herbivores in the park, and should be considered an important food species for ungulates and some waterfowl, primarily geese and coots.'

Fortunately, good sense prevailed upon the authorities; the outcome would otherwise have been highly controversial and embarrassing for the park management as well as the state government.

GOING DOWN THE PARK'S MEMORY LANE

Indira Gandhi, the then Prime Minister of India, visited the Ghana-Keoladeo Bird Sanctuary on 8 February 1976, along with her elder son Rajiv Gandhi, his wife Sonia and two children, Rahul and Priyanka, both were not even in their teens and Sanjay, her younger son and his wife Maneka. They reached the sanctuary on the evening before and stayed at the newly-constructed Forest Lodge, a hotel of the India Tourism Development

On the occasion of the then Prime Minister's historic visit, Chief Minister of Rajasthan, Harideo Joshi, presenting a gift to Sonia Gandhi. Also seen in the photograph are Rajiv Gandhi, Sanjay Gandhi and V.S. Saxena

HARSH VARDHAN

Corporation. Dr Salim Moizuddin Abdul Ali, father of Indian ornithology, was invited to escort them. On behalf of Rajasthan state, V.S. Saxena, a learned birder and ex-Divisional Forest Officer of Bharatpur (including Ghana-Keoladeo Sanctuary) was assisting the party.

Apart from the sanctuary personnel, much to the disappointment of her own party's leaders of the region, no one was allowed to be seen roaming around in the sanctuary throughout the Prime Minister's visit. However, to ensure adequate arrangements, the Chief Secretary of Rajasthan and the Secretary to the Chief Minister of Rajasthan were present at the Forest Lodge. Harsh Vardhan, a great birder and officer in the Government of Rajasthan, was handpicked by the Chief Secretary to assist him on this special occasion. The Gandhi family visited the sanctuary by road in a station wagon kind of vehicle and then again by boat after breakfast. The Prime Minister, in particular, showed keen interest in the rare Siberian cranes and the other migratory and heronry birds here. She wrote in the visitors' book, 'A delightful and peaceful experience, made enjoyable and interesting by having Shri Salim Ali with us. I hope something will be done about the arterial road, which brings buses and noise into the middle of the sanctuary.'

It was her visit that paved the way for the closure of the arterial road passing through the heart of the sanctuary, for all kinds of traffic except with the permission of the sanctuary management. The elevation of the status of the sanctuary to a national park and the consequent enforcement of the total ban on cattle grazing, too, were probably the outcome of this memorable visit when the Prime Minister and her family came to spend time at this serene wonderland of nature.

Dr Salim Moizuddin Abdul Ali, known as the Bird Man, decorated with a Padma Bhushan and a Padma Vibhushan by the Government of India for his unforgettable contribution to nature conservation, had a great fascination for the park. In fact, it would be appropriate to remember him as the 'Architect of Keoladeo'. He visited the park on 16 March 1981, a few days after Keoladeo's status was raised to that of a national park.

Keoladeo is one of the favourite water bird reserves of George Archibald and Ronald J. Sauey, Co-founders and Directors, International Crane Foundation. Sauey has conducted invaluable research on the behaviour and ecology of the rare Siberian crane and hence spent a huge amount of time at Keoladeo. On 10 February 1983, Archibald wrote in the visitors' book, 'KGNP is heaven on Earth for man, bird and wildlife alike. Its preservation stands as a monument to India's past, present and future in conservation. I have had the great privilege to visit Keoladeo National Park each winter since 1976. This winter I am absolutely amazed by the massive improvements that have been implemented both in the management of visitors and the fragile eco-system upon which survival of so many rare and beautiful creatures is based. With the cessation of grazing by domestic herds, we can expect to see an immediate recovery of the plant community, then an upsurge in the members of forest and grassland animal species. I feel that in the near future, the wild animal populations will be just as visible as the remarkable assemblage of birds. We outsiders consider India's management of this park

---

Dr Salim Ali (**above**)*, fondly remembered as the Bird Man and George Archibald* (**below**) *of the International Crane Foundation*

to be exemplified worldwide, and an added significance considering the local pressures that threaten the survival of this global treasure, Keoladeo National Park.'

On 12 December 1982, the internationally-renowned conservationist Peter Jackson wrote in the visitors' book, 'I came first to the Ghana with Salim Ali in 1956 and have been a frequent visitor ever since. It has been a special pleasure to be here again with Salim, to whom we all owe so much—for his efforts to save the Ghana and to ensure its conservation. Much has changed, it used to be a lonely place and it was wonderful that way. But it is gratifying now to see people coming from all over India and other parts of the world. Their interest will surely promote the conservation of nature. The birds have not changed. May they always find a perfect sanctuary here.'

In the winter of 1976, a seminar was jointly organised at Keoladeo by the Government of India and the Rajasthan Government through their forest and tourism departments. The basic object was to promote eco-tourism in India, especially in Rajasthan. The members of Audubon, a US-based nature conservation society, were invited to participate in this seminar. A painted stork was released in the sky and a postage stamp featuring this stork was also released by the dignitaries.

An International Crane Workshop was organised by the International Crane Foundation from 5–11 February, 1983. Its co-sponsors were the Governments of India and Rajasthan, BNHS, International Council for Bird Preservation, National Audubon Society–USA, Tourism and Wildlife Society of India, United States Fish and Wildlife Services, WWF-India, WWF International and the Zoological Survey of India. This

HARSH VARDHAN

HARSH VARDHAN

Left: *A painted stork was released by the dignitaries during the Audubon seminar. L-R: Dr S. Dillon Ripley, Head, Smithsonian Institution, Raj Bahadur, Union Minister, Government of India, Fateh Singh Rao Gaekwad, President, WWF-India and Dr Salim Ali, President, BNHS.* **Right:** *A stamp of the stork was released by Jujhar Singh, Cabinet Minister, Tourism, Government of Rajasthan and Fateh Singh Rao Gaekwad*

workshop was attended by 187 delegates from 24 nations. Indira Gandhi, the then Prime Minister of India, met the organisers in Delhi and extended her best wishes to them. The Maharaja of Bharatpur, along with his family, also attended the event. Dr Salim Ali, then 86, was an active participant and several resolutions pertaining to crane conservation were passed during this historic workshop. In 1993, on the behest of the International Crane Foundation, under the Convention of Migratory Species (CMS), also known as the Bonn Convention, a memorandum of understanding was prepared for all the 12 Siberian crane range countries. The second meeting of this convention was held at the Keoladeo National Park in November 1996 and was attended by most of the tiger range countries including Iran, Kazakhstan, Russia, Azerbaijan, Turkmenistan and Uzbekistan. The agreement's objective is to coordinate efforts to save the central and western population of the highly-endangered Siberian crane species. Since then, commendable work has been done in this field, raising hopes for the revival of this magnificent species.

Acknowledgements

I am indebted to the personnel (past and present) of the Keoladeo National Park who have generously assisted me in learning birdwatching and wetland management. Abrar Khan (alias Bholu), Sohan Lal and Dharam Singh deserve special mention. The mammoth operation of *Prosopis juliflora* eradication would not have been possible without the dedication and hard work of the park's personnel of all ranks. I hold them in high esteem. Rajendra Gupta, Narayan Singh, Vasudeo, Nawab Singh, Parminder, Amar Singh, Puran and Ranno are a few names coming to my memory, but there were many. I am thankful to all of them. I am also grateful to my dear friends Dinesh Durrani, Dhirendra Godha and wildlife enthusiasts such as Deen Dayal Sharma (a banker), Navin Sharma and Kailash Navrang (both photojournalists) for their constant motivational support in rejuvenating this diminishing birds' paradise.

I want to convey my deep gratitude to Maharaj Kumar Vishwendra Singh, Bharatpur, for his constant encouragement and friendly support in fighting the unprecedented drought and the *Prosopis juliflora* menace in the park. The support I received from V.P. Singh (the then Chairman of the State Steering Committee for Wildlife and Forests), Dr Digamber Singh (then Cabinet Minister, Government of Rajasthan) and Rajpal Singh (then Member of the V.P. Singh Committee) in rescuing the park from this crisis is unforgettable. I am extremely grateful to all of them.

Lifting Keoladeo out of the crisis required emergency-like operations and there was simply no time to strictly follow the procedural formalities. Higher bureaucracy could have nailed down my pace but for R.N. Mehrotra, the then Chief Wildlife Warden of Rajasthan and P.S. Somshekhar (Conservator Wildlife) who not only stood by me throughout but also encouraged me. I am forever thankful to them. Undoubtedly, R.N. Mehrotra is the all-time best warden that Rajasthan could ever have.

Several researchers have studied the various ecological aspects of the park and their work has contributed immensely to the cause of nature conservation and has helped enhance scientific knowledge about Keoladeo, for which we conservationists are grateful. The services of the country's premier institutions such as the Wildlife Institute of India, BNHS Mumbai and WWF-India deserve special mention for their invaluable contribution to this cause. Ravi Singh (Secretary General and CEO, WWF-India), Dr Parikshit Gautam (Ex-Director, Fresh Water Bodies, WWF), Dr V.B. Mathur (Director, WII) and Dr V.S. Vijayan (BNHS) will always be remembered for their love, support and contribution to the park, whose glory they have helped enhance. WWF-India, under the leadership of Ravi Singh, has always played the role of an important partner to the Keoladeo National Park, especially during moments of crisis. The creation of an invaluable asset such as the Nature Interpretation Centre at Keoladeo is just one example. I will remain indebted to Ravi Singh for his support throughout my crusade of pulling the park out from the deep trouble of water crisis and weed menace.

Dr Asad Rahmani, former Director of BNHS Mumbai, a great ornithologist of international repute, has not only contributed immensely to Keoladeo but to nature conservation as a whole. He has been a great scholar and renowned teacher of ornithology, yet he is far too modest. He has generously guided me on various tricky management issues pertaining to avian fauna throughout my long career as a wildlife manager serving in the Thar Desert to the Keoladeo wetlands.

Harsh Vardhan, Founder Director, Tourism and Wildlife Society of India, Jaipur, with his undying passion for wildlife, will always be remembered for not only inculcating the love and respect for nature and its wild inhabitants in thousands of school children but also for fighting to save Keoladeo, Sambhar, Mansagar and many other important wetlands. For years, he tried to convince the central and state governments and judiciary to revive the water supply to Keoladeo from the Gambhiri river. He even compelled the Government of India to deter the powerful Sheikh of Saudi Arabia from hunting the great Indian bustard on Indian soil. It was his crusade for the protection of this bird that led the Government of Rajasthan to declare it its state bird. I have very high regard for his unparalleled contribution to the pious cause of nature conservation. He has helped me in not only saving Keoladeo from the menace of *Prosopis juliflora* but also in motivating bureaucrats and political bosses to provide funds for the creation of the 'New Canal' for channelising Chiksana Canal water into Keoladeo lakes. I am indebted to Harsh Vardhan for not only inspiring me to write this book but for also providing some rare knowledge and pictures.

Dr Anita Kothari, a close family friend, helped me immensely in correcting and adding literary inputs in the initial drafts of this book. I owe a lot to her for this invaluable support. Pushp Jain, Chief Analyst, EIA Resource and Response Centre, New Delhi, is a hardcore wildlifer, a writer on wildlife, and works on the conservation and protection of forests and the environment. He is one of the most travelled wildlifers in the country and his knowledge about wildlife and its management is immense. I have no words to express my gratitude for his generous support in editing and guiding me throughout this book, right till its finalisation. I feel blessed to have such a great friend. Dr M.M. Trigunayat, a Bharatpur-based expert on entomology, has educated me on insect life in Keoladeo and also generously vetted the chapter on butterflies. I am indebted to him. I am also extremely grateful to Dr Abhishek Bhatnagar, Landscape Coordinator, WWF-India, who has been of immense help in providing relevant maps and checklists (Hindi/local names) of the birds at Keoladeo. For not only generously sharing relevant information on the park, but also facilitating my stay and visits here, my special thanks to Ajit Uchoi, Bijoy and Anoop K.R.

All Keoladeo lovers and the fraternity of conservationists are grateful to Belinda Wright and Stanley Breeden for showcasing the unique beauty and richness of the Keoladeo National Park by making a wonderful film, titled 'Birds of the Indian Monsoon'. Kailash Sankhala, Rajpal Singh and the Bittoo Sehgal-Bikram Garewal duo will always be remembered for creating such outstanding books on Keoladeo.

I pay my tribute to my revered guru, H.S. Pawar, a Padma Bhushan recipient and Founder Director of the Wild Life Institute of India, for his ever-lasting contribution to the worthy cause of nature conservation. He has always inspired me to give it my best.

There are numerous wildlife lovers and friends who have also inspired me to write this book. I am extremely thankful to them. I also thank my wife, Renu, for being a constant source of inspiration to me to write this book. My son Manish, daughter Bhawna and grandchildren Sumera, Shivansh and Suryansh have all lovingly supported me in this endeavour. Finally, I salute the former Prime Minister, Indira Gandhi, the remarkable ornithologist, Salim Ali and the great wildlife conservationist, Kailash Sankhala, for their invaluable contribution to the development of Keoladeo and placing it among the top bird sanctuaries in the world.

APPENDIX

Flora of Keoladeo National Park

Family and Species/Synonyms		Common Name
Menispermaceae		
1	*Cocculus hirsutus (L.) Diels/Cocculus villosus DC.*	Jal-jamni
2	*Tinospora cordifolia (Willd.) Miers*	(Heart leaved moonseed)/ Gulbel
Nymphaeaceae		
3	*Nymphaea nouchali Burm. f./Nymphaea stellata Willd.*	Kamal
4	*Nymphaea pubescens Willd./Nymphaea lotus auct. non L.*	Kamal
Papaveraceae		
5	*Argemone mexicana L.*	Mexican Poppy/Satyanashi
6	*Argemone ochroleuca*	Satyanashi
Brassicaceae (Cruciferae)		
7	*Cochlearia cochlearioides (Roth) Santapau & Mahesh./Cochlearia flava Buch.-Ham. ex Roxb.*	
8	*Coronopus didymus (L.) Sm./Senebiera pinnatifida DC.*	
9	*Rorippa indica (L.) Hiern/Nasturtium indicum DC.*	
Cleomaceae		
10	*Cleome gynandra L./Gynandropsis pentaphylla (L.) DC.*	Bagro
11	*Cleome viscosa L.*	
Capparaceae (Capparidaceae)		
12	*Capparis decidua (Forsk.) Edgew./Capparis aphylla Roth*	Karil
13	*Capparis sepiaria L.*	Wild Capper Bush/Heens
14	*Crataeva magna (Lour.) DC./Crataeva religiosa auct. non Forst., Crataeva nurvala Buch.-Ham.*	Barna
15	*Maerua oblongifolia (Forsk.) A. Rich./Maerua arenaria Hook. f. & Thoms.*	Desert maerua/Jangle Jalebi
Caryophyllaceae		
16	*Spergula arvensis L.*	
Portulacaceae		
17	*Portulaca quadrifida L.*	
Tamaricaceae		
18	*Tamarix aphylla (L.) Karst./Tamarix articulata Vahl*	Athel pine/Pharash/Jhau
Elatinaceae		
19	*Bergia ammannioides Roxb.*	
20	*Elatine triandra Schk./Elatine americana Arn.*	
Malvaceae		
21	*Abelmoschus ficulneus (L.) Wt. & Arn./Hibiscus ficulneus L.*	Jungali Bhindi
22	*Abutilon indicum (L.) Sweet*	Kanghi/Kakahi/Kanghi
23	*Abutilon ramosum Guill. & Perr.*	

Family and Species/Synonyms		Common Name
24	*Althaea ludwigii L.*	
25	*Gossypium arboreum L.*	Bun
26	*Hibiscus amblyocarpus Hochst/Hibiscus obtusilobus Garcke, Hibiscus punctatus Dalz.*	
27	*Hibiscus caesius Gracke/Hibiscus gibsoni Stocks ex Ham & Sond.*	
28	*Hibiscus ovalifolius (Forsk.) Vahl/Hibiscus micranthus L. f.*	Okda
29	*Malva parviflora L.*	
30	*Malvastrum coromandelianum (L.) Garcke/ Malvastrum tricuspidatum A. Gray*	
31	*Sida cordata (Burm. f.) Borss./Sida humilis Cay.*	Heart leaf sida/Bhuini
32	*Sida rhombifolia L./Sida orientalis Cay.*	Jelly leaf/Sahdeo
33	*Sida spinosa L./Sida alba L.*	
34	*Thespesia populnea (L.) Soland. ex Corr.*	Parus Peepal
Sterculiaceae		
35	*Melochia corchorifolia L.*	
Tiliaceae		
36	*Corchorus aestuans L./Corchorus acutangularis Lamk.*	Hade-ka –Khet
37	*Corchorus capsularis L.*	
38	*Corchorus fascicularis Lamk.*	
39	*Corchorus olitorius L.*	
40	*Corchorus tridens L.*	
41	*Grewia tenax (Forsk.) Fiori/Grewia populifolia Vahl*	
Zygophyllaceae		
42	*Tribulus terrestris L.*	Gokhru
Oxalidaceae		
43	*Oxalis corniculata L.*	Tipatti
Balanitaceae		
44	*Balanites aegyptiaca (L.) Del./Balanites roxburghii Planch.*	Hingot
Meliaceae		
45	*Azadirachta indica A. Juss./Melia azadirachta L.*	Neem
Rhamnaceae		
46	*Ziziphus mauritiana Lamk./Ziziphus jujuba (L.) Gaertn. non Mill.*	Ber
47	*Ziziphus nummularia (Burm. f.) Wt. & Arn./Ziziphus rotundifolia Lamk.*	Jhad Beri
Vitaceae		
48	*Cayratia trifolia (L.) Domin/Cayratia carnosa Gagnep., Vitis carnosa Wall., Vitis trifolia L.*	
Sapindaceae		
49	*Cardiospermum halicacabum L.*	
Fabaceae (Papilionaceae)		
50	*Abrus precatorius L.*	Rathi
51	*Aeschynomene indica L.*	

Family and Species/Synonyms		Common Name
52	*Alghai pseudalhagi (M. Bieb.) Desv/Alghai camelorum Fisch., Alghai maurorum auct. non Desv*	Javasa
53	*Alysicarpus longifolius (Roth.) Wt. & Arn.*	
54	*Alysicarpus vaginalis DC.*	
55	*Clitoria ternatea L.*	Gokarni
56	*Crotalaria medicaginea Lamk.*	Gulali
57	*Dalbergia sissoo Roxb.*	Shisham
58	*Goniogyna hirta (Willd.) All/Heylandia latebrosa DC.*	
59	*Indigofera cordifolia Heyne ex Roth*	
60	*Indigofera tinctoria L.*	Sankh Buti
61	*Indigofera trita L. f.*	
62	*Lathyrus aphaca L.*	Sattar
63	*Medicago polymorpha L./Medicago denticulata Willd.*	
64	*Melilotus indica All./Melilotus parviflora Desf.*	Morara
65	*Pongamia pinnata (L.) Pierre /Pongamia glabra Vent., Derris indica (Lamk.). Bennet*	Pongam tree/Karanj
66	*Rhynchosia minima (L.) DC*	Kulta
67	*Sesbania bispinosa (Jacq.) W. F. Wight/Sesbania aculeata Pers.*	Dhadon
68	*Teramnus labialis (L.) Spreng.*	Kalian
69	*Trigonella hamosa L. subsp. uncata (Boiss. & Noe) Townsend*	
70	*Trigonella occulta Del.*	
71	*Vicia sativa L.*	
72	*Vigna trilobata (L.) Verdcourt/Phaseolus trilobus Ait.*	
Caesalpiniaceae		
73	*Cassia fistula L.*	Amaltash
74	*Cassia occidentalis L.*	
75	*Cassia pumila Lamk.*	
76	*Cassia siamea Lamk.*	Cassia Siamea
77	*Cassia surattensis Burm. f./Cassia glauca Lamk.*	
78	*Cassia tora L./Cassia obtusifolia L.*	Puvad
79	*Delonix regia (Boj.) Raf./Poinciana regia Boj. ex Hook.*	Gulmohar
80	*Parkinsonia aculeata L.*	Jerusalem thorn/Parkinsonia
81	*Tamarindus indica L.*	Imli
Mimosaceae		
82	*Acacia leucophloea (Roxb.) Willd.*	Ronjh
83	*Acacia nilotica (L.) Del. sub sp. indica (Benth.) Brenan/Acacia arabica Willd.*	Babool
84	*Albizia lebbeck (L.) Benth.*	Siras
85	*Dichrostachys cinerea (L.) Wt. & Arn.*	
86	*Leucaena latisiliqua (L.) Gillis/Leucaena leucocephala (Lamk.) de Wit., Leucaena glauca Benth.*	

Family and Species/Synonyms		Common Name
87	*Neptunia oleracea Lour.*	Chhui-mui
88	*Pithecellobium dulce (Roxb.) Benth.*	
89	*Prosopis cineraria (L.) Druce/Prosopis spicigera L.*	Khejadi
90	*Prosopis juliflora (Sw.) DC.*	Vilayati Babool
Rosaceae		
91	*Potentilla supina L.*	Bushy cinquefoil
Myrtaceae		
92	*Callistemon lanceolatus DC.*	Bottle Brush
93	*Syzygium cumini (L.) Skeels/Eugenia jambolana Lamk.*	Jamun
Lythraceae		
94	*Ammannia auriculata Willd./Ammannia senegalensis Lamk.*	
95	*Ammannia baccifera L.*	Jar Bangro
96	*Lawsonia inermis L./Lawsonia alba lamk.*	Mehndi
97	*Rotala densiflora (Roth. ex Roem. & Schult.) Koehne/Ammannia pentandra auct. non Roxb*	
98	*Rotala indica (Willd.) Koehne./Ammannia peploides Spreng.*	
Onagraceae		
99	*Ludwigia perennis L./Ludwigia parviflora Roxb., Jussiaea perennis (L.) Brenan*	
Trapaceae		
100	*Trapa natans L. var. bispinosa (Roxb.) Makino/ Trapa bispinosa Roxb.*	Singhada
Cucurbitaceae		
101	*Coccinia grandis (L.) J. 0. Voigh./Coccinia cordifolia (L.) Cogn., Coccinia indica Wt. & Arn., Cephalandra indica Naud.*	Ivy Gourd/Kundaru/Gulkakad
102	*Cucumis melo L./Cucumis callosus (Rottl.) Cogn.*	
103	*Luffa acutangula (L.) Roxb. var. amara (Roxb.) Clarke Luffa*	Jungali Torai
104	*Luffa echinata Roxb.*	Karai Banyar
105	*Momordica charantia L. var. muricata (Willd.) Chakravarty*	Rumia Karela
106	*Mukia maderaspatana (L.) M. Roem./Mukia scabrella Arn., Melathria maderaspatana Cogn.*	
107	*Trichosanthes cucumerina L.*	Ankh Phod
Cactaceae		
108	*Opuntia elatior Mill.*	Nagphani
Molluginaceae		
109	*Glinus lotoides L./Mollugo hirta Thunb.*	Bakada
110	*Glinus oppositifolia (L) A. DC./Molugo oppositifolia L., Mollugo spergula L.*	
Aizoaceae		
111	*Trianthema portulacastrum L./ Trianthema monogyna L.*	Santi
112	*Trianthema triquetra Rottl. & Willd./Trianthema crystaNna auct.non Vahl*	
113	*Zaleya govindia (Buch.-Ham. ex G. Don) N. C. Nair/Trianthema govindia Buch.-Ham. ex G. Don, Trianthema pentandra auct. non L.*	
114	*Seseli diffusum (Roxb. ex Sm.) Santapu & Wagh/Seseli indicum Wt. & Arn.*	

Family and Species/Synonyms		Common Name
Rubiaceae		
115	*Catunaregam spinosa (Thunb.) Tiruv./Xeromphis spinosa (Thunb.) Keay, Randia dumetorum Lamk.*	
116	*Dentella repens (L.) Forst.*	
117	*Mitragyna parvifolia (Roxb.) Korth./Stephegyne parvifolia Korth.*	Kadam/Kalam
118	*Oldenlandia corymbosa L.*	Daman Papar
119	*Oldenlandia pseudocorymbosa (Bakh. f.) C. R. Babu Asteraceae (Compositae)/ Hedyotis pseudocorymbosa Bakh. f.*	
120	*Ageratum conyzoides L.*	
121	*Bidens biternata (Lour.) Merr. & Sherff/Bidens pilosa auct. non L.*	
122	*Blumea eriantha DC.*	
123	*Blumea laciniata (Roxb.) DC.*	
124	*Blumea membranacea DC.*	
125	*Blumea mollis (D. Don) Merr./Blumea wightiana DC.*	
126	*Blumea obliqua (L.) Druce/ Blumea amplectens DC.*	
127	*Caesulia axillaris Roxb.*	
128	*Conyza bonariensis (L.) Cronq./Erigeron bonariensis L., Erigeron linifolius Willd.*	
129	*Cotula anthemoides L.*	
130	*Echinops echinatus Roxb.*	
131	*Eclipta prostata (L.) L./Eclipta alba (L.) Hassk., Eclipta erecta L.*	Cucur Bhangra, Kara Bhangra
132	*Gnaphalium luteo-album L. subsp. affine (D. Don) Koster/Gnaphalium luteo-album L. var. multiceps Hook. f.*	
133	*Gnaphalium polycaulon Pers./Gnaphalium indicum auct. non L.*	
134	*Gnaphalium pulvinatum Del.*	
135	*Gnaphalium purpureum L.*	
136	*Grangea maderaspatana (L.) Poir.*	Asteraceae/Mustaru
137	*Laggera aurita (Willd.) Sch.-Bip. ex Cl.*	
138	*Launaea procumbens (Roxb.) Ramayya & Rajagopal/ Launaea nudicaulis Hook. f.,Launaea fallax (Jaub. & Spach.) 0. Kuntze*	Creeping launaea/Jangigobhi
139	*Oligochaeta ramosa (Roxb.) Wagen./Volutarella divaricata Benth. & Hook. f., Volutarella ramosa (Roxb.) Santapau, Amberboa ramosa (Roxb.) Jafri*	
140	*Pluchea lanceolata (DC.) Cl.*	
141	*Pluchea wallichiana DC.*	
142	*Pulicaria crispa Sch.-Bip.*	
143	*Sonchus asper (L.) Hill.*	
144	*Sonchus oleraceus L.*	
145	*Sphaeranthus indicus L.*	
146	*Tridax procumbens L.*	
147	*Vernonia cinerea (L.) Less.*	
148	*Vicoa indica (L.) DC./Vicoa auriculata Cass., Inula indica L.*	
149	*Xanthium strumarium L.*	
Campanulaceae		
150	*Wahlenbergia marginata (Thunb.) DC./Wahlenbergia gracilis (Forst.) DC.*	

Family and Species/Synonyms		Common Name
Sphenocleaceae		
151	*Sphenoclea zeylanica Gaertn.*	
Plumbaginaceae		
152	*Plumbago zeylanica L.*	
Primulaceae		
153	*Anagallis arvensis L.*	
Ebenaceae		
154	*Diospyros cordifolia Roxb.*	Pasendu
Salvadoraceae		
155	*Salvadora oleoides Dence.*	Pilu
156	*Salvadora persica L.*	Pilu/Khadyar
Asclepiadaceae		
157	*Calotropis procera (Ait.) R. Br.*	Akada/Aak
158	*Ceropegia bulbosa Roxb. var. lushii (Grah.) Hook. f./Oxystelma esculentum (L. f.) R. Br.*	Rosy milkweed wine/Barbatta
159	*Oxystelma secamone (L.) Karst./Pentatropis spiralis sensu Dence.*	
160	*Pentatropis nivalis (Gmel.) Field & Wood/Pentatropis cynanchoides R. Br.*	Leafed milkweed
161	*Pergularia daemia (Forsk.) Chiov./Daemia extensa R. Br.*	
162	*Wattakaka volubilis (L. f.) Stapf/Dregea volubilis Benth. ex Hook., Marsdenia volubilis (L. f.) Cooke*	
Periplocaceae		
163	*Cryptostegia grandiflora R. Br.*	Chamchari
Gentianaceae		
164	*Centaurium centaurioides (Roxb.) Rao & Hem./Erythraea roxburghii G. Don*	
165	*Nymphoides cristata (Roxb.) Kuntze/Limnanthemum cristatum Griseb.*	
166	*Nymphoides indica (L.) Kuntze/Limnanthemum indicum Thwaites*	
Hydrophyllaceae		
167	*Hydrolea zeylanica (L.) Vahl*	
Boraginaceae		
168	*Coldenia procumbens L.*	
169	*Heliotropium ovalifolium Forsk.*	
170	*Heliotropium strigosum Willd.*	Arkali
171	*Trichodesma amplexicaule Roth*	
Ehretiaceae		
172	*Cordia dichotoma Forst. f./Cordia obliqua Willd.*	Nisoda
173	*Ehretia aspera Roxb.*	Apho
Convolvulaceae		
174	*Convolvulus microphyllus Sieb. ex Spreng./Convolvulus pluricaulis Choisy*	
175	*Evolvulus alsinoides (L.) L.*	Shankh Pushpi
176	*Ipomoea aquatica Forsk./Ipomoea reptans (L.) Poir.*	Nari

Family and Species/Synonyms		Common Name
177	*Ipomoea carnea Jacq. sub sp. fistulosa (Mart. ex Choisy) Austin/Ipomoea fistulosa Mart. ex Choisy*	Vilaiti Aak
178	*Ipomoea dichroa (Roem. & Schult.) Choisy/Ipomoea pilosa Sweet*	
179	*Ipomoea hederifolia L./Ipomoea angulata Lamk., Quamoclit phoenicia Choisy*	
180	*Ipomoea nil (L.) Roth*	
181	*Ipomoea pes-tigridis L.*	Ghiabathi
182	*Ipomoea sindica Stapf*	
183	*Merremia emarginata Hall. f./Merremia gangetica (L.) Cufodont., Ipomoea reniformis Choisy*	Moosa Kaani
Cuscutaceae		
184	*Cuscuta reflexa Roxb.*	Amarbel
Solanaceae		
185	*Datura innoxia Mill.*	Dhatura
186	*Lycopersicon esculentum Mill.*	Tamatar
187	*Nicotiana alata Link & Otto*	
188	*Nicotiana plumbaginifolia Viv.*	Junjali tamaku
189	*Physalis minima L.*	Chin Mitti
190	*Solanum nigrum L.*	Black night shade/Makoy
191	*Solanum surattense Burm. f./Solanum xanthocarpum Schrad. & Wendl.*	Phal kateri
192	*Withania somnifera (L.) Dunal*	Askand
Scrophulariaceae		
193	*Glossostigma diandrum (L.) Kuntze/Glossostigma spathulatum/(Hook. ex Wt.) Arn. Ex Benth.*	
194	*Limnophila indica (L.) Druce/Limnophila gratioloides R. Br.*	Gulabi
195	*Lindernia ciliata (Colsm.) Penn./Bonnaya brachiata Link & Otto*	
196	*Lindernia crustacea (L.) F. Muell./Vandellia crustacea Benth.*	
197	*Lindernia parviflora (Roxb.) Haines/Illysanthes parviflora (Roxb.) Benth.*	
198	*Peplidium maritimum (L. f.) Asch./Peplidium humifusum Del.*	
199	*Verbascum chinense (L.) Santapau/Celosia coromandeliana Vahl*	
Lentibulariaceae		
200	*Utricularia aurea Lour./Utricularia flexuosa Vahl*	
201	*Utricularia exoleta R. Br.*	
202	*Utricularia stellaris L. f./Utricularia inflexa Forsk. Var. stellaris (L. f.) P. Taylor*	
Bignoniaceae		
203	*Millingtonia hortensis L. f.*	Neem-Chameli
Pedaliaceae		
204	*Pedalium murex L.*	Vilayti Gokhru
Acanthaceae		
205	*Adhatoda zeylanica Medic./Adhatoda vasica Nees, Justicia adhatoda L.*	Adushta
206	*Barleria cristata L.*	
207	*Blepharis maderaspatensis (L.) Heyne ex Roth/Blepharis boerhaviaefolia Pers.*	

	Family and Species/Synonyms	Common Name
208	*Dicliptera verticillata (Forsk.) Christen/Dicliptera micranthes Nees*	
209	*Dipteracanthus prostratus (Poir.) Nees/Ruellia prostrata Poir.*	
210	*Elytraria acaulis (L. f.) Kuntze/Tubiflora acaulis (L. f.) Kuntze*	Pattharchatta
211	*Hemiadelphis polyspermus (Roxb.) Nees/Hygrophila polysperma (Roxb.) T. Anders.*	
212	*Hygrophila auriculata (Schum.) Heine/Hygrophila spinosa T. Anders., Asteracantha longifolia (L.) Nees*	Marsh barbell/ Bhankari/Unt katera
213	*Justicia heterocarpa T. Anders.*	
214	*Peristrophe paniculata (Forssk.) Brummitt/ Peristrophe bicalyculata (Retz.) Nees*	
215	*Rostellularia quinqueangularis (Koen.) Nees var. peploides (Nees) Raizada/ Justicia quinqueangularis Koen. var. peploides (Nees) Raizada*	
216	*Ruellia tuberosa L.*	Minnieroot/Chatakni Phali
217	*Rungia pectinata (L.) Nees*	
218	*Rungia repens (L.) Nees*	
Verbenaceae		
219	*Clerodendrum phlomidis L. f./Clerodendrum multiflorum (Burm. f.) Kuntze*	Inni
220	*Lantana camara L. var. aculeata (L.) Mold.*	Lantana
221	*Phyla nodiflora (L.) Greene/Lippia nodiflora A. Rich.*	Jal Pipali
222	*Vitex negunda L.*	Ningand
Lamiaceae (Labiatae)		
223	*Leucas urticaefolia (Vahl) R. Br.*	
224	*Ocimum basilicum L.*	
225	*Salvia plebeia R. Br.*	
Nyctaginaceae		
226	*Boerhavia diffusa L./Boerhavia procumbens Roxb.*	Lal Sata
227	*Commicarpus chinensis (L.) Heimerl./Boerhavia chinensis (L.) Asch. & Schweinf., Boerhavia repanda Willd.*	Diffuse hogweed
228	*Commicarpus helenae (Schultes) Meikle/Boerhavia verticillata auct. non Poir.*	
Amaranthaceae		
229	*Achyranthes aspera L. var. argentea Hook. f.*	Chirchira/Devil'Hosewhip
230	*Achranthes aspera L. var. porphyristachya Hook. f.*	Onga
231	*Alternanthera paronychioides St. Hil.*	
232	*Alternanthera pungens H. B. & K.*	Kantewali Santi
233	*Alternanthera sessilis (L.) R. Br.*	Sessilie Joyweed/Garundi
234	*Amaranthus spinosus L.*	Jungali Choulai
235	*Amaranthus tricolor L.*	
236	*Amaranthus viridis L.*	Lasua
237	*Celosia argentea L.*	Chamkili
238	*Digera muricata (L.) Mart./Digera arvensis Forst.*	Lasua
239	*Gomphrena serrata L./Gomphrena celosioides Mart*	
240	*Nothosaerva brachiata (L.) Wt.*	
241	*Pupalia lappacea (L.) Juss.*	Chirchita

Family and Species/Synonyms		Common Name
Chenopodiaceae		
242	*Chenopodium album L.*	Bathua
243	*Chenopodium murale L.*	Kharthua
244	*Salsola baryosma (Roem. & Schult.) Dandy/Salsola foetida Del.*	Chir Chitti
245	*Suaeda fructicosa (L.) Forsk.*	
Basellaceae		
246	*Basella alba L./Basella rubra L.*	
Polygonaceae		
247	*Antigonon leptopus Hook. & Arn.*	
248	*Polygonum barbatum L.*	
249	*Polygonum glabrum Willd.*	
250	*Polygonum limbatum Meissn.*	
251	*Polygonum plebeium R. Br.*	
252	*Rumex dentatus L.*	Toothed dock/Jungli Palak
Euphorbiaceae		
253	*Acalypha ciliata Forsk.*	
254	*Acalypha indica L.*	
255	*Chrozophora rottleri (Geir.) Juss. ex Spreng./Chrozophora plicata Voigt*	Suryvarti/Shadevi/Shadevi
256	*Euphorbia hirta L./Euphorbia pilulifera Hook. f.*	
257	*Euphorbia orbiculata H. B. & K./Euphorbia microphylla Heyne*	
258	*Euphorbia parviflora L./Euphorbia hypericifolia L.*	
259	*Euphorbia thymifolia L.*	
260	*Kirganelia reticulata (Poir.) Baill./Phyllanthus reticulatus Poir.*	Makhi
261	*Phyllanthus amarus Schum. & Thonn.*	
262	*Phyllanthus fratemus Webster/Phyllanthus niruri Sensu Hook. f., non L.*	
263	*Phyllanthus maderaspatensis L.*	
264	*Phyllanthus virgatus Forst. f./Phyllanthus simplex Retz.*	Gujrati Bawal
Ulmaceae		
265	*Holoptelea integrifolia (Roxb.) Planch.*	Churel/Papdi
Moraceae		
266	*Ficus benghalensis L.*	Bargad/Bad
267	*Ficus racemosa L./Ficus glomerata Roxb.*	Indian fig tree/Gular
268	*Ficus religiosa L.*	Peepal
269	*Morus alba L.*	Shahtut
Cannabinaceae		
270	*Cannabis sativa L.*	Ganja
Ceratophyllaceae		
271	*Ceratophyllum demersum L.*	Hornwort
Hydrochariataceae		
272	*Hydrilla verticillata (L. f.) Royle*	

Family and Species/Synonyms		Common Name
273	*Vallisneria natans (Lour.) Hara/Vallisneria spiralis L.*	
Liliaceae		
274	*Asparagus racemosus Willd.*	Shatavar
Pontederiaceae		
275	*Eichhornia crassipes (Mart.) Solms.*	Jal Kumbhi
276	*Monochoria vaginalis (Burm. f.) Presl.*	
Commelinaceae		
277	*Commelina benghalensis L.*	Bokna
278	*Commelina forskalei Vahl*	Kana
279	*Commelina hasskarlii Clarke*	
280	*Murdannia nudiflora (L.) Brenan*	
281	*Tonningia axillaris (L.) Kuntze/Amischophacelus axillaris (L.) Rolla Rao & Kammathy, Cyanotis axillaris Schult.*	Kana
Arecaceae (Palmae)		
282	*Phoenix sylvestris (L.) Roxb.*	Date palm/Khajur
Typhaceae		
283	*Typha angustata Bory & Chaub./Typha angustifolia auct. non L.*	Patera
Lemnaceae		
284	*Lemna perpusilla Torrey/Lemna paucicostata Hegelm*	Lemna/Chhoti Kai
285	*Spirodela polyrhiza (L.) Schleid./Lemna polyrhiza L.*	Common duck weed/kai
286	*Wolffia globosa (Roxb.) Hartog & Plas/Wolffia arrhiza auct. non Horkel ex Wimmer*	
Alismataceae		
287	*Limnophyton obtusifolium (L.) Miq.*	
288	*Sagittaria guayanensis H. B. & K.*	
Butomaceae		
289	*Butomopsis latifolia (D. Don) Kunth/Tenagocharis latifolia (D. Don) Buchen, Butomopsis lanceolata (Roxb.) Kunth*	
Aponogetonaceae		
290	*Aponogeton natans (L.) Engl. & Krause*	
Potamogetonaceae		
291	*Potamogeton crispus L.*	
292	*Potamogeton nodosus Poir./Potamogeton indicus Roxb.*	
293	*Potamogeton pectinatus L.*	
Najadaceae		
294	*Najas graminea Del.*	
295	*Najas minor All.*	
Cyperaceae		
296	*Cyperus alopecuroides Rottb./Juncellus alopecuroides Clarke*	Motha-Patera
297	*Cyperus alulatus Kern*	
298	*Cyperus iria L.*	
299	*Cyperus bulbosus Vahl*	

Family and Species/Synonyms		Common Name
300	*Cyperus compressus L.*	
301	*Cyperus difformis L.*	Small flower umbrella/Mothi/ Bada Nagarmotha
302	*Cyperus pygmaeus Rottb./Cyperus michelianus (L.) Del. subsp. pygmaeus Aschers. & Graebn.,Juncellus pygmaeus Clarke*	
303	*Cyperus rotundus L.*	Nut sedge/Motha
304	*Cyperus triceps (Rottb.) Endl./Kyllinga triceps Rottb.*	
305	*Eleocharis acutangula (Roxb.) Schult./Eleocharis fistulosa Schult.*	
306	*Eleocharis atropurpurea (Retz.) Kunth*	
307	*Eleocharis dulcis (Burm. f.) Henschel/Eleocharis plantaginea R. Br.*	Pola
308	*Eleocharis palustris R. Br.*	Poly
309	*Fimbristylis bisumbellata (Forssk.) Bubani/Fimbristylis dichotoma (non Vahl) Kunth*	
310	*Fimbristylis falcata (Vahl) Kunth/Fimbristylis junciformis (Nees) Kunth*	
311	*Fimbristylis ferruginea (L.) Vahl*	
312	*Fimbrstylis miliacea (L.) Vahl/Fimbristylis quinquangularis Kunth*	
313	*Scirpus articulatus L.*	
314	*Scirpus lateriflorus Gmel./Scirpus supinus L. var. lateriflorus (Gmel.) Koyama*	
315	*Scirpus littoralis Schrad.*	
316	*Scirpus roylei (Nees) Parker/Scirpus quinquefarius Buch.-Ham. ex Boeck.*	
317	*Scirpus supinus L.*	
318	*Scirpus tuberosus Desf./Scirpus maritimus L.*	Motha
Poaceae (Gramineae)		
319	*Acrachne racemosa (Heyne) Ohwi/Eleusine verticillata Roxb.*	
320	*Alloteropsis cimicina (L.) Stapf/Axonopus cimicinus P. Beauv.*	
321	*Aristida adscensionis L.*	
322	*Arundo donax L.*	Narkul Ghas
323	*Brachiaria distachya (L.) Stapf*	
324	*Brachiaria ramosa (L.) Stapf/Panicum ramosum L.*	
325	*Brachiaria reptans (L). Gard. & Hubb./Panicum prostratum Lamk.*	
326	*Cenchrus ciliaris L./Pennisetum cenchroides Rich.*	Safed Dhaman Ghas
327	*Cenchrus setigerus Vahl/Cenchrus biflorus sensu Hook. F., non Roxb.*	Kali Dhaman Ghas
328	*Chloris dolichostachya Lagasca/Chloris incompleta Roth*	
329	*Chloris quinquesetica Bhide*	
330	*Coix lacryma-jobi L.*	
331	*Crypsis schoenoides (L.) lamk./Heleochloa schoenoides Host*	
332	*Cynodon dactylon (L.) Pers.*	Dub Ghas
333	*Dactyloctenium aegyptium (L.) P. Beauv.*	Ganthi, Makra Ghas
334	*Desmostachya bipinnata (L.) Stapf/Eragrostis cynosuroides P. Beauv.*	Dab Ghas
335	*Dichanthium annulatum (Forssk.) Stapf*	Gerga Ghas
336	*Digitaria ciliaris (Retz.) Koel./Digitaria adscendens (H. B. & K.) Henr.*	
337	*Diplachne fusca (L.) P. Beauv.*	

Family and Species/Synonyms		Common Name
338	*Echinochloa colonum (L.) Link/Panicum colonum L.*	Homa, Soma
339	*Echinochloa crusgalli (L.) P. Beauv. var. breviseta (Doell.) Nielr.*	Sama
340	*Echinochloa crusgalli (L.) P. Beauv. var. crusgalli/Panicum crusgalli L.*	Sama
341	*Eragrostis cilianensis (All.) Vignolo-Lutati/Eragrostis major (L.) Host*	
342	*Eragrostis ciliaris (L.) R. Br.*	Underpuncha-choti
343	*Eragrostis gangetica (Roxb.) Steud./Eragrostis stenophylla Hochst. ex Miq.*	
344	*Eragrostis japonica (Thunb.) Trin.*	
345	*Eragrostis minor Host/Eragrostis poaeoides P. Beauv.*	
346	*Eragrostis tenella (L.) P. Beauv.*	
347	*Erianthus ravennae (L.) P. Beauv./Saccharum ravennae (L.) Murray*	Baru-sarpatho
348	*Eriochloa fatmensis (Hochst. & Steud.) Clayton/Eriochloa nubica (Steud.) Hack. & Stapf ex Thell.*	
349	*Eriochloa procera (Retz.) Hubb./Eriochloa polystachya Hook. f.*	
350	*Hemarthria compressa (L. f.) R. Br./Rottboellia compressa L. f.*	
351	*Iseilema laxum Hack.*	Gandhel
352	*Leptochloa panicea (Retz.) Ohwi/Leptochloa filiformis sensu Hook. f. non P. Beauv.*	
353	*Oplismenus burmanii (Retz.) P. Beauv.*	
354	*Oryza rufipogon Griff.*	Jungli Chawal
355	*Panicum antidotale Retz.*	Murut
356	*Panicum paludosum Roxb./Panicum proliferum sensu Hook. f. non Lamk.*	
357	*Panicum psilopodium Trin.*	
358	*Paspalidium punctatum (Burm.) A. Camus/Panicum punctatum Burm.*	Egyptian panic grass/ Paspaldium/Phatairo
359	*Paspalum distichum L.*	Aincha Ghas
360	*Paspalum scrobiculatum L.*	
361	*Phalaris minor Retz.*	
362	*Polypogon monospeliensis (L.) Desf.*	Kayvaye
363	*Pseudoraphis spinescens (R. Br.) Vickery/Panicum spinescens R. Br.*	
364	*Saccharum spontaneum L.*	Kans
365	*Sacciolepis indica (L.) A. Chase/Panicum indicum L.*	
366	*Setaria intermedia Roem. & Schult./Setaria tomentosa (Roxb.) Kunth*	
367	*Setaria verticillata (L.) P. Beauv.*	Chirchitta
368	*Sporobolus coromandelianus (Retz.) Kunth*	
369	*Sporobolus helvolus (Trin.) Th. Dur. & Schinz/Sporobolus glaucifolius Hochst. ex Steud.*	Khencha
370	*Sporobolus ioclados (Nees ex Trin.) Nees/Sporobolus marginatus Hochst.*	Usari
371	*Tragus roxburghii Panigrahi/Tragus biflorus (Roxb.) Schult., Tragus racemosus sensu Hook. f., non Scop.*	Sita Ghas
372	*Vetiveria zizanioides (L.) Nash*	Khus Ghas

Birds of Keoladeo National Park

Species	Scientific Name	Jan	Feb	Mar	Apr	May	Jun	Jul	Aug	Sep	Oct	Nov	Dec
Family Podicipedidae (Grebes)													
Little Grebe (Dabchick)	*Tachybaptus ruficollis*	*	*	Ï	Ï	*	*	Ï	Ï	Ï	*	*	*
Great Crested Grebe	*Podiceps cristatus*	*									*	*	*
Black-necked Grebe	*Podiceps nigricollis*	*	*								*	*	*
Family Pelecanidae (Pelicans)													
Great White Pelican (Rosy Pelican)	*Pelecanus onocrotalus*	*	*	*								*	*
Spot-billed Pelican (Grey Pelican)	*Pelecanus philippensis*	*	*									*	*
Dalmatian Pelican	*Pelecanus crispus*	*	*	*	*							*	*
Family Phalacrocoracidae (Cormorants/Shags)													
Little Cormorant	*Phalacrocorax niger*	*	*	*	*	*	*	Ï	Ï	Ï	*	*	*
Indian Cormorant (Indian Shag)	*Phalacrocorax fuscicollis*	*						Ï	Ï	Ï	*	*	*
Great Cormorant	*Phalacrocorax carbo*	*	*					Ï	Ï	Ï	Ï	Ï	*
Family Anhingidae (Darters)													
Darter (Snake-bird)	*Anhinga melanogaster*	*	*	*	*	*	*	Ï	Ï	Ï	*	*	*
Family Ardeidae (Herons, Egrets and Bitterns)								Ï	Ï	Ï			
Little Egret	*Egretta garzetta*	*	*	*	*	*	Ï	Ï	Ï	Ï	Ï	*	*
Western Reef-Egret	*Egretta gularis*	*	*						*	*			*
Grey Heron	*Ardea cinerea*	Ï	Ï	Ï	Ï	Ï	*	*	Ï	Ï	Ï	*	*
Purple Heron	*Ardea purpurea*	Ï	Ï	Ï	Ï	Ï		*	Ï	Ï	Ï	*	*
Great Egret (Large Egret)	*Casmerodius albus*	Ï	Ï	Ï	Ï	Ï	*	*	Ï	Ï	Ï	*	*
Intermediate Egret (Median Egret)	*Mesophoyx intermedia*	Ï	Ï	Ï	Ï	Ï	*	*	Ï	Ï	Ï	*	*
Cattle Egret	*Bubulcus ibis*	*	*	*	*	*	*	Ï	Ï	Ï	*	*	*
Indian Pond-Heron	*Ardeola grayii*	*	*	*	*	*	*	*	*	*	*	*	*
Little Heron (Little Green Heron)	*Butorides striatus*	*	Ï	Ï	*	*	*	Ï	Ï	*	*	*	*
Black-crowned Night-Heron	*Nycticorax nycticorax*	*	Ï	Ï	*	*	*	Ï	Ï	*	*	*	*
Little Bittern	*Ixobrychus minutus*	*	*	*	*	*	*	Ï	Ï	*	*	*	*
Yellow Bittern	*Ixobrychus sinensis*	*	*									*	*

Species	Scientific Name	Jan	Feb	Mar	Apr	May	Jun	Jul	Aug	Sep	Oct	Nov	Dec
Cinnamon Bittern (Chestnut Bittern)	*Ixobrychus cinnamomeus*	*	Ï	Ï	*	*	*	Ï	Ï	*	*	*	*
Black Bittern	*Dupetor flavicollis*	*	Ï	Ï	*	*	*	Ï	Ï	Ï	*	*	*
Great Bittern (Tiger Bittern)	*Botaurus stellaris*	*	*										
Family Ciconiidae (Storks)													
Painted Stork	*Mycteria leucocephala*	*	*	*	*	*	*		Ï	Ï	Ï	Ï	Ï
Asian Openbill (Asian Openbill-Stork)	*Anastomus oscitans*	*					*	Ï	Ï	Ï	*	*	*
Black Stork	*Ciconia nigra*	*	*	*	*	*							*
Woolly-necked Stork (White-necked Stork)	*Ciconia episcopus*	*	*	*	*	*	*	*	Ï	Ï	*	*	*
White Stork (European White Stork)	*Ciconia ciconia*		*	*									
Black-necked Stork	*Ephippiorhynchus asiaticus*	*	*	*	*	*	*	*	Ï	Ï	Ï	Ï	Ï
Lesser Adjutant-Stork	*Leptoptilos javanicus*			*	*	*	*	*					
Greater Adjutant Stork	*Leptoptilos dubius*		*	*	*								
Family Threskiornithidae (Ibises and Spoonbills)													
Glossy Ibis	*Plegadis falcinellus*	*	*	*						*	*	*	*
Black-headed Ibis (Oriental White Ibis)	*Threskiornis melanocephalus*	*	*	*	*	*	*	Ï	Ï	Ï	*	*	*
Black Ibis	*Pseudibis papillosa*				*	*	*						
Eurasian Spoonbill	*Platalea leucorodia*	*	*	*	*	*	*	*	Ï	Ï	Ï	Ï	*
Family Phoenicopteridae (Flamingos)													
Greater Flamingo	*Phoenicopterus ruber*			*	*					*	*		
Lesser Flamingo	*Phoenicopterus minor*			*	*					*	*		
Family Anatidae (Swans, Geese and Ducks)													
Lesser Whistling-Duck	*Dendrocygna javanica*	*	Ï	Ï	*	*	*	Ï	Ï	*	*	*	*
Greater White-fronted Goose	*Anser albifrons*	*	*										*
Lesser White-fronted Goose	*Anser erythropus*	*	*										
Greylag Goose	*Anser anser*	*	*								*	*	*
Bar-headed Goose	*Anser indicus*	*	*	*	*						*	*	*
Ruddy Shelduck (Brahminy Shelduck)	*Tadorna ferruginea*	*	*	*	*						*	*	*
Common Shelduck	*Tadorna tadorna*	*	*	*								*	*

Species	Scientific Name	Jan	Feb	Mar	Apr	May	Jun	Jul	Aug	Sep	Oct	Nov	Dec
Comb Duck	*Sarkidiornis melanotos*	*	*	*	*	*	*	*	Ï	Ï	*	*	*
Cotton Pygmy-Goose (Cotton Teal)	*Nettapus coromandelianus*	*	*	*	*	*	*	Ï	Ï	Ï	*	*	*
Gadwall	*Anas strepera*	*	*	*							*	*	*
Falcated Duck	*Anas falcata*	*	*	*							*	*	*
Eurasian Wigeon	*Anas penelope*	*	*	*							*	*	*
Mallard	*Anas platyrhynchos*	*	*									*	*
Spot-billed Duck	*Anas poecilorhyncha*	*	*	Ï	Ï	*	*	Ï	Ï	*	*	*	*
Northern Shoveller	*Anas clypeata*	*	*	*	*						*	*	*
Northern Pintail	*Anas acuta*	*	*	*							*	*	*
Garganey	*Anas querquedula*	*	*	*	*				*	*	*	*	*
Baikal Teal	*Anas formosa*	*	*									*	*
Common Teal	*Anas crecca*	*	*	*							*	*	*
Marbled Teal	*Marmaronetta angustirostris*	*	*									*	*
Red-crested Pochard	*Rhodonessa rufina*	*	*										*
Common Pochard	*Aythya ferina*	*	*									*	*
Ferruginous Pochard	*Aythya nyroca*	*	*									*	*
Tufted Pochard	*Aythya fuligula*	*	*								*	*	*
Family Accipitridae (Raptors)													
Oriental Honey-Buzzard	*Pernis ptilorhynchus*	*	*	*	Ï	Ï	Ï	*	*	*	*	*	*
Black-shouldered Kite	*Elanus caeruleus*	*	*	Ï	Ï	Ï	*	*	*	Ï	Ï	*	*
Black Kite	*Milvus migrans*	*	*	*	*	*	*	*	*	*	*	*	*
Brahminy Kite	*Haliastur Indus*								*	*	*	*	*
Pallas's Fish-Eagle	*Haliaeetus leucoryphus*	*	*	*	*				Ï	Ï	Ï	*	*
White-tailed Eagle (White-tailed Sea-Eagle)	*Haliaeetus albicilla*	*	*								*	*	*
Lesser Fish Eagle	*Ichthyophaga humilis*	*	*								*	*	*
Grey-headed Fish Eagle	*Ichthyophaga ichthyaetus*										*	*	*
Egyptian Vulture	*Neophron percnopterus*	*	*	Ï	Ï	Ï	*	*	*	*	*	*	*
White-rumped Vulture	*Gyps bengalensis*	Ï	Ï	Ï	Ï	*	*	*	*	*	*	*	*
Long-billed Vulture	*Gyps indicus*	*	*	*	*	*	*	*	*	*	*	*	*
Eurasian Griffon	*Gyps fulvus*	*	*									*	*
Cinereous Vulture	*Aegypius monachus*	*	*									*	*

Species	Scientific Name	Jan	Feb	Mar	Apr	May	Jun	Jul	Aug	Sep	Oct	Nov	Dec
Red-headed Vulture	*Sarcogyps calvus*	Ï	Ï	*	*	*	*	*	*	*	*	*	*
Short-toed Snake-Eagle	*Circaetus gallicus*	*	Ï	Ï	*	*	*	*	*	*	*	*	*
Crested Serpent-Eagle	*Spilornis cheela*	*	*	*							*	*	*
Eurasian Marsh Harrier	*Circus aeruginosus*	*	*	*					*	*	*	*	*
Hen Harrier	*Circus cyaneus*	*	*	*						*	*	*	*
Pallid Harrier	*Circus macrourus*	*	*	*						*	*	*	*
Pied Harrier	*Circus melanoleucos*	*	*	*						*	*	*	*
Montagu's Harrier	*Circus pygargus*	*	*	*							*	*	*
Shikra	*Accipiter badius*	*	Ï	Ï	*	*	*	*	*	*	*	*	*
Besra (Besra Sparrowhawk)	*Accipiter virgatus*	*	*	*							*	*	*
Eurasian Sparrowhawk	*Accipiter nisus*	*	*	*							*	*	*
Northern Goshawk	*Accipiter gentilis*	*	*	*							*	*	*
White-eyed Buzzard	*Butastur teesa*	*	*	*	*	*			*	*	*	*	*
Common Buzzard	*Buteo buteo*	*	*	*						*	*	*	*
Long-legged Buzzard	*Buteo rufinus*	*	*	*							*	*	*
Lesser Spotted Eagle	*Aquila pomarina*	*	*	Ï	Ï	Ï	*	*	*	*	*	*	*
Greater Spotted Eagle	*Aquila clanga*	*	*	*							*	*	*
Tawny Eagle	*Aquila rapax*	*	*	*								*	*
Steppe Eagle	*Aquila nipalensis*	*	*	*								*	*
Imperial Eagle (Eastern Imperial Eagle)	*Aquila heliaca*	*	*	*								*	*
Bonelli's Eagle	*Hieraaetus fasciatus*	*	*									*	*
Booted Eagle	*Hieraaetus pennatus*	*	*	*							*	*	*
Family Pandionidae (Osprey)													
Osprey	*Pandion haliaetus*	*	*	*						*	*	*	*
Family Falconidae (Falcons)													
Common Kestrel	*Falco tinnunculus*	*	*	*							*	*	*
Red-necked Falcon (Red-headed Falcon)	*Falco chicquera*	*	*	*							*	*	*
Merlin	*Falco columbarius*	*	*	*							*	*	*
Laggar Falcon (Laggar)	*Falco jugger*	*	*								*	*	*
Shaheen Falcon (Saker)	*Falco peregrinus peregrinus*	*	*									*	*
Peregrine Falcon	*Falco peregrinus japonensis*	*	*	*								*	*

Species	Scientific Name	Jan	Feb	Mar	Apr	May	Jun	Jul	Aug	Sep	Oct	Nov	Dec
Family Phasianidae (Pheasants, Partridges, Quails)													
Black Francolin	*Francolinus francolinus*	*	*	Ï	Ï	Ï	*	*	*	*	*	*	*
Grey Francolin	*Francolinus pondicerianus*	*	*	Ï	Ï	Ï	*	*	Ï	Ï	Ï	*	*
Jungle Bush-Quail	*Perdicula asiatica*	*	*	Ï	Ï	Ï	*	*	*	*	*	*	*
Indian Peafowl	*Pavo cristatus*	*	*	*	*	*	*	Ï	Ï	Ï	*	*	*
Family Turnicidae (Buttonquails/Bustardquails)													
Barred Buttonquail (Common Buttonquail)	*Turnix suscitator*	*	*	*	Ï	Ï	Ï	Ï	*	*	*	*	*
Rain Quail	*Coturnix-coromandelica*				*	*	*	*	*				
Family Gruidae (Cranes)													
Siberian Crane	*Grus leucogeranus*	*	*	*								*	*
Sarus Crane	*Grus antigone*	*	Ï	Ï	Ï	Ï	*	*	Ï	Ï	Ï	Ï	*
Demoiselle Crane	*Grus virgo*	*									*	*	*
Common Crane	*Grus grus*	*	*	*							*	*	*
Family Otididae													
Lesser Florican	*Eupodotis indica*												
Family Rallidae (Rails, Crakes, Moorhens, Coots)													
Water Rail	*Rallus aquaticus*	*	*	*					*	*	*	*	*
Brown Crake	*Amaurornis akool*	*	*	*	*	*	*	*	*	*	*	*	*
White-breasted Waterhen	*Amaurornis phoenicurus*	*	Ï	Ï	*	*	*	Ï	Ï	Ï	Ï	*	*
Baillon's Crake	*Porzana pusilla*	*	*	*					*	*	*	*	*
Spotted Crake	*Porzana porzana*	*							*	*	*	*	*
Ruddy-breasted Crake	*Porzana fusca*	*	*	*					*	*	*	*	*
Watercock	*Gallicrex cinerea*						*	*	Ï	Ï	*	*	
Purple Moorhen	*Porphyrio porphyrio*	*	*	*	*	*	*	*	Ï	Ï	*	*	*
Common Moorhen	*Gallinula chloropus*	*	*	*	*	*	*	Ï	Ï	Ï	*	*	*
Common Coot	*Fulica atra*	*	*	*					*	*	*	*	*
Family Jacanidae (Jacanas)													
Pheasant-tailed Jacana	*Hydrophasianus chirurgus*	*	Ï	Ï	*	*	*	*	Ï	Ï	*	*	*
Bronze-winged Jacana	*Metopidius indicus*	*	Ï	Ï	*	*	*	*	Ï	Ï	*	*	*
Family Rostratulidae (Painted-Snipes)													
Greater Painted-Snipe	*Rostratula benghalensis*	*	Ï	Ï	Ï	Ï	*	*	*	*	*	*	*

Species	Scientific Name	Jan	Feb	Mar	Apr	May	Jun	Jul	Aug	Sep	Oct	Nov	Dec
Family Charadriidae (Plovers, Dotterels, Lapwings)													
Pacific Golden-Plover	*Pluvialis fulva*	*	*							*	*	*	*
Common Ringed Plover	*Charadrius hiaticula*	*	*	*							*	*	*
Little Ringed Plover	*Charadrius dubius*	*	*	*							*	*	*
Kentish Plover	*Charadrius alexandrinus*	*	*	*							*	*	*
Northern Lapwing	*Vanellus vanellus*	*	*										*
Yellow-wattled Lapwing	*Vanellus malabaricus*	*	*	Ï	Ï	Ï	*	*	*	*	*	*	*
River Lapwing	*Vanellus duvaucelii*	*	*	*	*	*	*	*	*	*	*	*	*
Grey-headed Lapwing	*Vanellus cinereus*	*	*	*								*	*
Red-wattled Lapwing	*Vanellus indicus*	*	*	Ï	Ï	Ï	Ï	Ï	Ï	*	*	*	*
Sociable Lapwing	*Vanellus gregarius*	*	*									*	*
White-tailed Lapwing	*Vanellus leucurus*	*	*	*					*	*	*	*	*
Family Scolopacidae (Sandpipers, Stints, Snipes, Godwits and Curlews)													
Eurasian Woodcock	*Scolopax rusticola*	*	*									*	*
Pintail Snipe	*Gallinago stenura*	*	*	*									*
Common Snipe	*Gallinago gallinago*	*	*	*	*					*	*	*	*
Jack Snipe	*Lymnocryptes minimus*	*	*	*					*	*	*	*	*
Black-tailed Godwit	*Limosa limosa*	*	*	*	*				*	*	*	*	*
Eurasian Curlew	*Numenius arquata*	*	*	*					*	*	*	*	*
Spotted Redshank	*Tringa erythropus*	*	*	*	*	*			*	*	*	*	*
Common Redshank	*Tringa totanus*	*	*	*	*				*	*	*	*	*
Marsh Sandpiper	*Tringa stagnatilis*	*	*	*					*	*	*	*	*
Common Greenshank	*Tringa nebularia*	*	*	*					*	*	*	*	*
Green Sandpiper	*Tringa ochropus*	*	*	*	*				*	*	*	*	*
Wood Sandpiper	*Tringa glareola*	*	*	*	*				*	*	*	*	*
Common Sandpiper	*Actitis hypoleucos*	*	*	*	*				*	*	*	*	*
Long-billed Dowitcher	*Limnodromus scolopaceus*	*	*										
Little Stint	*Calidris minuta*	*	*	*					*	*	*	*	*
Temminck's Stint	*Calidris temminckii*	*	*	*					*	*	*	*	*
Dunlin	*Calidris alpina*	*	*	*					*	*	*	*	*
Curlew Sandpiper	*Calidris ferruginea*	*	*	*					*	*	*	*	*
Spoonbill Sandpiper	*Calidrispygmea*	*	*	*					*	*	*	*	*
Ruff	*Philomachus pugnax*	*	*	*					*	*	*	*	*

Species	Scientific Name	Jan	Feb	Mar	Apr	May	Jun	Jul	Aug	Sep	Oct	Nov	Dec
Family Recurvirostridae (Ibisbill, Avocets and Stilts)													
Black-winged Stilt	*Himantopus himantopus*	*	*	*	*	*	*	*	*	*	*	*	*
Pied Avocet	*Recurvirostra avosetta*	*	*										*
Family Burhinidae (Stone Curlew, Stone Plovers and Thick Knees)													
Eurasian Thick-Knee (Stone-Curlew)	*Burhinus oedicnemus*	*	*	Ï	Ï	Ï	*	*	*	*	*	*	*
Great Thick-Knee (Great Stone-Plover)	*Esacus recurvirostris*	*	*									*	*
Family Glareolidae (Coursers and Pratincoles)													
Indian Courser	*Cursorius coromandelicus*	*	*	Ï	Ï	Ï	*	*	*	*	*	*	*
Collared Pratincole	*Glareola pratincola*	*					*	*	*	*	*	*	*
Small Pratincole	*Glareola lacteal*	*	*	*							*	*	*
Oriental Prntincole	*Glareola maldivarum*		*	*									
Family Laridae (Gulls, Terns and Noddies)													
Herring Gull	*Larus artentatus*	*	*	*								*	*
Brown-headed Gull	*Larus brunnicephalus*	*	*	*	*					*	*	*	*
Black-headed Gull	*Larus ridibundus*	*	*									*	*
Gull-billed Tern	*Gelochelidon nilotica*	*	*	*	*						*	*	*
River Tern	*Sterna aurantia*	*	*	*						*	*	*	*
Little Tern	*Sterna albifrons*	*	*	*	*			*	*	*	*	*	*
Black-bellied Tern	*Sterna acuticauda*	*	*	*					*	*	*	*	*
Whiskered Tern	*Chlidonias hybridus*	*	*	*						*	*	*	*
Family Rynchopidae (Skimmers)													
Indian Skimmer	*Rynchops albicollis*	*	*									*	*
Family Pteroclididae (Sandgrouse)													
Chestnut-bellied Sandgrouse (Common Sandgrouse)	*Pterocles exustus*	*	*	Ï	Ï	Ï	Ï	*	*	*	*	*	*
Family Columbidae (Pigeons and Doves)													
Rock Pigeon (Blue Rock Pigeon)	*Columba livia*	*	*	*	Ï	Ï	Ï	*	*	*	*	*	*
Oriental Turtle-Dove (Rufous Turtle Dove)	*Streptopelia orientalis*	*	*	*								*	*
Laughing Dove (Little Brown Dove)	*Streptopelia senegalensis*	*	*	*	Ï	Ï	Ï	Ï	*	*	*	*	*
Spotted Dove	*Streptopelia chinensis*	*	*	*							*	*	*
Red Collared-Dove (Red Turtle Dove)	*Streptopelia tranquebarica*	*	*	Ï	Ï	Ï	Ï	Ï	*	*	*	*	*

Species	Scientific Name	Jan	Feb	Mar	Apr	May	Jun	Jul	Aug	Sep	Oct	Nov	Dec
Eurasian Collared-Dove (Ring Dove)	*Streptopelia decaocto*	*	*	Ï	Ï	Ï	Ï	Ï	*	*	*	*	*
Yellow-legged Green-Pigeon	*Treron phoenicoptera*	*	*	Ï	Ï	Ï	Ï	Ï	*	*	*	*	*
Family Psittacidae (Parakeets)													
Rose-ringed Parakeet	*Psittacula krameri*	*	Ï	Ï	Ï	Ï	Ï	*	*	*	*	*	*
Plum-headed Parakeet	*Psittacula cyanocephala*	*	*	*							*	*	*
Family Cuculidae (Cuckoos, Malkohas and Coucals)													
Pied Cuckoo (Pied Crested Cuckoo)	*Clamator jacobinus*					*	Ï	Ï	Ï	Ï	*	*	
Common Hawk Cuckoo (Brainfever Bird)	*Hierococcyx varius*	*	Ï	Ï	Ï	Ï	Ï	Ï	*	*	*	*	*
Eurasian Cuckoo (Cuckoo)	*Cuculus canorus*						*	*	*				
Grey-bellied Cuckoo (Indian Plaintive Cuckoo)	*Cacomantis passerinus*					*	*	*	*	*			
Drongo Cuckoo	*Surniculus lugubris*	*	*										*
Asian Koel	*Eudynamys scolopacea*	*	*	*	*	Ï	Ï	Ï	Ï	*	*	*	*
Sirkeer Malkoha	*Phaenicophaeus leschenaultii*	*	Ï	Ï	Ï	Ï	Ï	*	*	*	*	*	*
Greater Coucal (Crow Pheasant)	*Centropus sinensis*	*	Ï	Ï	Ï	Ï	Ï	Ï	Ï	Ï	*	*	*
Family Tytonidae (Barn Owls)													
Barn Owl	*Tyto alba*	*	*	*	*	*	*	*	*	*	*	*	*
Family Strigidae (Owls)													
Oriental Scops-Owl	*Otus sunia*	*	*	*								*	*
Collared Scops-Owl	*Otus bakkamoena*	*	*	Ï	Ï	*	*	*	*	*	*	*	*
Eurasian Eagle-Owl (Indian Great Horned Owl)	*Bubo bubo*	*	*									*	*
Dusky Eagle-Owl (Dusky Horned Owl)	*Bubo coromandus*	Ï	Ï	*	*	*	*	*	*	*	Ï	Ï	Ï
Brown Fish-Owl	*Ketupa zeylonensis*	*	*	*	*	*	*	*	*	*	*	*	*
Mottled Wood-Owl	*Strix ocellata*	*	Ï	Ï	Ï	Ï	Ï	*	*	*	*	*	*
Spotted Owlet	*Athene brama*	*	*	Ï	Ï	Ï	Ï	*	*	*	*	*	*
Brown Hawk Owl	*Ninox scutulata*	*	*	*							*	*	*
Short-eared Owl	*Asio flammeus*	*	*	*							*	*	*

Species	Scientific Name	Jan	Feb	Mar	Apr	May	Jun	Jul	Aug	Sep	Oct	Nov	Dec
Family Caprimulgidae (Nightjars)													
Grey Nightjar (Indian Jungle Nightjar)	*Caprimulgus indicus*	*	*	*							*	*	*
Large-tailed Nightjar	*Caprimulgus macrurus*	*	*	*							*	*	*
Indian Nightjar (Common Indian Nightjar)	*Caprimulgus asiaticus*	*	*	*							*	*	*
Savanna Nightjar (Franklin's Nightjar)	*Caprimulgus affinis*		*	Ï	Ï	Ï	*	*	*	*	*		
Family Apodidae (Swifts)													
Asian Palm-Swift	*Cypsiurus balasiensis*	*	Ï	Ï	Ï	Ï	Ï	*	*	*	*	*	*
House Swift	*Apus affinis*	*	*	*	*	*	*	*	*	*	*	*	*
Family Alcedinidae (Kingfishers)													
Common Kingfisher (Small Blue Kingfisher)	*Alcedo atthis*	*	Ï	Ï	Ï	Ï	*	*	*	*	*	*	*
Stork-billed Kingfisher	*Halcyon capensis*	*	*									*	*
White-throated Kingfisher (White-breasted Kingfisher)	*Halcyon smyrnensis*	*	*	Ï	Ï	Ï	Ï	*	*	*	*	*	*
Black-capped Kingfisher	*Halcyon pileata*	*	*	*							*	*	*
Pied Kingfisher (Lesser Pied Kingfisher)	*Ceryle rudis*	*	*	*	*	*	*	*	*	*	*	*	*
Family Meropidae (Bee-eaters)													
Green Bee-eater (Small Bee-eater)	*Merops orientalis*	*	*	Ï	Ï	Ï	Ï	*	*	*	*	*	*
Blue-cheeked Bee-eater	*Merops persicus*									*	*	*	
Blue-tailed Bee-eater	*Merops philippinus*	*	*	*	*	*	*	*	*	*	*	*	*
Family Coraciidae (Rollers)													
European Roller	*Coracias garrulus*	*	*	*							*	*	*
Indian Roller	*Coracias benghalensis*	*	*	Ï	Ï	Ï	Ï	*	*	*	*	*	*
Family Upupidae (Hoopoes)													
Common Hoopoe	*Upupa epops*	*	Ï	Ï	Ï	Ï	*	*	*	*	*	*	*
Family Bucerotidae (Hornbills)													
Indian Grey Hornbill	*Ocyceros birostris*	*	*	Ï	Ï	Ï	Ï	*	*	*	*	*	*

Species	Scientific Name	Jan	Feb	Mar	Apr	May	Jun	Jul	Aug	Sep	Oct	Nov	Dec
Family Capitonidae (Barbets)													
Brown-headed Barbet	*Megalaima zeylanica*	*	*	Ï	Ï	Ï	Ï	Ï	*	*	*	*	*
Coppersmith Barbet	*Megalaima haemacephala*	*	*	Ï	Ï	Ï	Ï	Ï	*	*	*	*	*
Family Picidae (Woodpeckers)													
Eurasian Wryneck	*Jynx torquilla*	*	*	*							*	*	*
Brown-capped Pygmy Woodpecker	*Dendrocopos nanus*	*	*	Ï	Ï	Ï	*	*	*	*	*	*	*
Yellow-crowned Woodpecker (Yellow-fronted Pied Woodpecker)	*Dendrocopos mahrattensis*	*	*	Ï	Ï	Ï	Ï	*	*	*	*	*	*
Black-rumped Flameback (Lesser Golden-backed Woodpecker)	*Dinopium benghalense*	*	*	Ï	Ï	Ï	Ï	*	*	*	*	*	*
Family Pittidae (Pittas)													
Indian Pitta	*Pitta brachyuran*						*	*	*	*			
Family Alaudidae (Larks)		*	*	*							*	*	*
Singing Bush-Lark	*Mirafra cantillans*	*	*	*	*	*	*	*	*	*	*	*	*
Indian Bush-Lark (Red-winged Bush-Lark)	*Mirafra erythroptera*	*	*	Ï	Ï	*	*	*	*	*	*	*	*
Ashy-crowned Sparrow-Lark	*Eremopterix grisea*	*	Ï	Ï	Ï	Ï	*	*	*	*	*	*	*
Rufous-tailed Lark (Rufous-tailed Finch-Lark)	*Ammomanes phoenicurus*	*	*	Ï	Ï	Ï	*	*	*	*	*	*	*
Greater Short-toed Lark	*Calandrella brachydactyla*												
Crested Lark (Common Crested Lark)	*Galerida cristata*	*	*	Ï	Ï	*	*	*	*	*	*	*	*
Sykes's Crested Lark	*Galerida deva*	*	*									*	*
Eurasian Skylark	*Alauda arvensis*	*	*	*								*	*
Bimaculated Lark (Calandra Lark)	*Melanocorypha bimaculata*	*	*	*								*	*
Oriental Skylark (Eastern Skylark)	*Alauda gulgula*	*	*	*	*	*	*	*	*	*	*	*	*
Family Hirundinidae (Swallows and Martins)													
Sand Martin	*Riparia riparia*	*	*	*								*	*
Plain Martin	*Riparia paludicola*	*	*	*								*	*
Dusky Crag-Martin	*Hirundo concolor*	*	*	*	*	*	*	*	*	*	*	*	*

Species	Scientific Name	Jan	Feb	Mar	Apr	May	Jun	Jul	Aug	Sep	Oct	Nov	Dec
Barn Swallow (Common Swallow)	*Hirundo rustica*	*	*	*							*	*	*
Wire-tailed Swallow	*Hirundo smithii*	*	*	Ï	Ï	*	*	*	Ï	Ï	Ï	*	*
Red-rumped Swallow (Striated Swallow)	*Hirundo daurica*			*	*	*	*	*	*				
Streak-throated Swallow (Indian Cliff Swallow)	*Hirundo fluvicola*			*	*	*	*	*	*				
Family Motacillidae (Wagtails and Pipits)													
Forest Wagtail	*Dendronanthus indicus*		*	*	*	*							
White Wagtail	*Motacilla alba*	*	*	*							*	*	*
White-browed Wagtail (Large Pied Wagtail)	*Motacilla maderaspatensis*	*	*	Ï	Ï	Ï	*	*	*	*	*	*	*
Citrine Wagtail	*Motacilla citreola*	*	*	*							*	*	*
Yellow Wagtail	*Motacilla flava*	*	*	*							*	*	*
Grey Wagtail	*Motacilla cinerea*	*	*	*							*	*	*
Richard's Pipit	*Anthus richardi*	*	*	*							*	*	*
Paddyfield Pipit	*Anthus rufulus*	*	*	Ï	Ï	Ï	*	*	*	*	*	*	*
Tawny Pipit	*Anthus campestris*	*	*	*							*	*	*
Tree Pipit (Eurasian Tree Pipit)	*Anthus trivialis*	*	*	*							*	*	*
Olive-backed Pipit (Oriental Tree Pipit)	*Anthus hodgsoni*	*	*	*							*	*	*
Rosy Pipit	*Anthus roseatus*	*	*	*							*	*	*
Long-billed Pipit	*Anthus similis*	*	*	*							*	*	*
Water Pipit	*Anthus spinoletta*	*	*	*							*	*	*
Family Campephagidae (Cuckoo-Shrikes, Flycatcher-Shrikes, Trillers, Minivets, Woodshrikes)													
Large Cuckoo-Shrike	*Coracina macei*	*	*	*					*	*	*	*	*
Black-winged Cuckoo-Shrike	*Coracina melaschistos*	*	*	*				*	*	*	*	*	*
Small Minivet	*Pericrocotus cinnamomeus*	*	*	Ï	Ï	Ï	*	*	*	*	*	*	*
White-bellied Minivet	*Pericrocotus erythropygius*	*	*	*							*	*	*
Long-tailed Minivet	*Pericrocotus ethologus*	*	*	*							*	*	*
Scarlet Minivet	*Pericrocotus flammeus*	*	*	*							*	*	*
Short-billed Minivet	*Pericrocotus brevirostris*	*	*	*							*	*	*
Common Woodshrike	*Tephrodornis pondicerianus*	*	*	Ï	Ï	Ï	Ï	Ï	*	*	*	*	*

Species	Scientific Name	Jan	Feb	Mar	Apr	May	Jun	Jul	Aug	Sep	Oct	Nov	Dec
Family Pycnonotidae (Bulbuls and Finchbills)													
Red-whiskered Bulbul	*Pycnonotus jocosus*	*	*	*							*	*	*
White-eared Bulbul	*Pycnonotus leucotis*	*	*	Ï	Ï	Ï	Ï	Ï	*	*	*	*	*
Red-vented Bulbul	*Pycnonotus cafer*	*	*	Ï	Ï	Ï	Ï	Ï	*	*	*	*	*
Family Irenidae (Ioras, Chloropsis/Leafbird, Fairy-Bluebird)													
Common Iora	*Aegithina tiphia*	*	*	*							*	*	*
Marshall's Iora	*Aegithina nigrolutea*	*	*	Ï	Ï	Ï	Ï	*	*	*	*	*	*
Family Laniidae (Shrikes)													
Red-backed Shrike	*Lanius collurio*	*	*									*	*
Rufous-tailed Shrike (Isabeline Shrike)	*Lanius isabellinus*	*	*	*								*	*
Brown Shrike	*Lanius cristatus*	*	*	*							*	*	*
Bay-backed Shrike	*Lanius vittatus*	*	*	Ï	Ï	Ï	Ï	Ï	*	*	*	*	
Long-tailed Shrike (Rufous-backed Shrike)	*Lanius schach*	*	*	Ï	Ï	Ï	Ï	Ï	*	*	*	*	*
Southern Grey Shrike	*Lanius meridionalis*	*	*	*	*	*	*	*	*	*	*	*	*
Family Turdinae (Thrushes, Shortwings, Robins, Forktails, Wheaters)													
Blue-capped Rock Thrush (Blue-headed Rock-Thrush)	*Monticola cinclorhynchus*	*	*									*	*
Blue Rock-Thrush	*Monticola solitarius*	*	*	*	*	*	*	*	*	*	*	*	*
Orange-headed Thrush	*Zoothera citrina*	*	*	*								*	*
Scaly Thrush	*Zoothera dauma*	*	*	*								*	*
Tickell's Thrush	*Turdus unicolor*	*	*	*								*	*
Black-breasted Thrush	*Turdus dissimilis*	*	*									*	*
Grey-winged Blackbird	*Turdus boulboul*	*	*	*								*	*
Siberian Rubythroat	*Luscinia calliope*	*	*	*								*	*
White-tailed Rubythroat	*Luscinia pectoralis*	*	*	*								*	*
Bluethroat	*Luscinia svecica*	*	*	*		*						*	*
Oriental Magpie-Robin	*Copsychus saularis*	*	*	*	Ï	Ï	*	*	*	*	*	*	*
Indian Robin	*Saxicoloides fulicata*	*	*	*	Ï	Ï	*	*	*	*	*	*	*
Black Redstart	*Phoenicurus ochruros*	*	*	*							*	*	*
Common Stonechat	*Saxicola torquata*	*	*	*							*	*	*

Species	Scientific Name	Jan	Feb	Mar	Apr	May	Jun	Jul	Aug	Sep	Oct	Nov	Dec
White-tailed Stonechat	*Saxicola leucura*	*	*	*							*	*	*
Pied Bushchat	*Saxicola caprata*	*	*	*	Ï	Ï	Ï	*	*	*	*	*	*
Grey Bushchat	*Saxicola ferrea*	*	*	*							*	*	*
Variable Wheatear	*Oenanthe picata*	*	*	*							*	*	*
Desert Wheatear	*Oenanthe deserti*	*	*	*							*	*	*
Isabelline Wheatear	*Oenanthe isabellina*	*	*	*							*	*	*
Pied Wheatear	*Oenan the pleschanka*	*	*	*							*	*	*
Brown Rock-Chat (Indian Chat)	*Cercomela fusca*	*	*	*	Ï	Ï	Ï	*	*	*	*	*	*
Family Timaliinae (Babblers, Laughingthrushes, Yuhinas)													
Yellow-eyed Babbler	*Chrysomma sinense*	*	*	*	*	*	Ï	Ï	Ï	*	*	*	*
Common Babbler	*Turdoides caudatus*	*	*	Ï	Ï	Ï	*	*	*	*	*	*	*
Large Grey Babbler	*Turdoides malcolmi*	*	*	*	*	*	Ï	Ï	Ï	Ï	*	*	*
Jungle Babbler	*Turdoides striatus*	*	*	*	*	*	Ï	Ï	Ï	Ï	*	*	*
Family Sylviinae (Goldcrest, Prinias, Tesias, Warblers)													
Ziting Cisticola (Streaked Fantail-Warbler)	*Cisticola juncidis*	*	*	*	*	*	Ï	Ï	Ï	Ï	*	*	*
Ashy Prinia	*Prinia socialis*	*	*	Ï	Ï	Ï	Ï	Ï	Ï	Ï	*	*	*
Plain Prinia	*Prinia inornata*	*	*	Ï	Ï	Ï	Ï	Ï	Ï	Ï	*	*	*
Cetti's Bush-Warbler	*Cettia cetti*	*	*	*								*	*
Lanceolated Warbler (Streaked Grasshopper-Warbler)	*Locustella lanceolata*	*	*	*								*	*
Paddyfield Warbler	*Acrocephalus agricola*	*	*	*								*	*
Blyth's Reed-Warbler	*Acrocephalus dumetorum*	*	*	*								*	*
Clamorous Reed Warbler (Indian Great Reed-Warbler)	*Acrocephalus stentoreus*	*	*	*								*	*
Booted Warbler	*Hippolais caligata*	*	*	*								*	*
Common Tailorbird	*Orthotomus sutorius*	*	*	Ï	Ï	Ï	Ï	Ï	*	*	*	*	*
Common Chiffchaff	*Phylloscopus collybita*	*	*	*								*	*
Plain Leaf-Warbler	*Phylloscopus neglectus*	*	*	*								*	*
Dusky Warbler	*Phylloscopus fuscatus*	*	*	*								*	*
Tickell's Leaf Warbler	*Phylloscopus affinis*	*	*	*								*	*

Species	Scientific Name	Jan	Feb	Mar	Apr	May	Jun	Jul	Aug	Sep	Oct	Nov	Dec
Sulphur-bellied Warbler (Olivaceous Leaf-Warbler)	*Phylloscopus griseolus*	*	*	*								*	*
Brooks's Leaf-Warbler	*Phylloscopus subviridis*	*	*	*								*	*
Hume's Warbler	*Phylloscopus humei*	*	*	*								*	*
Greenish Warbler (Greenish Leaf-Warbler)	*Phylloscopus trochiloides*	*	*	*								*	*
Lesser Whitethroat (Common Lesser Whitethroat)	*Sylvia curruca*	*	*	*								*	*
Orphean Warbler	*Sylvia hortensis*	*	*	*								*	*
Moustached Warbler	*Acrocephalus melanopogon*	*	*	*								*	*
Yellow-browed Warbler	*Phylloscopus inornatus*	*	*	*								*	*
Family Muscicapinae (Flycatchers)													
Rusty-tailed Flycatcher	*Muscicapa ruficauda*	*	*									*	*
Red-throated Flycatcher	*Ficedula parva*	*	*	*								*	*
Ultramarine Flycatcher	*Ficedula superciliaris*	*	*	*								*	*
Verditer Flycatcher	*Eumyias thalassina*	*	*	*								*	*
Tickell's Blue-Flycatcher	*Cyornis tickelliae*	*	*	*								*	*
Grey-headed Canary Flycatcher	*Culicicapa ceylonensis*	*	*	*								*	*
Family Monarchinae (Monarch-Flycatchers and Paradise-Flycatchers)													
Asian Paradise-Flycatcher	*Terpsiphone paradisi*	*	*	*	*	Ï	Ï	Ï	Ï	*	*	*	*
Family Rhipidurinae (Fantail-Flycatchers)													
White-browed Fantail (White-browed Fantail-Flycatcher)	*Rhipidura aureola*	*	*	*								*	*
Family Remizidae (Penduline-Tits)													
Fire-capped Tit	*Cephalopyrus flammiceps*	*	*	*								*	*
Family Paridae (Tits)													
Great Tit	*Parus major*	*	*									*	*

Species	Scientific Name	Jan	Feb	Mar	Apr	May	Jun	Jul	Aug	Sep	Oct	Nov	Dec
Family Sittidae (Nuthatches, Wallcreeper)													
Chestnut-bellied Nuthatch	*Sitta castanea*	*	Ï	Ï	Ï	*	*	*	*	*	*	*	*
Family Certhiidae (Tree-Creepers, Creepers)													
Spotted Creeper	*Salpornis spilonotus*	*	*	*	*	*	*	*	*	*	*	*	*
Family Nectariniidae (Sunbirds and Spiderhunters)													
Purple Sunbird	*Nectarinia asiatica*	*	Ï	Ï	Ï	Ï	*	*	*	*	*	*	*
Family Zosteropidae (White-eyes)													
Oriental White-eye	*Zosterops palpebrosus*	*	*	*	*	*	*	Ï	Ï	Ï	*	*	*
Family Emberizinae (Buntings)													
Crested Bunting	*Melophus lathami*	*	*	*	*	*						*	*
White-capped Bunting	*Emberiza stewarti*	*	*	*								*	*
Black-headed Bunting	*Emberiza melanocephala*	*	*	*	*							*	*
Red-headed Bunting	*Emberiza bruniceps*	*	*	*	*							*	*
Family Fringillidae (Finches)													
Common Rosefinch	*Carpodacus erythrinus*	*	*	*	*	*							
Family Estrildidae (Munias [Estrildid Finches])													
Red Avadavat (Red Munia)	*Amandava amandava*	*	*	*	*	*	*	*	*	Ï	Ï	*	*
Indian Silverbill (White-throated Munia)	*Lonchura malabarica*	*	*	*	*	*	*	*	*	Ï	Ï	*	*
Scaly-breasted Munia (Spotted Munia)	*Lonchura punctulata*	*	*	*	*	*	*	*	*	Ï	Ï	*	*
Black-headed Munia	*Lonchura malacca*	*	*	*	*	*	*	*	*	*	*	*	*
Family Passerinae (Sparrows)													
House Sparrow	*Passer domesticus*	*	Ï	Ï	Ï	Ï	Ï	Ï	*	*	*	*	*
Spanish Sparrow	*Passer hispaniolensis*	*	*									*	*
Chestnut-shouldered Petronia (Yellow-throated Sparrow)	*Petronia xanthocollis*	*	*	Ï	Ï	Ï	*	*	*	*	*	*	*
Family Ploceinae (Weavers)													
Black-breasted Weaver	*Ploceus benghalensis*	*	*	*	*	*	*	*	Ï	Ï	*	*	*
Streaked Weaver	*Ploceus manyar*	*	*	*	*	*	*	*	*	*	*	*	*
Baya Weaver	*Ploceus philippinus*	*	*	*	*	*	*	Ï	Ï	Ï	*	*	*

Species	Scientific Name	Jan	Feb	Mar	Apr	May	Jun	Jul	Aug	Sep	Oct	Nov	Dec
Family Sturnidae (Starlings and Mynas)													
Brahminy Starling	*Sturnus pagodarum*	*	*	Ï	Ï	Ï	Ï	*	*	*	*	*	*
Rosy Starling	*Sturnus roseus*	*	*	*					*	*	*		
Common Starling	*Sturnus vulgaris*	*	*									*	*
Asian Pied Starling	*Sturnus contra*	*	*	*	Ï	Ï	Ï	Ï	Ï	*	*	*	*
Common Myna	*Acridotheres tristis*	*	*	*	Ï	Ï	Ï	Ï	Ï	Ï	*	*	*
Chestnut-tailed Starling (Grey-headed Myna)	*Sturnus malabaricus*	*	*									*	*
Bank Myna	*Acridotheres ginginianus*	*	*	*	Ï	Ï	Ï	Ï	Ï	Ï	*	*	*
Family Oriolidae (Orioles)													
Eurasian Golden Oriole	*Oriolus oriolus*	*	*	*	*	*	Ï	Ï	Ï	*	*	*	*
Black-headed Oriole	*Oriolus xanthornus*	*	*	*							*	*	*
Black-naped Oriole	*Oriolus chinensis*	*	*	*									
Family Dicruridae (Drongos)													
Black Drongo	*Dicrurus macrocercus*	*	*	*	Ï	Ï	Ï	Ï	*	*	*	*	*
Ashy Drongo	*Dicrurus leucophaeus*	*	*									*	*
White-bellied Drongo	*Dicrurus caerulescens*	*	*									*	*
Spangled Drongo	*Dicrurus hottentottus*	*	*									*	*
Greater Racket-tailed Drongo	*Dicrurus paradiseus*	*	*										*
Family Corvidae (Crows, Jays, Treepies, Magpies)													
Rufous Treepie (Indian Treepie)	*Dendrocitta vagabunda*	*	*	Ï	Ï	Ï	Ï	*	*	*	*	*	*
House Crow	*Corvus splendens*	*	Ï	Ï	Ï	Ï	Ï	*	*	*	*	*	*
Large-billed Crow (Jungle Crow)	*Corvus macrorhynchos*	*	Ï	Ï	Ï	Ï	Ï	*	*	*	*	*	*

Mammals of Keoladeo National Park

Common Name	Scientific Name	Local Name	Remarks
Family Felidae			
Tiger	*Panthera tigris*	Bagh	One tiger stayed here from 2000 to 2005
Leopard	*Panthera pardus*	Baghera	Extirpated in 1988
Fishing Cat	*Prionailurus viverrinus*	Machhali Billi	Rare
Jungle Cat	*Felis chaus*	Jungali Billi	Common
Family Canidae			
Jackal	*Canis aureus*	Gidad	Common
Indian Fox	*Vulpes bengalensis*	Lomadi	Extirpated
Family Hyaenidae			
Striped Hyaena	*Hyaena hyaena*	Jarakh	Rare
Family Viverridae			
Small Indian Civet	*Viverricula indica*	Chhoti Civet Billi	Rare
Common Palm Civet	*Paradoxurus hermaphroditus*	Palm Civet Billi	Common
Family Herpestidae			
Small Indian Mongoose	*Herpestes javanicus*	Chhota Nevla	Rare
Common Mongoose	*Herpestes edwardsii*	Nevla	Common
Family Mustelidae			
Smooth Indian Otter	*Lutra perspicillata*	Jal Manush	Extirpated
Family Cercopithecidae			
Rhesus Macaque	*Macaca mulatta*	Lal Muh ka Bandar	
Hanuman Langur	*Semnopithecus entellus*	Langoor	Occasional Visitor
Family Cervidae			
Sambar	*Cervus unicolor*	Sambar	Common
Chital	*Axis axis*	Chital	Common
Hog Deer	*Axis porcinus*		Rare
Family Bovidae			
Feral Cow	*Bos taurus*	Jungali Gai	Common
Bluebull	*Boselaphus tragocamelus*	Nil Gai	Common
Black Buck	*Antilope cervicapra*	Kala Hiran	Extirpated 2008
Family Suidae			
Indian Wild Boar	*Sus scrofa*	Jungali Suar	Common
Family Hystricidae			
Indian Porcupine	*Hystrix indica*	Sehie	Rare

Common Name	Scientific Name	Local Name	Remarks
Family Leporidae			
Rufous-tailed Hare	*Lepus nigricollis ruficaudatus*	Jungali Khargosh	Common
Family Erinaceidae			
Indian Hedgehog	*Hemiechinus micropus*	Jhau Chuha	Rare
Family Sciuridae			
Five-striped Palm Squirrel	*Funambulus pennantii*	Gilahari	Common
Family Soricidae			
Musk Shrew	*Suncus murinus*		Rare
Family Muridae			
Indian Long-tailed Tree Mouse	*Vandeleuria oleracea*		Rare
House Mouse	*Mus musculus*	Chuha	Common
Indian Bush Rat	*Golunda ellioti*	Jungali Chuha	Common
House Rat	*Rattus rattus*	Chuha	Common
Indian Gerbile	*Tatera indica*	Chhachhundar	Common
Family Pteropodidae			
Indian Flying Fox	*Pteropus giganteus*	Udan Gilahari	Extinct
Family Vespertilionidae			
Asiatic Greater Yellow House Bat	*Scotophilus heathii*	Chamgadad	Rare
Family Rhinolophidae			
Fulvus Leaf-nosed Bat	*Hipposideros fulvus*	Chamgadad	Rare, roosts in python burrows

Ichthyofauna (Fishes) of Keoladeo National Park

Common Name	Scientific Name
Family Schilbeidae	
Gangetic ailia	*Ailia coila*
Garua bachcha, Guarchcha	*Clupisoma garua*
Batchwa vacha	*Eutropiichthys vacha*
Indian potasi	*Pseudeutropius atherinoides*
Family Cyprinidae	
Mola carplet, Pale carplet	*Amblypharyngodon mola*
Pearl Danio	*Brachydanio albolineatus*
Catla	*Catla catla*
Chaguni	*Chagunius chagunio*
Large razorbelly minnow	*Chela bacaila*
Silver hatchet chela	*Chela cachinus*
Mrigal	*Cirrhinus mrigala*
Reba-carp	*Cirrhinus reba*
Gangetic latia	*Crossocheilus latius latius*
Scale-carp	*Cyprinus carpio comminus*
Dangila danio	*Danio dangila*
Flying barb	*Esomus danricus*
Bata labeo	*Labeo bata*
Kalbasu, Black rohu	*Labeo calbasu*
Fringed-lipped peninsula carp	*Labeo fimbriatus*
Kuria labeo	*Labeo gonius*
Rohu	*Labeo rohita*
Cotio	*Osteobrama cotio cotio*
Olive barb	*Puntius sarana sarana*
Spotfin swamp barb	*Puntius sophore*
Ticto barb, Firefin barb, Two-spot barb	*Puntius ticto*
Blackline rasbora	*Rasbora daniconius*
Chilwa	*Salmostoma bacaila*
Gora-chela	*Securicula gora*
Family Bagridae	
Long-whiskered catfish	*Aorichthys aor*
Giant river-catfish	*Aorichthys seenghala*
Gangetic mystus	*Mystus cavasius*
Tengara mystus	*Mystus tengara*
Striped dwarf catfish	*Mystus vittatus*

Common Name	Scientific Name
Family Cobitidae	
Y-loach	*Botia lohachata*
Guntea loach, Zebra fish	*Lepidocephalus guntea*
Stone loach	*Noemachelius botia botia*
Loach	*Noemachelius corica*
Family Chandidae	
Elongated glass-perchlet	*Chanda nama*
Indian glassy fish	*Chanda ranga*
Family Channidae	
Giant snakehead	*Channa marulius*
Spotted snakehead	*Channa punctatus*
Striped or Banded snakehead	*Channa striatus*
Asiatic snakehead	*Channa gachua*
Family Clariidae	
Magur	*Clarias batrachus*
Thailand magur, African magur	*Clarias gariepinus*
Family Sisoridae	
Huddah nangra	*Gagata viridescens*
Family Belontidae	
Striped gourami, Giant gourami	*Colisa fasciatus*
Family Clupeidae	
Indian river shad	*Gudusia chapra*
Family Heteropneustidae	
Stinging catfish	*Heteropneustes fossilis*
Family Mastacembelidae	
Spotted spiny eel	*Macrognathus aculeatus*
Tire-track spiny eel	*Mastacembelus armatus armatus*
Striped spiny eel	*Mastacembelus pancalus*
Family Notopteridae	
Humped featherback	*Notopterus chitala*
Grey featherback	*Notopterus notopterus*
Family Siluridae	
India butter-catfish	*Ompok bimaculatus*
Boal	*Wallago attu*
Family Belonidae	
Freshwater garfish	*Xenentodon cancila*

Reptiles of Keoladeo National Park, Bharatpur

Common Name	Scientific Name
Family Bataguridae (Hardshell turtles, pond turtles)	
Spotted Pond Turtle	*Geoclemys hamiltonii*
Crowned River Turtle	*Hardella thurjii*
Indian Roofed Turtle	*Kachuga tecta*
Indian Tent Turtle	*Kachuga tentoria*
Family Trionychidae (Softshell turtles)	
Indian Softshell Turtle	*Aspideretes gangeticus*
Indian Peacock Softshell Turtle	*Aspideretes hurum*
Indian Flapshell Turtle	*Lissemys punctata*
Family Gekkonidae (Geckos)	
Brook's House Gecko	*Hemidactylus brookii*
Yellow-green House Gecko	*Hemidactylus flaviviridis*
Termite Hill Gecko	*Hemidactylus triedrus*
Family Agamidae (Garden lizards)	
Indian Garden Lizard	*Calotes versicolor*
Fan-throated Lizard	*Sitana ponticeriana*
Family Scincidae (Skinks)	
Spotted Supple Skink	*Lygosoma punctata*
Striped Grass Skink	*Mabuya dissimilis*
Family Varanidae (Monitor lizards)	
Bengal Monitor	*Varanus bengalensis*
Family Typhlopidae (Worm snake)	
Common Worm Snake	*Ramphoryphlops braminus*
Family Boidae (Earth snakes)	
Common Sand Boa	*Eryx conicus*
Red Sand Boa	*Eryx johnii*
Indian Rock Python	*Python molurus*
Family Colubridae	
Common Indian Cat Snake	*Boiga trigonatus*
Common Wolf Snake	*Lycodon aulicus*
Banded Kukri Snake	*Oligodon armensis*
Pakistan Ribbon Snake	*Psammophis leithii*
Western Rat Snake	*Ptyas mucosus*
Checkered Keelback Water Snake	*Xenochrophis piscator*
Family Elapidae	
Common Indian Krait	*Bungarus caeruleus*
Spectacled Cobra	*Naja naja*
Family Viperidae (Vipers)	
Russell's Viper	*Daboia russelii*
Indian Saw-scaled Viper	*Echis carinatus*

Butterflies of Keoladeo National Park

1. Plain Tiger
Danaus chrysippus

2. Dorippus Tiger
Danauschrysippus f dorippus

3. Striped tiger
Danus genutia

4. Common Crow
Euploea core (Sch-IV)

5. Blue Tiger
Tirumala limniace

6. Dark Blue Tiger
Tirumala septentrionis

7. Glassy Tiger
Parantica aglea

8. Common Rose
Pachliopta aristolochiae

9. Crimson Rose
Pachliopta hector

10. Lime Butterfly
Papilio demoleus

11. Common Mormon
Papilio polytes

12. Angled Castor
Acriadne ariadne

13. Common Castor
Acriadn emerione

14. Tawny Coster
Acraea violae

15. Indian Fritillary
Argyneus hyperbius

16. Painted Lady
Cynthia cardui

17. Blue Moon Butterfly
Hypolimnias Bolina

18. Danaideggfly
Hypolimnias missippus

19. Yellow Pansy
Junoni ahierta

20. Peacock Pansy
Junonia Almana

21. Lemon Pansy
Junonia lemonias

22. Blue Pansy
Junonia orithya

23. Common Leopard
Phalantha phalantha

24. Chocolate Pansy
Prescis iphita

25. Common Evening Brown
Melanitis leda

26. Dark Evening Brown
Melanitis phedima bela

27. Pioneer White
Anaphaeis aurota

28. Common Emigrant
Catospsilia pomana

29. Lemon Emigrant
Catospsilia f. crocale

30. Mottled Emigrant
Catospsilia pyranthe

31. Common Gull
Cepora nesissa

32. Small Salmon Arab
Colotis amata

33. Crimson Tip
Colotis danae danae

34. Crimson Tip
Colotis danae dulcis

35. Little Orange Tip
Colotis etrida

36. Large Salmon Arab
Madais fausta

37. White Arab
Colotis vestalis

38. Common Jezebel
Delias eucharis

39. Sulphur Orange Tip
Colotis eucharis

40. White Orange Tip
Lxias mariamme

41. Yellow Oange Tip
Lxias pyrene

42. Common Grass Yellow
Eurema hecabe

43. Spotless Grass Yellow
Terias laeta laeta

44. Small Grass Yellow
Eurema brigitta rubella

45. One Spot Grass Yellow
Eurema andersoni

46. Common Wanderer
Parenonia hippie

47. Large Cabbage White
Pieris brassicae

48. Indian Cabbage White
Pieris canidia

49. Psyche
Leptosia nina

50. Great Black Vein
Aponia agathon

51. Clouded Yellows
Colias electrofieldi

52. Bright Babul Blue
Azanus ubaldus

53. Lime Blue
Chilades laius

54. Plains Cupid
Chilades pandava

55. Lycaenidae Family
Euchrysops enejus

56. Grass Jewel
Fryeria trochylus

57. Common Cerulean
Jamaide sceleno

58. Pea Blue
Lampides boeticus

59. Pale Grass Blue
Pseudozizeeria maha

60. Common Silverline
Spindasis vulcanus

61. Zebra Blue
Syntarucus plinius

62. Dark Grass Blue
Zizeeria karsandra

63. Lesser Grass Blue
Zizina otis

64. Gaika Blue
Zizula gaika

65. Tiny Grass Blue
Zizula hylax

66. Grass Blues
Zizeeria trochylus

67. Blue Pierrots
Tarcus venosus

68. Plain Banded Awl
Hasora vitta

69. Brown Awl
Bademia exclmationis

70. Blank Swift
Caltoris kumara

71. African Straight
Parnara nasobeda

72. Skippers
Taractrocera maevius

73. Grass Demon
Udaspus folus

74. Indian Palm Bob
Suastus gremius

75. Figure Of Swift
Baoris kumara

References

Numbers 31,33,35,40,41,45,48,52,53,62,67,69 have been taken from www.ifoundbutterflies.org
Numbers 1,3,4-30,32,36-39,42,44,47,49,51,54,55-59,61,63,64,65,71,72 have been taken from Wikipedia
Number 60 has been taken from www.wikiwind.com
Number 43 has been taken from the Australian Museum
Number 2 has been taken from http://butterflycircle.blogspot.com/
Numbers 66,73,74 have been taken from butterflycircle.com

Dragonflies and Damselflies of Keoladeo National Park

1. Brown Spreadwing
Lestes umbrinus Selys

2. Wandering Midget
Agriocnemis pygmaea (Rambur)

3. Yellow Waxtail
Ceriagrion coromandelianum

4. Little Blue
Enallagma parvum Selys

5. Golden Dartlet
Ischnura aurora

6. Pixie Dartlet
Ischnura nursei

7. Senegal Golden Dartlet
Ischnura senegalensis

8. Three-lined Dart
Pseudagrion decorum

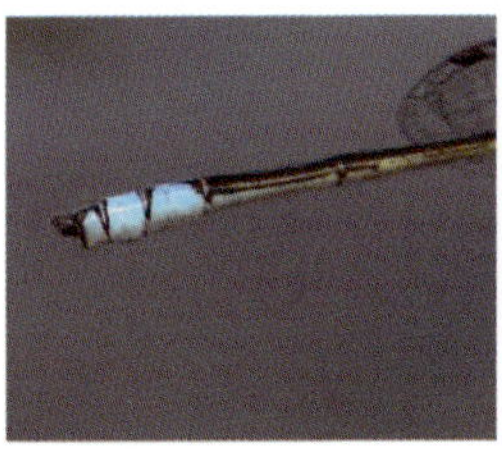

9. *Pseudagrion spencei Fraser*

10. Rusty Darner
Anaciaeschna jaspidea (Burmeistar)

11. Blue-tailed Green Darner
Anax guttatus (Burmeistar)

12. Blue Darner
Anax immaculifrons (Rambur)

13. Blue Emperor
Anax imperator (Leach)

14. Lesser Emperor
Anax parthenope (Selys)

15. Vagrant Emperor
Hemianax ephippiger (Burmeistar)

16. Asian Pintail
Acisoma panorpoides (Rambur)

17. Libellulidae
.Brachydiplax sobrina (Rambur)

18. Ditch Jewel
Brachthemis contaminate (Rambur)

19. Granite Ghost
Bradinopyga geminate (Rambur)

20. Ruddy Marsh Skimmer
Crocothemis servilia (Drury)

21. Black Percher
Diplacodes lefebvrii (Rambur)

22. Chalky Percher
Diplacodes trivialis (Rambur)

23. Pied Paddy Skimmer
Neurothemis tullia (Drury)

24. Crimson-tailed Marsh Hawk
Orthet rumpruinosum interjectum (Rambur)

25. Slender Skimmer
Orthetrum sabina (Drury)

26.Asian Freshwater Dragonfly
Orthetrum taeniolatum (Schneider)

27. Asian Widow
Palpopleura sexmaculata (Fabricius)

28.Globe Skimmer
Pantala flavescens (Fabricius)

29. Dragonfly
Potamarcha congener (Rambur)

30. Rufous Marsh Glider
Rhodothemis rufa (Rambur)

31. Common Picture Wing
Rhyothemis variegate (Linnaeus)

32. Coral-tailed Cloud Wing
Tholymis tillarga (Fabricius)

33. Keyhole Glider
Tramea basilaris burmeisteri
(Palisot de Beauvois)

34. Black Marsh Trotter
Tramea limbata
(Desjardins)

35. Crimson Marsh Glider
Trithemis urora
(Burmeistar)

36. Indigo Dropwing
Trithemis festiva
(Rambur)

37. Dancing Dropwing
Trithemis pallidinervis
(Kirby)

References

Numbers 1-5,13-37 have been taken from Wikipedia
Numbers 6-12 have been taken from www.ifoundbutterflies.org

Turtles of Keoladeo National Park

Crowned River Turtle

Indian Flapshell Turtle

Indian Peacock Softshell Turtle

Indian Roofed Turtle

Indian Softshell Turtle

Spotted Pond Turtle

Three-striped Roofed Turtle

Source: WWF-India Field Guide to Fresh Water Turtles and Tortoises of India (October 1999)

BIBLIOGRAPHY

Anoop K.R. Management Plan of Keoladeo National Park Bharatpur (2010–14), Department of Forests and Wild Life, Rajasthan.

Archibald, George. *The Cranes: Status Survey and Conservation Action Plan*, IUCN/SSC Crane Specialist Group, 1996.

Bhupati S. and Vijayan V.S. A paper on the 'Status, Distribution and General Ecology of the Indian Python in KNP'. BNHS, October 1988.

Choudhary, B.C. Article, 'Are the Bharatpur Pythons Doomed'. WII Newsletter, Wild Life Institute of India, Vol. 6 No. 1, Jan–March, 1991.

Ecology of a Semitropical Monsoonal Wetland in India, The Keoladeo National Park, Bharatpur Rajasthan. Final Report. September 1988.

Grewal Bikram and Sahgal Bittu. *The Bharatpur Inheritance*. Mumbai: Sanctuary Asia, 2006.

Hanfee, Fahmeeda. Field Guide to Freshwater Turtles and Tortoise of India. Traffic India/ WWF-India, 1999.

Perennou, C. and Ramesh B.R. Explanatory Notes on the Vegetation Map of Keoladeo National Park Bharatpur. The French Institute, Puducherry and the Bombay Natural History Society.

Sankhala, Kailash. *Gardens of God: The Waterbird Sanctuary at Bharatpur*. New Delhi: Vikas Publishing House, 1990.

Sharma Shruti and Praveen B. Management Plan of Keoladeo National Park Bharatpur (2002–06), Department of Forests and Wild Life, Rajasthan.

Singh, D.B. and J.T. Hermans. Dragonflies and Damselflies (Odonata: Insecta) of Keoladeo National Park, Journal of Threatened Taxa 9 (7): 10445–10452; http://doi.org/10.11609/jott.3689.9.7.10445-10452. 2017.

Singh, Rajpal. *Birds of Bharatpur*. New Delhi: Prakash Books India, 2005.

Dr Trigunayat, M.M., MSJ College Bharatpur. 'Butterflies in Rajasthan', article published in the book *Conserving Biodiversity of Rajasthan* by Ashok Verma, 2008.

Verma, Ashok. Harriers in India, Introduction and Identification Booklet. Wild Life Institute of India, Dehradun, 2007.

Vijayan, V.S. Keoladeo National Park Ecology Study 1980–90. Final Report. Bombay Natural History Society.

INDEX

A

Acacia nilotica (babool) trees, 35
African catfish *(Clarias gariepinus),* 156
Agra, 30–31
Ajan Dam, 29, 31, 34, 37, 39, 43, 84, 155, 186, 188–192, 196, 209, 213–214, 221
Ali, Dr Salim, 36, 76, 88, 101, 175, 224, 226–227, 232–235
Ali, Humayun Abdul, 224
Ali, Zafar Fateh, 224
Anoop, K.R., 147
Archibald, George, 230, 233
Arora, V.M., 105
Asian paradise flycatcher, 133

B

babool, 36, 50, 132, 207
Babur, Emperor, 30
Banganga river, 37
bar-headed geese, 80, 87–89
baya weaver, 131
ber tree, 36, 193, 207
Bhainsamori, 122, 185
Bharatpur, 29
 drainage system, 17
 subtropical region, 36–37
 swamps, 78
 township, 23
bird shoot, 33, 35
blacknecked stork, 54
black-rumped flame-backed (golden-backed) woodpecker, 134–135
blue jay or Indian roller, 135–136
Bonelli's eagle, 116
Brar, A.S., 98, 108
breeding colonies, 49–64
 habitat and availability of food, 63
bronze-winged jacana, 72–74
bulbuls, 131
butterflies, 164–167, 271–275

C

Capparis aphylla, 131
cattle egret, 56–57
Ceratophyllum, 82
Chambal-Dholpur-Bharatpur Drinking Water Supply Project, 212
Chambal river, 212–213
Chand, Mool, 105
Channa marulius, 156
Channa punctatus, 156–157
Channa striatus, 156–157
Chansoria, Vijay, 172
Chara, 65, 67, 84
Chief Wildlife Warden (CWLW), 175
Chiksana Canal, 34, 213–215
Choudhary, Dr B.C., 218
Clarias batrachus, 156–157
common babbler, 133
common pochard, 87
common shelduck, 85
common teal, 84
Convention of Migratory Species (CMS), 235
coot, 85–86
Copper Age, in the Indian subcontinent, 27–29
coppersmith barbet, 136, 139
cotton teal, 65
cranes
 breeding, 95–97
 common, 97
 demoiselle, 100
 hunting of, 229–230
 migration recorded, 95, 97–98
 migration routes of common, 99
 nests, 95
 sarus crane, 13, 42, 87, 95–98, 110, 225
 Siberian, 98, 101
crested honey buzzard, 117
crested serpent eagle, 115
cuckoos, 138
Curzon, Lord, 33
Cyperus alopecuroides, 67, 178
Cyperus rotundus, 101

D

D. Swarovski & Co (Austria), 174
dalmatian pelican, 91–92
damselflies, 169, 276–278
 Agriocnemis pygmaea, 169
 Ceriagrion coromandelianum, 169
 Ischnura aurora, 169
 Ischnura senegalensis, 169
Delhi–Sawai Madhopur (Ranthambore Tiger Reserve), 23, 30–31
demoiselle crane, 100
Devendra, 173
Dey, Hemal, 172
Dharmendra, 172
dragonflies, 168–169, 276–278
ducks
 common shelduck, 85
 dimorphism of sexes, 81
 nakta or comb-duck, 66
 pintail, 82
 ruddy shelduck, 84
 shoveller, 83
 spot-bill duck, 65
 tufted duck, 87
 wigeon, 82–83
duck shoot, 33, 35
Durrani, Dinesh Verma, 172

E

eagles, 113–116
 Bonelli's eagle, 116
 crested serpent eagle, 115
 golden eagles, 116
 imperial eagles, 116
 short-toed snake eagle, 114
 Tawny and Steppy, 115
Eco Development Committees, 200–201
Egyptian vulture, 119
Eleocharis, 67, 101
Eleocharis plantaginea, 67, 97
Eurasian collared dove, 132

F

Fauzdar, Rakesh, 105
feeding method of species, 50
 blacknecked stork, 54
 cormorants, 58
 openbill stork, 53
 oriental darter, 58
fish fauna, 154–157, 269
 air breathers and non-air breathers, 157
fishing machines, 57
fish species of Keoladeo lakes, 53
flamingos, 92–93
floodplains of Bharatpur, 32, 39
flowerpecker, 136

G

Gambhiri river, 37
Gandhi, Indira, 225, 231
Gandhi, Maneka, 181
Gandhi, Priyanka, 231
Gandhi, Rahul, 231
Gandhi, Rajiv, 231
Gandhi, Sonia, 231

garganey teal (blue-wing teal), 81
Gautam, Dr Parikshit, 218
General Engineering Works, 171
Ghana forests, 29–32, 35–36
Ghana/Jatoli Canal, 31
Ghana Keoladeo Natural History Society, 97
Ghasola village, 26, 31
golden eagles, 116
golden oriole, 138
Gopal, Brij, 218
grasslands, 115–116
    of Keoladeo, 37
    of Koladahar, 114, 127–130
Grass seeds, 67
grazing, 19–20, 36, 55, 71, 81, 101, 145, 178, 181–182, 223–230, 232–233
greater flamingo, 93
great grey, bay-backed and long-tailed breed, 136
great white pelican, 90–91
green, blue-cheeked and blue-tailed bee-eaters, 140
grey heron, 60
grey hornbill, 136
greylag geese, 88, 90
greylag teal, 81
grey partridge (grey francolin), 142
Gujjar community, 199
Gupta, Krishn Kumar, 97, 172
Gupta, Rajesh, 206

H

Harbhanji of Morvi (Gujarat), Prince, 31–32
harriers, 116–117
Hermans, J.T., 169
heronries, 49
heronry breeders, 50
Heteropneustes fossilis, 157
Heteropneustes fossils, 156
Hume, A.O., 101
Hydrilla, 65
Hydrilla verticillata, 101, 169

I

Icornia cresipus (jal kumbhi), 116
imperial eagles, 116
Indian moorhen, 69–71
insects, 167–168
intermediate egret, 55
intermediate or medium cormorant, 57
International Crane Foundation (ICF), USA, 102, 229
International Crane Workshop, 234
International Union for Conservation of Nature (IUCN), 18, 113
    classification, 163, 165
Ipomea, 82, 84–85
Ipomea aquatica, 67
Ipomoea aquatica, 169

J

Jackson, Peter, 234
Jain, Pradeep, 172
jamun, 36
Jamwa Ramgarh lake, 189
Jat kingdom, 30
Jatoli-Bhainsamori track, 25
Jatoli village, 31
*jheel*s, 67
jungle babblers, 133

K

Kadam Kunj, 34, 116, 209, 226
kadam tree, 36, 193, 196, 207
Kanjar community, 185
Keoladeo National Park (KNP), 23
    area, 24–25
    birds, 251–266
    climate, 39–43
    counter-fire techniques, 184
    deterioration of, 107
    fish fauna, 154–157, 269
    flora, 239–250
    impact of periodic drying, 40–41
    mammals, 267–268
    marshes at, 26–27, 29
    organic farming around, 97
    protection of, 177–186
    rainy season, 41–42
    reptiles, 270
    species, 25
    vegetation at, 24
    as World Heritage Site, 36–37, 170–171, 192
Keoladeo swamps, 39, 50–51, 60, 78, 88, 95, 106, 113, 178
khajur *(Phoenix sylvestris),* 132
Khan, Ansar, 156
Khan, Bholu Abrar, 105, 172
koel *(Eudynamys scolopacea),* 127–128
Koladahar, 34, 37
Kostyukov, 106
Krishna, Lord, 26

L

Lal, Sohan, 172
large cormorant, 57
large egret, 55
large grey babblers, 133
Leape, Jim, 204
lesser pied kingfisher, 140–141
lesser whistling teal, 67
Libellulidae, 169
Limnophyton species, 101
little cormorant, 57
little egret, 55
Lohagarh (iron) fort of Bharatpur, 31
long-tailed minivet, 129

M

Maharaja of Bharatpur, 25, 30–31, 34, 36, 76, 235
Mal, Maharaja Suraj, 23, 29–30
Malah or Mallah village, 26
mallard, 86
Manohar, 172
marbled teal, 87
marshes, 24, 27, 29, 32, 35, 39–40, 43, 46, 66, 101, 134, 178
marsh harrier, 117
Mathura oil refinery, 186
migration of birds, 75–79
    bird ringing programme, 76–78
    route map, 77
    theory about, 78–79
migratory birds, 32–33
Mudgal, Laxmi Narayan, 172
mynas, 132

N

Najas, 67
Najas minor, 169
nakta or comb-duck, 66
National Chambal Gharial Sanctuary, 212
'Nature Guide' licences, 173
Nehru, Jawahar Lal, 36
nesting places, 50
night heron, 60
non-avian fauna
    blackbuck, 144
    blue bull, 145
    fishing cat, 149
    hog deer, 145
    hyenas, 147, 149
    jackal, 148–149
    jungle cat, 149

leopard, 151
mongoose, 161
monitor lizards, 161
otter, 151
palm civets, 149
pangolin, 146–147
porcupine, 146
sambar, 145
spotted deer, 144
tigers, 152–154
unproductive cows, 146
wild boar, 145
Notopterus notopterus, 156
Nut community, 185
Nymphaea, 65, 67, 82
Nymphaea pubescens, 169
Nymphaea species, 97, 101
Nymphoides, 65, 82
Nymphoides cristatum, 169
Nymphoides indicum, 169
Nymphoides seeds, 67

O
openbill stork, 53
oriental darter, 58
owls, 120–124, 184
barn owl, 122–123
brown fish owl, 124
collared scops owl, 122
dusky-horned owl, 122
eagle owl, 123
spotted owlet, 121–123

P
painted snipe *(Rostratula benghalensis),* 78
painted stork, 53–54
Panchana Dam, 191–192, 210
parakeets, 133–134, 137
park management, 17, 19–20, 37, 50, 55, 71, 153, 156, 173, 176, 181–183, 190, 193, 207, 225, 230
Paspalum distichum, 65, 67, 145, 157, 169, 178, 226, 228–230
Paspalum-Ipomoea, 169
passerine and non-passerine birds, 127
peacock *(Pavo cristatus),* 134
peeloo *(Salvadora persica),* 131
pheasant-tailed jacana, 71–72
pied and common hawks, 138
pilu tree, 193
pintail duck, 82
Platform Terminal Transmitter (PTT), 98
plum-headed parakeet, 133
poaching
of animals and birds, 180, 185
of Siberian crane *(Grus leucogeranus),* 102–103
Potamogeton species, 101
Potamogeton nodosus, 169
Prakash, Dr Vibhu, 218
Prasad, Arun, 218
predatory birds (raptors)
buzzards, 117–118
eagles, 113–116
harriers, 116–117
kites, 124
owls, 120–124
shikra, 118
vultures, 118–119
Prosopis juliflora, 37, 145, 185, 199–200, 207
eradication of, 199–201, 203
menace, 193–196
Pseudoraphis spinescens, 229
Public Health Engineering Department (PHED), 212
purple heron, 60–61
purple moorhen (lipstick bird), 67–69

Q
quails, 142

R
Raju (Sikh), 173
Ramakrishna, R., 183
Ramsar Site, 36
Rana Sanga of Mewar, King, 30
Rathore, Fateh Singh, 195
red-crested pochard, 87
reptiles, 270
rose-ringed parakeet, 133
rosy pastor, 129, 139
ruddy shelduck, 84

S
Salim Ali Visitor Interpretation Centre, 175–176
salt production, 29
Sankhala, Kailash, 36, 171, 224–225
Sansi community, 185
Sariska Tiger Reserve, 206, 216
sarus crane, 13, 42, 87, 95–98, 110, 225
Sauey, Ronald J., 230, 233
Saxena, V.S., 146, 232
scarlet minivet, 139
Schaller, George, 144
Scirpus littoralis, 67, 101, 169
Scirpus tuberosus, 97, 101, 169
Shanti Kutir, 174, 176
Sharma, K.K., 218
Sharma, L.K., 186
Sharma, Pravin, 172
Sharma, Shruti, 175
Sharma, V.D., 226
shikra, 118
Shiva temple, 35
short-toed snake eagle, 114
shoveller, 83
Siberian crane, 37
Siberian crane *(Grus leucogeranus),* 98, 101
breeding habitat of, 106–107
captivity rearing, 109–111
disappearance from Bharatpur, 101–103
feeding behaviour, 106
feeds of, 101
migration route of, 104, 106–107
poaching of, 102–103
SIMCO Railway Wagon Factory, 171
Singh, Bane, 173
Singh, Bharat, 183
Singh, Brijendra, 169, 172
Singh, Dharam Kumar, 36, 199–200
Singh, Dheerendra, 169
Singh, Dr Digamber, 201–202, 217
Singh, Hari, 173
Singh, Maharaj Kumar Vishwendra, 201–202
Singh, Raj, 172
Singh, Randhir, 172
Singh, Ratan, 31, 173
Singh, Ravi, 205
Singh, Udai, 172
Singh, V.P., 216, 220
Singh, Vijay Pal, 172
smaller flamingo, 92–93
snake fauna
cobra, 161
pythons, 158–161
vipers, 161
soil profile of KNP, 26
Soran, 172
Sorokin, Alexander, 106, 108–109
Spanish sparrows, 127
species of odonata order, 169
Spirilla, 65
spoonbill, 61–62

spot-bill duck, 65
starlings *(Sturnus vulgaris),* 139
stone curlew, 141–142
streaked weavers, 131
Sujan Ganga, 150
sun birds, 136
Suri, Dr, 181

T
Talab-i-Shahi, 105
Tal Chhapar Sanctuary, 144
Talsur injection, 181
Talwar, Dr, 181
Thanvi, S.N., 214–215
Thorat, Yashwant, 217
tortoise beetle *(Cassida circumdata),* 168
tortoises, 162
Tourism and Wildlife Society of India, 215
transportation inside KNP, 172–173
tree-borne colony, 57
treepie, 136–137
tufted duck, 87
turtles, 143, 162–165, 279
    crowned river turtle *(Hardella thurjii),* 163
    Indian flapshell turtle *(Lissemys punctata),* 163
    Indian peacock soft-shell turtle *(Aspideretus hurum),* 165
    Indian roofed turtle *(Kachuga tecta),*163
    Indian soft-shell turtle *(Aspideretus gangeticus),* 165
    spotted pond turtle *(Geoclemys hamiltonii),* 163
    three-striped roofed turtle *(Kachuga dhongoka),* 163
Typha angustata, 67, 157, 168

U
United Nations Educational, Scientific and Cultural Organisation (UNESCO), 36
uprooting of plants, 199, 202–203, 207
Utricularia, 169

V
Vallisneria spiralis, 101
Vardhan, Harsh, 214, 232
V.D. Sharma Committee of 1983, 186
Vijayan, Dr, 101–102, 218, 226, 228–229
visitors, 174–175
vultures, 118–120

W
wagtails *(Motacilla spp),* 139
Watchtower of Koladahar Chowki, 183
water hyacinth *(Eichhornia crassipes),* 178
water resources
    Chiksana Canal, 213–215, 218–219
    Govardhan drain, 17, 156, 186, 215–222
    KP drain, 215
    new, 222
    New Canal, 219
    shallow borewells, 209–211
weaver birds, 131–132
wetland plants, 44–48
    Algae, 44
    Ceratophyllum, 44
    Cynodon dacttylon, 44
    Cyperus alopecuroides, 44
    Cyperus bulbous/rotundus, 44
    Cyperus littoralis, 44
    Cyperus rotundus, 44
    Eichornia crassipus, 44
    Hydrilla, 44
    Hydrilla verticillata, 44
    Ipomea aquatic, 44
    Najas, 44
    Nymphaea nouchali/stellata, 44–45
    Nymphaea stellata, 46
    Nymphoides cristata, 44, 46–47
    Nymphoides indica, 44
    Nymphoides indicum, 46
    Oriza sativa, 47–48
    Oryza rufipogon, 47–48
    Panicum paludosum, 44
    Paspalidium punctatum, 44
    Paspalum distichum, 44
    Potamogeton crispus, 44
    Potamogeton indicus, 44
    Pseudoraphis spinescens, 44
    Scirpus littoralis, 44
    Scirpus tuberosus, 44
    Sporobolus helvolus, 44
    Typha, 47
    Typha angustata, 44
    Vallisneria, 44
Wetlands Links International (WLI), 175
wetlands of Bharatpur, 37
white-breasted kingfisher, 140, 142
white eye, 138
white-eye buzzard *(Butastur teesta),* 117–118
white-fronted goose, 87
white ibis, 62
white stork *(Ciconia ciconia),* 78
wigeon duck, 82–83
Wildlife (Protection) Act, 163, 199, 201
wild Sibes, 109–110
wood collection, 178
World Heritage Centre/IUCN mission report, 205
World Wide Fund for Nature (WWF)-India, 174–175

Y
Yamuna floodplains/depressions of Bharatpur, 26–27

Z
Zygoptera, 169